EMERSON & THOREAU

American Philosophy

John J. Stuhr, editor

Emerson & Thoreau

FIGURES OF FRIENDSHIP

EDITED BY

John T. Lysaker & William Rossi

Indiana University Press
Bloomington & Indianapolis

This book is a publication of

Indiana University Press
601 North Morton Street
Bloomington, IN 47404-3797 USA

www.iupress.indiana.edu

Telephone orders 800-842-6796
Fax orders 812-855-7931
Orders by e-mail iuporder@indiana.edu

⊜ The paper used in this publication meets the minimum requirements of the American National Standard for Information Sciences—Permanence of Paper for Printed Library Materials, ANSI Z39.48-1992.

Manufactured in the United States of America

Library of Congress Cataloging-in-Publication Data

Emerson and Thoreau : figures of friendship / edited by John T. Lysaker and William Rossi.
p. cm. — (American philosophy)
Includes bibliographical references and index.
ISBN 978-0-253-35388-7 (cloth : alk. paper) — ISBN 978-0-253-22143-8 (pbk. : alk. paper) 1. Emerson, Ralph Waldo, 1803–1882—Friends and associates. 2. Thoreau, Henry David, 1817–1862—Friends and associates. 3. Friendship—United States—History—19th century. 4. Authors, American—19th century—Biography. I. Lysaker, John T. II. Rossi, William John.
PS1633.E44 2010
814'.3—dc22
[B]

2009020513

1 2 3 4 5 15 14 13 12 11 10

To two friendships that began in Nashville and continue to render the wide world habitable: Thank you Joseph Helm and Michael Sullivan. —J. T. L.

To Lynne, Julia, and Rachel: Everything with you and nothing that matters without. —W. R.

I had three chairs in my house; one for solitude,
two for friendship, three for society.

THOREAU

CONTENTS

ACKNOWLEDGMENTS

The editors are grateful for permission to publish John T. Lysaker's "On the Faces of Emersonian 'Friendship,'" which has been revised from an earlier version in Lysaker's *Emerson and Self-Culture* (Bloomington: Indiana University Press, 2008), 141–167; and William Rossi's "'In Dreams Awake': Loss, Transcendental Friendship, and Elegy," an earlier version of which appeared in *The New England Quarterly* 81 (2008): 252–277, as "Performing Loss, Elegy, and Transcendental Friendship."

ABBREVIATIONS FOR EMERSON, THOREAU, AND CARLYLE CITATIONS

Emerson

CE — *The Complete Works of Ralph Waldo Emerson.* Centenary Edition. 12 vols. Ed. Edward Waldo Emerson. Boston: Houghton Mifflin, 1903–1904.

CEC — *The Correspondence of Emerson and Carlyle.* Ed. Joseph Slater. New York: Columbia University Press, 1964.

CL — *The Letters of Ralph Waldo Emerson.* 10 vols. Ed. Ralph L. Rusk and Eleanor M. Tilton. New York: Columbia University Press, 1939–1995.

CS — *Complete Sermons of Ralph Waldo Emerson.* 4 vols. Ed. Albert J. von Frank, et al. Columbia: University of Missouri Press, 1989–1992.

CW — *The Collected Works of Ralph Waldo Emerson.* 7 vols. to date. Ed. Robert E. Spiller et al. Cambridge, Mass.: Harvard University Press, 1971–.

EAW — *Emerson's Antislavery Writings.* Ed. Len Gougeon and Joel Myerson. New Haven, Conn.: Yale University Press, 1995.

EL — *The Early Lectures of Ralph Waldo Emerson.* Ed. Stephen E. Whicher et al. Cambridge, Mass.: Harvard University Press, 1959–1972.

JMN — *The Journals and Miscellaneous Notebooks of Ralph Waldo Emerson.* Ed. William H. Gilman et al. Cambridge, Mass.: Harvard University Press, 1960–1982.

LL *The Later Lectures of Ralph Waldo Emerson.* 2 vols. Ed. Ronald A. Bosco and Joel Myerson. Athens: University of Georgia Press, 2001.

MMF *The Memoirs of Margaret Fuller Ossoli.* Ed. Ralph Waldo Emerson et al. Boston: Phillips, Sampson, 1852.

PN *The Poetry Notebooks of Ralph Waldo Emerson.* Ed. Ralph H. Orth et al. Columbia: University of Missouri Press, 1986.

TN *The Topical Notebooks of Ralph Waldo Emerson.* 3 vols. Ed. Ralph H. Orth et al. Columbia: University of Missouri Press, 1990–1994.

Thoreau

AW *A Week on the Concord and Merrimack Rivers.* Ed. Carl F. Hovde, William L. Howarth, and Elizabeth Hall Witherell. Princeton, N.J.: Princeton University Press, 1980.

CC *Cape Cod.* Ed. Joseph J. Moldenhauer. Princeton, N.J.: Princeton University Press, 1988.

Corr *The Correspondence of Henry David Thoreau.* Ed. Walter Harding and Carl Bode. New York: New York University Press, 1958.

EE *Early Essays and Miscellanies.* Ed. Joseph J. Moldenhauer and Edwin Moser, with Alexander C. Kern. Princeton, N.J.: Princeton University Press, 1975.

EX *Excursions.* Ed. Joseph J. Moldenhauer. Princeton, N.J.: Princeton University Press, 2007.

J *The Journal of Henry D. Thoreau.* 14 vols. Ed. Bradford Torrey and Francis Allen. Boston: Houghton Mifflin, 1906.

PJ *Journal.* 8 vols. to date. Ed. John C. Broderick, Robert Sattelmeyer et al. Princeton, N.J.: Princeton University Press, 1981–.

Wa *Walden.* Ed. J. Lyndon Shanley. Princeton, N.J.: Princeton University Press, 1971.

Carlyle

LDP *Carlyle's Latter-day Pamphlets.* Ed. M. K. Goldberg and J. P. Seigel. Ottawa: Canadian Federation for the Humanities, 1983.

LTJWC *The Collected Letters of Thomas and Jane Welsh Carlyle.* 35 vols. to date. Ed. Charles Richard Sanders, Kenneth J. Fielding, et al. Durham, N.C.: Duke University Press, 1970–.

WTC *The Works of Thomas Carlyle.* Centenary Edition. 30 vols. Ed. H. D. Traill. London: Chapman and Hall, 1896–1899.

EMERSON & THOREAU

INTRODUCTION

JOHN T. LYSAKER & WILLIAM ROSSI

"The office of the scholar," Emerson writes, "is to cheer, to raise, and to guide men by showing them facts amidst appearances" (*CW* 1: 62). Our volume takes this charge to heart. By attending to the intricacies of friendship, we aim to stoke the fires of our affections for those whose presence is, as Aristotle claims in book eight of the *Nicomachean Ethics,* "most necessary for life," to the point that "no one would choose to live without friends, despite having all the rest of the goods" (1155a3–4).

In attending to matters close to home, this volume also proves responsive to another Emersonian charge, namely, to address everyday life, what he terms "the near, the low, the common" (*CW* 1: 67). That said, such inquiries still seek "facts amidst appearances"; that is, in addressing friendship, this volume aims to articulate the logic by which friendship unfolds as well as the benefits and hurts, challenges and rewards that friendship introduces.

For many who are compelled to speak on its behalf, friendship produces ecstatic testimonials whose intensity can embarrass a reader unused to discourses of praise. But we take the fact that friendship inspires manifold celebration as a principal character of its appearance. Like few folds in mortal life, friendship seems a necessary part of the good. We are thus unsurprised that Aristotle's *Nicomachean Ethics* devotes two of its ten books to friendship, or that Aristotle locates it so near the heart of human flourishing. Nor are we (or many others, for that matter) averse to his position. Experiences shared in friendship are often richer for being shared, and regardless of whether the mutual understanding is articulated. "To know someone here or there," Goethe writes, "with whom you can feel there is understanding in spite of distances or thoughts expressed—that can make life a garden." In fact, even in their absence, friends are a comfort. As Samuel Johnson writes to Bennet Langton: "It is pleasing in the silence of solitude to think, that there is one at least, however distant, of whose benevolence there is little doubt, and whom there is yet hope of seeing again." But friendship offers more than comfort. Friends stimulate us, coax us beyond ourselves, and accompany us into wider worlds. Because they broaden our lives and leave us richer for having known them, "friends do not live in harmony merely, as some say, but in melody," as Thoreau rightly observed (*AW* 266). That said, friends no doubt also offer a kind of security, a place to turn in times of need, as a Moroccan proverb attests: "Your truest friends are those who visit you in prison or in hospital." This is why the thought of friendship seems so bound to ideas of loyalty, even sturdiness, and why we turn to friends for counsel on matters we shield from others. But more than loans or sympathetic ears, friends offer recognition: they know us and still receive, even welcome us into their lives, which not only comforts but also allows us to simply be ourselves. "One's friends are a part of the human race with which one can be human," Santayana writes. And in difficult times, when our judgment is questioned or our peers regard us as woefully out of step, the knowing look of a friend can still our ensuing vertigo and help us persevere. Another proverb, this one from Spain, perhaps says this best: "It is good to have friends even in hell."[1]

Given its many benefits, and given the range of testimony on friendship's behalf, we find the theme of friendship ever-timely and especially pressing for humanist reflection. In contemporary Euro-American society, many feel an increased sense of isolation as adult life advances. In other words, we are doing more alone than simply bowling.[2] But perhaps the issue isn't only one of isolation. With the increased commercialization of every sphere of life, a certain degree of calculation infects even the most innocuous activities, e.g., what we wear, how we "spend" our free time, and with whom. What may be missing is thus less company than meaningful company—the kind of company with which we can share and even develop our humanity, to recall Santayana's remark. No doubt factors beyond our creeping, strategic alliances threaten to hollow us out. Nevertheless, we think it important to bring discussions of friendship into the forefront of our collective reflections on human flourishing, and we find Emerson and Thoreau equal to the occasion.

Friendship Theory: A Western Sketch

While Concord's most illustrious citizens have offered us brilliant writings on the matter of friendship, neither is unique in their essays. As several of our authors show, both Emerson and Thoreau remain in touch with a variety of sources which constitute, in part, the history of friendship as a Western, humanistic theme. A brief sketch of this history might prove useful, then, particularly if Emerson is correct that "every book is a quotation; and every house a quotation out of all the forests and mines and stone quarries; and every man is a quotation from all his ancestors" (*CW* 4: 24).

For Greek and Roman thinkers in antiquity, friendship was central to the good life and a training ground for citizenship. It not only helped center character but, because republican political action extended beyond the family, friendship also helped young men (in this case) cultivate allegiances outside of their most intimate milieu. Classical conceptions of friendship were thus ethical through and through, grounded in characters molded by shared conceptions of the good. As Cicero states in *Laelius:* "Friendship may be defined as a complete identity of feeling about all things in heaven and earth: an identity which is strengthened by mutual goodwill and affection." We should add, however, that for Plato and Aristotle, true friends do not simply agree upon but generate their conception of the good together, through dialogue and deliberation.[3]

In Europe's medieval period, Aristotle and Cicero remained principal figures, though in the context of Christianity friendship had to contend with the city of God as well as the cities of human beings.[4] This led many thinkers like Aelred (1109–1166) to use the notion of friendship (particularly Cicero's) to interpret God's relationship to humanity, and then not only to assess human friendships on the basis of that perfect love, but also to view friendship as an activity that is oriented toward deepening friends' relations to the divine. Aquinas (1225–1274), who had perhaps a better feel for the contingencies of mortal friendships, puzzled at some length about the kinds and degrees of disagreement friendships could endure. If Daniel Schwartz (2007) is correct in his *Aquinas and Friendship,* this portly saint allowed a wider range of dissonance among friends than his classical predecessors had. Yet, for Aquinas, friendship remained bound to the divine so that friends needed to remain united in their faith in God and in their commitment to aid one another in faith and good works. To some contemporary readers, then, Aquinas still expects friends to share remarkably deep commitments.

Europe's early modern period brought forth Montaigne's now famous essay "On Friendship." (M. A. Screech translates the title "On affectionate relationships," given the semantic breadth of *amitié,* which includes parent-child affection, brotherly or sisterly love, and even marriage.)[5] Like classical authors, Montaigne puts friendship at the center of human life, setting his essay at the midpoint of his first book, which he characterizes as a self-portrait—"it is my own self that I am painting." Montaigne's humanistic orientation differs from that of his medieval counterparts because it frees friends from the task of keeping one another on the path to salvation. At the same time, and possibly because it lacks a theistic core, he intensifies the union that friendship seems to involve. He terms friendship "indivisible" because "in the friendship which I am talking about, souls are mingled and confounded in so universal a blending that they efface the seam which joins them together so that it cannot be found." As blending of this sort is uncommon, Montaigne finds, in distinction to classical and medieval authors, that genuine friendship is an equally rare occurrence. "So many fortuitous circumstances are needed to make it, that it is already something if Fortune can achieve it once in three centuries."

Just as medieval theologians viewed divine-mortal relations in terms of friendship, so too the British and German Romantics understood friendship in terms of a joint pursuit of some greater whole to which both friends (and indeed all other things) belong. According to Robert J. Richards, the Jena circle of philosophers and lovers thought that humans had to "face the fragmented and contending elements of life, yet as progressive creatures, they continued to strive toward the ideal of unity" (Richards 2002, 203). For many Romantics, in both theory and practice, friendship was both a means to and an example of that unity. This may explain why the Romantic period produced some of the most famous (if troubled) literary friendships: those of Coleridge and Wordsworth, Byron and Shelley, and Goethe and Schiller may be the period's most important contributions to the history of friendship as a humanist concern.

Looking more closely at British Romanticism, we find the figure of the friend in two related but distinguishable contexts. Some Romantics, like Coleridge, used the figure of the friend to articulate the writer-reader relationship, which he took to be central to the pursuit of an elevated consciousness in which friends mutually participate. Aiming to engage his reader in cultivating the "nobler and permanent parts of our Nature," Coleridge named his sporadic journal of 1809 and 1810 *The Friend* (it was expanded and republished in 1818), promising to justify "that sacred title" by combining "open-heartedness" with truth-telling, and thus to be a benefactor to whoever would read it (1969, 2: 20 n. 2, 1: 39). Coleman (1988) has suggested that this promise was not kept, since Coleridge's address in those years was full of condescension. But Taussig (2002) argues that because Coleridge took to heart Blake's belief that "opposition is true friendship," he located the beneficence of friends precisely in their ability to challenge and contradict one another, presuming, of course, that a wellspring of goodwill flowed between them.

For William Wordsworth, like his German and medieval counterparts, friendship is both a means to and an instance of unity, although unlike his medieval predecessors, Wordsworth's *deus sive natura* is pantheistic. In a letter to an eighteen-year-old Thomas De Quincey, Wordsworth describes the roots of friendship in terms of a spontaneity that is more a matter of "growth of time and circumstance" than of willful association—more wildflower than cultivated self-consciousness. But should friendship take root, then Wordsworth believes it can right us, even return us to genuine selves, as he tells his sister Dorothy in *The Prelude.*

> . . . but for thee, dear Friend!
> My soul, too reckless of mild grace, had stood
> In her original self too confident,
> Retained too long a countenance severe;
> A rock with torrents roaring, with the clouds
> Familiar, and a favourite of the stars:
> But thou didst plant its crevices with flowers,
> Hang it with shrubs that twinkle in the breeze,
> And teach the little birds to build their nests
> And warble in its chambers. . . .

For Romantics like Wordsworth, then, friendship played a quasi-ethical role. But whereas ancient writers took friendship to enrich and strengthen character, even to intensify a certain degree of self-control (and so make us better citizens), Wordsworth's conviction that friendship returns us to an enveloping source from which we have grown estranged seems closer to a medieval conception.

In our own day, friendship has focused the energies of several important thinkers and writers. As if reversing Coleridge's perspective, Hans-Georg Gadamer uses an implicit notion of friendship to orient interpretation—or so one can read his use of the notion of "good will." At the same time, Gadamer regards interpretation as a constitutive human activity that exceeds our relation to literary texts; and thus, in a classical vein, one could say that he takes friendship to name a basic, ethical relation. Intensifying Montaigne's sense that friendship is an unlikely occurrence (and playing on his predecessor's fondness for the plaint, attributed to Aristotle, "O my friend, there is no friend"), Jacques Derrida finds friendship bound to the manner in which we address others ("O my friend . . .") rather than in any agreement about extant beliefs. And he insists, as do Emerson and Thoreau, that such a manner must be proven again and again, such that the "friend" is always to come, which is to say, friendship is never a settled affair but a matter that must ever be reestablished.[6]

In feminist scholarship, friendship has also been a significant concern. Studying women's movements, scholars like Philippa Levine have noted that friendships underwrote solidarity among women seeking to address their oppression. Set beside Aristotle and Cicero, feminist friendships appear less a preparation for citizenship than a relationship that develops precisely because full citizenship is being denied. Nevertheless, it remains resolutely political in its rejection of what citizenship traditionally entails. In the context of feminist struggle, lessons learned in friendship, e.g., concerning the limits and abstraction of acquisitive individualism, offered a basis for political reconstruction (as opposed to simple political integration).[7]

Situating Emerson and Thoreau

In their efforts to express all that a full, rich, and noble life entails, Emerson and Thoreau also turned their attentions to those relations that seem to elevate us to our best. Beside the lifelong commentaries on the subject to be found in their journals, both produced key essays on friendship in *Essays: First Series* (1841) and *A Week on the Concord and Merrimack Rivers* (1849).[8] Moreover, because these reflections often arose out of their actual and occasionally tormented friendship, as well as their relations with others, friendship was at once a literary-philosophical and an existential concern for both men.

Set into the history we have just reviewed, Emerson's and Thoreau's work offers variations on its principal themes with a few notable differences. Since our essays engage this tradition from a variety of angles, we'll just note a few principal contrasts and overlaps. Like almost all their predecessors, Emerson and Thoreau consider friendship as an aspect of and factor in character development. But more than most, they consider it difficult to sustain the bonds that are forged in this process of mutual growth. Neither went as far as Samuel Johnson, however, who wrote in *The Rambler:* "So many qualities are indeed requisite to the possibility of friendship, and so many accidents must concur to its rise and its continuance, that the greatest part of mankind content themselves without it, and supply its place as they can, with interest and dependence." For no one, they believed, could do without it. "No word," Thoreau writes, "is oftener on the lips of men than Friendship, and indeed, no thought is more familiar to their aspirations" (*AW* 264). But they took its difficulty seriously, and thus set, at the very heart of friendship, the task of sustaining its unfolding melody. And furthermore—like Montaigne, but unlike classical conceptions and recent feminist thought—both hold friendship to be beyond the reach of politics, as if its more intimate stage enables a kind of growth that larger-scale social projects must forgo.

Interestingly, the question of a politics of friendship is not a matter that many of our authors directly pursue. David Robinson does discuss how friendship feeds utopian desires in Emerson, and Naoko Saito finds an incipient, cosmopolitan politics in the model of friendship that Emerson and Thoreau seem to share. But for the most part, the essays collected here move within the purportedly extra-political terrain traversed by their subjects.

We would like to consider one other point of intersection between Emerson and Thoreau and the ensemble of thought we have just rehearsed. Unlike all but their fellow Romantics, Emerson and Thoreau conceive of friendship as seamed by differences rather than as seamless. In fact, they propose that genuine friends should actively court each other's differences. (Coleridge seems to do the same, but it could be argued that the inquiring spirit that animates *The Friend* ultimately seeks to resolve those differences, whereas the Concord pair celebrate them as necessary.) This is worth underscoring, as several authors do, albeit in different ways. It suggests that, in their refusal to think friendship within a logic of identity, both Emerson and Thoreau anticipate later thinkers of difference even as they celebrate, without apology, the goods that friendship can provide.

Moving within and between disciplines such as literary criticism, philosophy, biography, and intellectual history, the nine essays collected in this volume focus variously on one of our authors or on both, on particular moments in their fraught relationship or on their engagements with others in their orbit, such as Margaret Fuller and Thomas Carlyle. But taken as a whole, the present collection's real concern is with friendship itself. Yes, the essays collected here enrich our understanding of powerful and perplexing texts and their authors. And thus, yes, this collection aims to contribute to Emerson and Thoreau scholarship as well as, more generally, to American Studies, where these themes have been a matter of recent interest and scrutiny.[9] Moreover, given the sharp focus and depth of the treatments collected here, as well as the striking ways in which they complement and contest one another, scholars and students of Romanticism, nineteenth-century American literature and philosophy, and Emerson or Thoreau will find much to consider. Yet as two other problematic friends would have it, if "in the end / the love you take / is equal to the love / you make," then we want this book to enrich our readers' collective sense of what friendship involves, what it requires, and how we might fare better on our paths.

This boldly humanistic purpose will strike some readers as odd, especially in light of what many regard as the failed relationship between Emerson and Thoreau. Wasn't their friendship a nettlesome and finally sour affair, producing bitterness in one and resentment in the other? While their writings jointly celebrate the promise of friendship, often ascending to lyric heights, they just as often despair of its sustainability and even its reality. Immediately following the observation that friendship is ever "on the lips of men," Thoreau suggests that while "all men are dreaming of it, . . . its drama . . . is always a tragedy" that is "enacted daily." As figures of friendship, therefore, Emerson's and Thoreau's writings and lives would seem to offer, at best, uncertain futures to those who would consider the friend on the basis of their words and experience.

Yet can we presume that their struggles with friendship were peculiar to them, or were as peculiar as these men and their circumstances may have been? This is unlikely. The conundrums that riddle texts like "Friendship" and *A Week* are not simply artifacts of Emerson's or Thoreau's temperament, or their psychic, sexual, and theoretical orientations. Friendship itself is a riddle, and an ongoing one for those who would have friendships between souls that become. Everyone has known the withering of friendship. And while all have thrilled to the charge and rested in the comfort friends bring, they have also fretted about how best to be a friend, and doubted that everything in the relationship was what it seemed. What puzzles Emerson and Thoreau in this regard is therefore what often puzzles us.

If friendship is something more than mutual usefulness or shared pleasure, what else is it that binds us? How many such friends have we really had?

Don't even the best of friends bore, trouble, and even repel each other? And once we realize this, how can or how do friendships survive the discovery, let alone the disclosure? Or consider this. If a certain degree of individualism, or an ability to think and act on one's own, is praiseworthy, how is it that two individuals can nevertheless intertwine their lives into the kind of "melody" that Thoreau claims friendship involves? These are thorny questions, which most everyone has considered. Precisely because such questions not only lie at the heart of their reflections on friendship, but also challenged them, repeatedly, as they struggled to remain more than occasional allies in their lifetimes, Emerson and Thoreau are worthy of our attention.

Of course, Emerson and Thoreau were not the only writers in nineteenth-century America to explore the subject of friendship. One can find thoughts as pertinent and bracing in the writings of Fuller, relating to her friendship with Caroline Sturgis, or in the works of Lydia Maria Child and Herman Melville, for example. Nor do we claim that the texts concentrated on here are necessarily the most insightful or progressive, but only that they are highly worthy of the kind of extensive, interdisciplinary review we have assembled here, since they set out the figure of the friend so luxuriantly. Finally, because Thoreau and Emerson were themselves friends—friends, moreover, who valued writing and silence above speech, even above friendship—they offer a figure of friendship that provides us with new avenues into the perils and pleasures of extended, non-sexualized intimacy.

The Essays

The two essays in part 1 examine the friendships between Emerson, Thoreau, and Carlyle in their biographical, social, and philosophical contexts, foregrounding both the problematic of Transcendentalist friendship theory and particular occasions in its fraught history. Noting that the relationship of Emerson and Thoreau represents "a case that is not only unique in the history of Transcendentalism" but also "strikingly original within world literary history," Lawrence Buell examines the historical record in light of Transcendentalist theories of friendship and of friendship theory generally. While both men idealized the figure of the friend, Thoreau, the more active seeker, also more willingly accepted the Derridean precondition of loving without evidence of being loved in return. Yet their awareness of a corollary of Transcendentalist idealization, observed both by Kant and later by Emerson's strongest European reader, Nietzsche—namely, that lived experience always falls short of the ideal—may explain the persistence of their affiliation, however it altered. In keeping with the relationship's well-documented breakdown, there is a common tendency to read Emerson's eulogy, "Thoreau," as a symptom of their estrangement. But given Emerson's "lifelong attempts to promote and defend Thoreau's work," as well as testimony from Thoreau's other friends, Buell argues that in the long term this friendship was more successful than the theories of either man might imply.

Barbara Packer incisively examines the dynamics of gift-giving and indebtedness in the friendships of Emerson, Carlyle, and Thoreau—from Emerson's early discipleship to the as-yet unknown Carlyle, an author of Victorian periodical essays, to Thoreau's repayment in *Walden* of Carlyle's response to his first book, *A Week on the Concord and Merrimack Rivers.* Throughout Emerson's visits to England, the Irish potato famine, Emerson's increasing participation in the abolitionist cause, and Carlyle's deepening skepticism about democracy, the two men exchanged gifts as various and vital as dried Indian corn, ideas, letters of introduction, publishing assistance, books, and money. Although Thoreau inhabited the margins of this exchange, he also gained and lost by it. As all three reciprocated their debts with generosity and guilt, malice and partiality, they learned that "it is dangerous both to give and to receive."

Three fine-grained analyses of Emerson's essay "Friendship" comprise part 2. Like Buell and Packer, David Robinson locates Transcendentalist friendship within the social relations that upheld it, identifying the deep interpersonal sources of Emerson's essay in his experience of an intimate community of friends which centered on the electric presence of Margaret Fuller during the late 1830s. Although chronologically an early work in Emerson's long career, the disillusionment this essay dramatizes regarding the transformative power of visionary experience and the efficacy of self-reliance foreshadows his later shift toward ethical discipline and pragmatic effort, which was initiated in "Experience." Whereas in the first half of "Friendship," Emerson entertains the claim that friendship is a fated relation or law of nature only to reject it, in the second movement he re-grounds friendship "on the firmer foundations of choice, will, and disciplined effort, a relation more created than given." In this respect "Friendship" can be read as a political essay—one rooted in a utopian experiment, but pointing "toward a larger vision of human mutuality and interdependent support."

While he remains attentive to thematic crosscurrents from other of Emerson's essays, Russell Goodman highlights Emerson's recurrent doubts about friendship in his essay on the topic. Emerson's abiding disappointment about our capacity to know others—what Stanley Cavell calls "lived skepticism"—strengthens him against what seem to be facile expressions of friendship. But as "Friendship" develops, rather than persist in his skepticism, Emerson recovers faith in the capacity of true friendship to offer glimpses of better relations and better moments, thereby tentatively (if ephemerally) restoring hope in it. While ranging through the experiential ebb and flow of the gift of friendship in our lives, Emerson nonetheless fails to address the death of friends, a failure he later amply redressed in "Experience."

Taking Emerson's essay personally, John Lysaker engages Emersonian friendship as a principal site of self-culture. In tracking the essay's mimetic fidelity to the bloom and fading of friendship and our capacity for it, Lysaker finds "Friendship" to be a text that is alive at once to friendship's fragility and to its ethical demands. The rare meeting point of friendship and self-culture produces a kind of ethical double consciousness, in which "we side with our emerging selves against the inertia of our foregoing hours, alert to the prophecy of one another, and loyal to our prospects"—as much for the others in our care, as for ourselves. At the same time, Emerson's theodicy—namely, his drift toward reliance on a bloodless impersonality—rings hollow or at best less than fortifying, for this twenty-first-century reader.

In part 3, the next essays turn to Thoreau, assessing in different ways his complementary divergence from his mentor. Sounding the truth of Lawrence Buell's pithy observation that Thoreau was a master of the "buried elegy" (2003, 117), William Rossi isolates the elegiac strain of his writing in the period before the falling out with Emerson. Thoreau's elegiac stance arose initially out of an attempt to negotiate his friendship with Emerson in their shared condition of family loss and grief, while he was living in the Emerson household. But by the end of this period, with a book publication seemingly imminent and authorial independence in sight, elegy had come to shape not only Thoreau's representation but his performance of transcendental friendship itself. Ironically forecasting the demise of his friendship with Emerson, Thoreau's essay also expresses a faith that even if such intimacy can never be sustained, neither can it be permanently lost.

More than is usually done, Alan Hodder's essay casts the religious dimensions of Transcendentalist friendship into bold relief. He traces the deep "philosophical rift" between Emerson and Thoreau, which is evident in their disparate representations of friendship, to their divergent attempts to accommodate the inherited metaphysical paradox on which Transcendentalist friendship was unstably founded: namely, that "the I and the thou are both separate and in some sense the same." Where Emerson's reliance on Platonic and Neo-Platonic idealism "allows the paradoxes of true friendship to stand, retreating little from even their most disturbing social implications," Thoreau's gravitation toward Confucian (and later Hindu) sources leads him to seek "an experiential resolution to the conflicts between real and ideal friendship in the natural world and the sphere of solitude itself."

The collection concludes with a pair of essays that pose the giving of friendship as both a vital gifting and a resilient model of global citizenship. Like Hodder, James Crosswhite plumbs the religious as well as the philosophical foundations of Transcendentalist friendship. But while Hodder reads Emerson's theory of friendship—and perhaps his capacity for it—as excessively constrained by Plato, Crosswhite, following Hans-Georg Gadamer, argues that Emerson's theory was equally entangled in an ontotheological model inherited from Aristotle. And in searching for an alternative, Thoreau took a direction that went "Plato one better." Moving into an altogether different, ontotheological register that Crosswhite (reviving an old Trinitarian word) terms "perichoretic," Thoreau represents friendship as existing "only in its being given and received." Thus, to be a friend is to give to another a new "way of being," one that is utterly incomprehensible as an exchange between self-generating and self-sufficient individuals. From the perichoretic perspective, individuality and self-sufficiency are themselves "achievements of friendship," made possible through a history of prior befriendings—the precedent friendships of families, former friends, fellow citizens, and neighbors.

But what then does it mean to "neighbor" others in a multicultural and globalized world? Drawing on the work of Stanley Cavell, Naoko Saito argues that the friendship theory of Emerson and Thoreau provides resources for countering a powerful force known as "Americanization," itself often fashioned out of an ersatz Emersonian individualism. In Saito's view, Emerson pursues and articulates the moral perfection of the self neither for its own sake nor in order to assimilate others, but as an activity that is integral to democratic social betterment. As a moral and social project ever in process, perfectionism not only necessarily requires the other; in Cavell's sense, it also "acknowledges" the other, accepting his or her unknowability while "still searching for connection with the other." In this way, rather than individualistically assimilating difference under the aegis of global Americanization, friendship provides a relationship of true mutuality and specifically of "mutual education."

As should be evident from this overview, common thoughts, themes, and questions move across the four parts of *Emerson and Thoreau: Figures of Friendship*, while each essay adds something to the others. However one chooses to peruse this collection, we are confident that provocations and insights will find you.

Notes

1. Many of these passages are taken from the useful and edifying compendium *The Oxford Book of Friendship* (1991). A contemporary volume from Norton, *The Norton Book of Friendship* (1991), also offers excellent selections.

2. The reference here is to Robert Putnam, *Bowling Alone: The Collapse and Revival of American Community* (1995).

3. Plato's *Lysis* is available in a fine translation by David Bolotin (Plato 1979), who also provides a thorough commentary. For a compelling translation of Aristotle's remarkable text, see Joe Sach's recent version (Aristotle 2002). Cicero's *Laelis* has been ably translated by Michael Grant and collected in *Cicero: On the Good Life* (1971). Michael Pakaluk has gathered several philosophical texts in *Other Selves: Philosophers on Friendship* (1991).

4. For surveys of this lengthy period, see Brian McGuire's *Friendship and Community: The Monastic Experience, 350–1250* (1988), Ulrich Langer's *Perfect Friendship: Studies in Literature and Moral Philosophy from Boccaccio to Corneille* (1994), and Reginald Hyatte's *The Arts of Friendship: The Idealization of Friendship in Medieval and Early Renaissance Literature* (1997).

5. M. A. Screech has translated and edited all of Montaigne's essays in *The Complete Essays* (Montaigne 1991).

6. For Gadamer's views, see his *Truth and Method* (1992). For the importance of friendship to his thought, see his interview in *Radical Philosophy* 69 (1995). Derrida develops his account in *The Politics of Friendship* (1997). For an intriguing if occasionally odd discussion wherein Derrida responds to Gadamer's conception of "good will," particularly as it functions in interpretation, see *Dialogue and Deconstruction* (Michelfelder and Palmer 1989).

7. Levine's discussion can be found in "Love, Friendship, and Feminism in Later 19th-century England" (1990). For a diverse and provocative feminist-philosophical discussion of friendship and community, see *Feminism and Community* (Weiss and Friedman 1995). Marilyn Friedman's view is developed in *What Are Friends For? Feminist Perspectives on Personal Relationships and Moral Theory* (1993). In a theological context, Mary E. Hunt (1991) uses friendship to figure in an ethically responsive orientation toward a vast range of human relations, including relations to the divine.

8. Thoreau assimilated several previously published stand-alone pieces into *A Week*, which function as meditative digressions from the boating narrative. In the same way that he incorporated essays such as "The Dark Ages" and "Aulus Persius Flaccus" or lectures like "Society," the discourse on friendship in "Wednesday" was

written as a separate lecture, as he reported in an 1848 letter to Emerson (*Corr* 208); see Johnson 1980, 444–465.

9. Recent studies include Harmon Smith, *My Friend, My Friend* (1999); Caleb Crain, *American Sympathy* (2001); Sharon Monteith, *Advancing Sisterhood?* (2000); Chris Packard, *Queer Cowboys* (2005); Rachel Cohen, *A Chance Meeting* (2004); Richard Lingeman, *Double Lives* (2006); Ivy Schweitzer, *Perfecting Friendship* (2006); and Jeffery Dennis, *We Boys Together* (2007).

PART ONE

Transcendental Contexts

ONE

Transcendental Friendship: An Oxymoron?

LAWRENCE BUELL

All that has been said of friendship is like botany to flowers.

THOREAU

My title both is and is not meant as a rhetorical question. However much the Transcendentalists valued solitude and independent-mindedness, the practice of friendship was also clearly important to them, not only in satisfying their human needs as social beings but in furthering the sense of intellectual affinity and mutuality that helped make possible such defining collaborative projects as the Transcendental Club and the Brook Farm commune. On the other hand, Transcendentalist friendship *theory*—especially as set out in Emerson's and Thoreau's disquisitions on the subject in *Essays: First Series* (1841) and *A Week on the Concord and Merrimack Rivers* (1849)—notoriously defines friendship in such exalted terms as to threaten to make it inoperable. "Friends, such as we desire," Emerson declares, "are dreams and fables" (*CW* 2: 125). Thoreau likens "The Friend" (the friend who is *wholly* worthy of the name) to "some fair floating isle of palms eluding the mariner in Pacific seas"—a beautiful mirage, "evanescent in every man's experience, and remembered like heat lightning in past summers" (*AW* 262, 261).

Not that Emerson or Thoreau thought friendship existentially impossible. But they feared it was impossible to achieve, much less sustain, at the level at which they considered the friendship to be ideal. Transcendentalist friendship discourse à la Emerson and Thoreau effectively defines friendship with a capital "F" in the same way it defines reality with a capital "R" or self with a capital "S"—that is, in terms of peak experience, by which standard quotidian experience yields a fitful flame that inevitably dwindles into scattered, memorable moments of exaltation.

The salience of this paradox of friendship in the Transcendentalists' life-records, versus their theoretical rarefaction of friendship virtually out of existence, can and often has been "explained" either psycho-biographically or psycho-culturally. Transcendentalism-watchers are quite familiar with such exegesis. Emerson and Thoreau were both in their own ways reticent and self-protective types, who seemed to many outsiders (and for that matter a number of closer acquaintances) cold fish. Both men knew this full well and berated themselves and each other for it. Furthermore, reserve was—as it still is—a stereotypical New England trait.[1] Temperamental reticence and regional decorum, together with the complications of a transitionally progressive but residually traditional gender ideology, underwrite the subtle element of denigration in Emerson's closest approximation to a portrait of the representative embodiment of his friendship ideal: Margaret Fuller. Emerson's sincere praise for Fuller as a friend is rendered ambiguous by his intimations of something dubiously overheated, possessive, disruptively exotic in her

> passionate wish for noble companions, to the end of making life [itself] altogether noble. With the firmest tact she led the conversation into the midst of their daily living & working, recognising the goodwill and intellectually all the points, that one seemed to see his life *en beau* or in a fine mirage, & was flattered by seeing what was ordinarily so tedious in its workaday weeds shining in so glorious costume. (*JMN* 11: 496)[2]

Again, that telltale "mirage" metaphor: Fuller as the orchestrator of luminous moments of encounter that leave you in limbo, feeling a certain sense of unreality about them and quotidian experience generally. But even though Emerson rather demystifies Fuller's charisma here, neither she nor the friendship ideal ceases to haunt him. As Thoreau wrote of "Economy," so too with both Emerson and Thoreau on "Friendship": it "admits of being treated with levity, but cannot be so disposed of" (*Wa* 29).

Mentorship and/versus Friendship

All this is simply preamble, however, to what I want now to argue about Transcendentalist friendship theory and practice vis-à-vis the Emerson-Thoreau relation specifically. The central underlying question I pose here is what the double helix of their friendship theory and actual life-history (insofar as we can reconstruct it) has to say about the prospect of a *bona fide* friendship evolving between a mentor and a mentee.

This is or ought to be a high-stakes issue for any thinking person, be they student or teacher, parent or child, supervisor or supervisee. I relate to this as a parent who is in the process of renegotiating his relations to much-loved and also much-respected grown-up children. I also relate to this as a teacher who is edging toward retirement, and who has felt close to a great many wonderful students (not to mention those I have admired as persons when they were less wonderful students), some of whose hair is now even grayer than my own. And I would very much like to believe that such transformations are possible at least sometimes—i.e., for mentor-mentee relationships to evolve into friend-friend relationships. I even dare to hope that this has happened in my own life. And I know that I am not alone. While I was drafting this very paragraph, I was called away to attend the memorial service of the late William R. Hutchison, to whose scholarship all of us interested today in the history of Transcendentalism as a religious movement are hugely indebted. At the service, one of his prize students of a few decades past, now himself a distinguished historian of religion, delivered an eloquent and compelling tribute to Bill as "mentor and friend, two in one."[3] Would that my former students thought so about me.

Scrolling back now to the nineteenth-century context of the subject at hand, in the archives of Emerson family history we find a similar testimony. Ronald Bosco and Joel Myerson's recent biographical study of the Emerson brothers prints for the first time an affectionate tribute delivered at the dinner following Emerson's 1837 Phi Beta Kappa oration by Edward Everett, whom Emerson later memorialized as the most charismatic Harvard professor of his day: a tribute not, however, to Ralph Waldo, but to his precocious brother Edward. "My relation with [him]," Everett affirms, "was one of the kindliest relations, that can subsist between man and man, that of a pupil grown up to be a friend" (Bosco and Myerson 2006, 69).

Yet both theory and history also testify against the likelihood of such outcomes, insofar as the highest kind of friendship presupposes a position of equality. Anthropologist Robert Brain asserts categorically that across cultures a position of "equality" is integral to the formation of friendship (1976, 20). Even if this over-generalizes, it seems broadly to hold for Western thinking. Aristotle deems equality in "excellence and virtue" to be "the perfect form of friendship." Mentor-mentee relations would fall, for Aristotle, into the lower category of instrumental friendship, friendship based on "the useful."[4] Montaigne insists peremptorily on "too great inequality" as a bar to friendship, disallowing the possibility of true friendship between parent and child and even between the sexes, inasmuch as—so he alleges—"the ordinary capacity of women is inadequate for that communion and fellowship which is the nurse of this sacred bond."[5] And for Simone Weil, "a bond of affection" which contains any degree of "necessity" as she calls it, such as dependence, fatally compromises that "autonomy" of individuals which is indispensable for friendship in the proper sense.[6] Although Montaigne and Weil stand at utterly opposite poles on the question of autonomy *per se*—he claims that true friends commingle their souls into one without reserve, whereas she likens friends to parallel lines that meet only in God—the principle of equality is indispensable to both.

And neither Emerson nor Thoreau contests this point. On the contrary, Emerson demands that the friend

> not cease an instant to be himself. The only joy I have in his being mine, is that the *not mine* is *mine*. I hate, where I looked for a manly furtherance, or at least a manly resistance, to find a mush of concession. Better be a nettle in the side of your friend than an echo. (*CW* 2: 122–123)

This last sentiment came back to haunt Emerson's relations with both Thoreau and Fuller when they *did* nettle him to the point that he reacted defensively, and then accused him of not practicing what he preached. But that does not mean that he did not believe what he says here; and Thoreau substantially agrees. Indeed, Thoreau goes even further in this Blakean vein wherein "Opposition is true Friendship," when he declares that "we have not so good a right to hate any as our Friend" (*AW* 282).[7]

On the other hand, another tradition of friendship theory allows for, even stresses, the inevitability and at times indeed the auspiciousness of inequality in friendship. For Jacques Derrida, friendship by definition begins *with* inequality; "it is to love *before* being loved."[8] And similarly, Nietzsche asserts that

> A good friendship originates when one party has a great respect for the other, more indeed than for himself, when one party likewise loves the other, though not as much as he does himself, and when, finally, one party knows how to facilitate the association by adding to it a delicate *tinge* of intimacy while at the same time withholding actual and genuine intimacy and the confounding of I and Thou.[9]

At first sight, this seems to be an uncannily precise description of how the Emerson-Thoreau friendship (if indeed that's the right word for it) historically began, as well as one that might apply more generally to mentor-mentee relations which blossom into something more.

So how *should* we size up the relation Emerson sustained with his various mentees? For in principle, we do need to talk also about mentees in the plural—there were dozens, if not hundreds—since Emerson was a perpetual encourager of youthful talent, indeed sometimes talent that was not so youthful that he took under his wing anyhow, like Bronson Alcott, who was even a little older than he. Each case turned out differently. At one extreme, the mercurial minor poet Ellery Channing, who never came near to living up to what Emerson fancied his early promise to be, became intimidated and demoralized by him. At the other extreme, Margaret Fuller started out much more intellectually and emotionally dependent on Emerson than she ended up, and he seems to have respected her for it. This does not in itself prove that they became true friends, according to the somewhat discrepant ideals the two of them held as to what counted as such. Fuller wished for a greater degree of intimacy than Emerson was willing to grant. Still, regardless of such complications, in my own judgment this was probably as close an approximation to a friendship of equals as Emerson ever formed with a significantly younger person who began as his admirer.[10] But the Emerson-Thoreau relationship is a case that is not only unique in the history of Transcendentalism; it is also strikingly original within world literary history: Thoreau as a protégé is intensely and carefully prepared from his earliest manhood to become a canonical figure in his own right—and he succeeds, to such an extent that his reputation has arguably eclipsed his mentor's. To what extent, though, is friendship a part of that story?

I would like to answer that friendship is involved to a significant degree. For not only is this the historical instance of an intimate mentor-mentee relation that I have studied most closely, it would also seem to be one of the most auspicious, considering (as I argue in my book *Emerson*) that Emerson was the quintessential "anti-mentor": one who disclaimed the desire to enlist disciples and cheerfully anticipated the prospect of his own supersession as American letters, culture, and thought continued to evolve.[11] Here in gist is my present view of the matter: On the one hand, the terms of the Transcendentalist theory of friendship both men espoused militated against the possibility of their ever becoming "friends." On the other hand, in their life-practice they arguably became so, however modern scholars have been predisposed to think otherwise. So my summary answer to the question my title posed is: Yes, Transcendental friendship *is* oxymoronic; but it does not follow from this that its theorists were less than friends in practice. I hope that this précis is both pointed enough to serve as a signpost for the rest of this essay, and tantalizing enough to keep my explication from seeming anticlimactic.

Friendship in Theory

The intertextual links between Thoreau's 1849 disquisition on friendship in *A Week* and Emerson's "Friendship" essay of 1841 are so thick that it is well to start by reminding ourselves that (almost certainly) neither man is the prototypical friend the other has chiefly in mind.

Emerson's essay was published in the wake of that moment in his life when he was most drawn by the idea of "a circle of godlike men and women variously related to each other, and between whom subsists a lofty intelligence." Here Emerson hints at a recurring dream he realized in part and never gave up on trying to realize more fully: to attract a critical mass of like-minded people of both sexes to Concord who would provide all the best pleasures of intellectual stimulation and sociality. The individuals he especially had in mind at this point were probably Margaret Fuller, Caroline Sturgis, Samuel Gray Ward, and Anna Barker—the latter two of whom, to both Emerson's and Fuller's chagrin, proceeded to get married and go their own way.[12] The real-life "ideal" reader that epistolary records suggest Emerson had most pointedly in mind, as the essay was in preparation, was young Samuel Ward—exactly Thoreau's age (fourteen years younger than Emerson), but from a higher socioeconomic class. Ward was a genteel and refined artistic dilettante who later blossomed (or faded, depending on your view) into the "wizard of Wall Street." While putting the finishing touches on "Friendship," Emerson alerted Ward that he hoped to send it to him—as evidently he later did—for "I would gladly provoke a commentary from so illuminated a doctor of the sweet science as yourself. I have written nothing with more pleasure, and the piece is already indebted to you and I wish to swell my obligations" (*CL* 7: 391–392).

As for Thoreau, whose essay on friendship in the "Wednesday" chapter of *A Week* was composed with a decade's experience of Emerson as his primary coach and encourager, the model imagined *reader* may well have been his mentor, whom the text explicitly lauds (as *Walden* studiously does not). But the model for the Friend of Thoreau's essay, to the extent it is based on a particular individual, is almost surely his late elder brother John, who accompanied him on the trip that his book memorializes.

But what I should especially stress about the two discourses is a telling difference in emphasis notwithstanding convergence on a number of points, e.g., that friendship should be conducted on the highest moral plane, that friends should be utterly sincere with each other, that so-called friendship is typically a shabby affair compared with what friendship ought to be, and that friendship of the very highest kind is rare, exceedingly hard to attain, and indeed is obtainable only in fleeting moments. ("Like the immortality of the soul," writes Emerson, it is "too good to be believed" [*CW* 2: 116].) Perhaps the single most revealing indicator of this underlying difference between the essays, however, is their different way of handling the device of the tortuous hypothetical letter to one's would-be friend. The tenor of the two letters differs sharply.

On the one hand, Emerson posits that "every man," "if he should record his true sentiment, . . . might write a letter like this, to each new candidate for his love":

> Dear Friend:—
>
> If I was sure of thee, sure of thy capacity, sure to match my mood with thine, I should never think again of trifles, in relation to thy comings and goings. I am not very wise: my moods are quite attainable: and I respect thy genius: it is to me as yet unfathomed; yet dare I not presume in thee a perfect intelligence of me, and so thou art to me a delicious torment. Thine ever, or never. (*CW* 2: 117)

On the other hand, Thoreau's (rather longer) letter, which he imagines being written by "the true and not despairing Friend," goes like this:

> I never asked thy leave to let me love thee,—I have a right. I love thee not as something private and personal, which is *your own*, but as something universal and worthy of love, *which I have found*. O how I think of you! You are purely good,—you are infinitely good. I can trust you forever. I did not think that humanity was so rich. Give me an opportunity to live.
>
> You are the fact in a fiction,—you are the truth more strange and admirable than fiction. Consent only to be what you are. I alone will never stand in your way.
>
> This is what I would like,—to be as intimate with you as our spirits are intimate,—respecting you as I respect my ideal. Never to profane one another by word or action, even by a thought. Between us, if necessary, let there be no acquaintance.

I have discovered you; how can you be concealed from me? (*AW* 269–270)

It is hard to imagine that when Thoreau resorted to this device of the imaginary letter, he would not have been thinking at least tangentially of Emerson's. Be that as it may, the key point for our present purposes is that amid the common ambience of shilly-shallying tentativeness and anxiety over whether the prospect of friendship will lead to anything, the Emerson persona presents himself as more guarded, wary, and ultimately judgmental about the capacity of the friend to meet his own standards, moods, and needs: Emerson assesses the potential friend as a "candidate for his love." Unlike the Emerson persona, Thoreau's persona meets the Derridean test of friendship as a condition of loving without (yet) knowing whether one is loved in return. The Thoreau persona also of course worries intensely about the problem of a bad fit between temperaments, but by contrast presents himself as the more active seeker *after* friendship, anxious all the while about whether he himself is sufficiently worthy of the friend he seeks. (As the hypothetical letter effuses: "O how I think of you! You are purely good,—you are infinitely good. I can trust you forever.")[13] The Emerson persona imagines himself alternately uplifted and harassed by a series of what might be called threshold-level friendship encounters which raise his hopes, click briefly, but soon weary him. Hence his peremptory verdict toward the close: "I do then with my friends as I do with my books. I would have them where I can find them, but I seldom use them." Even in the case of truly valued friends, "I cannot afford to talk with them and study their visions, lest I lose my own" (*CW* 2: 126).

It is easy to misconstrue such an apparently cold-hearted passage, first because of its deliberate hyperbole, and second because the analogy between book and friend, which sounds so callous to twenty-first-century ears, was a metaphor the nineteenth century took much more reverentially.[14] But the self-protective implication is clear: so-called friends all too easily become nuisances, distracting oneself from one's proper work.

This is precisely the kind of reaction we might expect from one who had become a celebrity mentor, a famous guru. Hawthorne, one of Emerson's successful targets of recruitment to expand the Concord circle—although he resisted being pulled emotionally into Emerson's orbit—captures deliciously in *Mosses from an Old Manse* the local scene of promiscuous importunity. "Never was a poor little country village infested with such a variety of queer" visitants. Emerson's "mind acted upon other minds, of a certain constitution, with wonderful magnetism, and drew many men upon long pilgrimages, to speak with him face to face"; "young visionaries," "gray-headed theorists," people of all sorts who "had lighted on a new thought, or a thought they fancied new, came to Emerson, as the finder of a glittering gem hastens to a lapidary."[15] Small wonder then that we find Emerson lamenting in his journal that "most of the persons whom I see in my own house I see across a gulf" (*JMN* 7: 301).

Fortifying a constitutional resistance to pesky interruptions, which lay behind the gracious face Emerson presented to the world, was the epistemological conviction that (as he puts it in "Experience"): "Never can love make consciousness and ascription equal in force."—"There will be the same gulf between every me and thee, as between the original and the picture" (*CW* 3: 44). This inevitably constrains Emerson's whole theory of Transcendental friendship, making friendship ancillary to self-culture. "I cannot deny it, O friend," his essay laments, "that the vast shadow of the Phenomenal includes thee, also, in its pied and painted immensity,—thee, also, compared with whom all else is shadow." In the last analysis, Emerson cannot conceive the prototypical friend as anything other than a transitional object: "the child of all my foregoing hours, the prophet of those to come, and the harbinger of a greater friend" (*CW* 1:116, 126). As one journal entry sweepingly declares,

> All loves, all friendships, are momentary. *Do you love me?* Means at last *Do you see the same truth I see?* If you do, we are happy together: but when presently one of us passes into the perception of new truth, we are divorced and the force of all nature cannot hold us to each other. (*JMN* 7: 532)

Honorifically regarded, Emerson's position here might be deemed a conscientious secularization of Augustine's view that friendship is ultimately intended to draw one up to God, while at the same time it chastely resists the sentimentalization of divine personhood (the "greater friend" referred to here) so characteristic of the Second Awakening. One finds the latter expressed in the much more untrammeled hymnody of the period, from the evangelical "What a Friend We Have in Jesus" to Theodore Parker's hymn, "O Thou Great Friend."[16]

Thoreau was capable of similar thoughts, when for example after his brother's death he writes a Harvard classmate:

> I do not wish to see John ever again—I mean him who is dead—but that other whom he would have wished to see, or to be, of whom he was the imperfect representative. For we are not what we are, nor do we treat or esteem each other for such, but for what we are capable of being. (*Corr* 62)

Similar, yes—but hardly identical. Despite or perhaps precisely because of the fact that Thoreau led a less social life than Emerson, he was far less likely to assert, as Emerson did to Fuller, that "we do not believe in any body's heart but our own" (*EL* 2: 62). Despite or perhaps precisely because Thoreau was less socially secure, he was much more likely to insist in principle on the importance of reciprocity in friendship, as when he wrote to Emerson that "a noble person confers no such gift as his whole confidence," and that it is "essential to friendship that some vital trust should have been reposed by one in the other" (*Corr* 86). "My Friend," as Thoreau's essay puts it, is "flesh of my flesh, bone of my bone. He is my real brother" (*AW* 284). Indeed, Thoreau never ceased believing that "the price of friendship" must be "the total surrender of yourself" (*J* 9: 479).

And again: despite or precisely because of the fact that Thoreau had fewer close friendships in his life outside of his family circle,[17] Thoreau also seems to have felt a greater need to ruminate about friendship, especially in his early years;[18] and he was commensurately more anguished and brittle both about friends letting him down and about his own failures to measure up to his high ideal. Then comes this:

> What avails it that another loves you, if he does not understand you? Such love is a curse. What sort of companions are they who are presuming always that their silence is more expressive than yours? How foolish, and inconsiderate, and unjust, to conduct as if you were the only party aggrieved! Has not your Friend always equal ground of complaint? (*AW* 278)

This passage beautifully scripts the intense frustration and anger that result from failures of mutuality. It is a stroke of genius here that Thoreau couches his point as an apostrophe, ambiguating the addressee so that it becomes unclear whom he is accusing, the other person or himself. Emerson is equally capable of blaming failed friendship on either self or other, but never does he reach this pitch of indignation about the actual betrayal of ideal possibility.

The difference was doubtless partly temperamental. It may also have been one of different life-stages, if Anthony Rotundo is right in claiming that nineteenth-century male-to-male friendships burned most brightly in adolescence and young manhood.[19] But partly too, the intenser emotions directed at the importance of trust and reciprocity (as well as the scandal of betrayal) that suffuse Thoreau's theory of Friendship were surely perpetuated (if not created) by having been a favored mentee of a caring and initially idealized mentor. Significantly, the closest counterpart in Emerson's own experience was his Aunt Mary Emerson, whose eccentricity and social marginality never made her anything like the shining model Emerson became for the young Thoreau—in a relation which, at the time Thoreau's Friendship essay was published, was on the verge of cooling down into something distinctly less intimate than it had been.

Friendship in Practice

I say "perpetuated (if not created)" because only after *A Week* did Thoreau start to complain vehemently about Emerson's patronizing and two-faced behavior toward him, although on Emerson's side the complaints about Thoreau's rigidity, truculence, and so forth start a couple of years earlier.[20] In any event, it doesn't take much imagination to connect up passages like these which were written some dozen years apart in Thoreau's *Journal:*

> There is no such general critic of men & things [as Emerson]—no such trustworthy & faithful man.— More of the divine realized in him than in any. . . . His personal influence upon young persons greater than any man's. (*PJ* 2: 223; in 1845–1846)
>
> One of the best men I know often offends me by uttering made words—the very best words of course or dinner speeches—most smooth and gracious & fluent repartee . . . a graceful bending—as if I were master Slingsby of promising parts from the University. (*PJ* 4: 209; in 1851)
>
> I say in my thought to my neighbor, who once was my friend, "It is of no use to speak the truth to you, you will not hear it. What, then, shall I say to you?" At the instant that I seem to be saying farewell forever to the one who has been my friend, I find myself unexpectedly near him, and it is our very nearness and dearness to each other that gives depth and significance to that forever. Thus I am a helpless prisoner, and these chains I have no skill to break. While I think I have broken one link, I have been forging another. (*J* 9: 276; in 1857)

Connect these up and they seem to suggest a story of an ideal mentorship which promised to blossom into friendship, but turned sour as a result of the master's failure to recognize a disciple's independent personhood and this disciple's inability to break the emotional tie. Such a story would tend not only to disconfirm the wish-fulfilling hope that mentors and mentees can be friends, but also ironically to bear out the bottom-line inferences of both Emerson's and Thoreau's version of Transcendentalist friendship theory: actuality will always fall sadly short of ideal.

But is all this really true? Certainly the Emerson-Thoreau relation cannot be said to attain the Ciceronian standard of perfect friendship—"complete agreement in policy, in pursuits, and in opinions" by two parties, each of whom is "so fortified by virtue and wisdom" as not to *need* the other's support to maintain their own self-sufficiency. Nor does it follow Montaigne's prescription for friendship *par excellence,* which stands at the opposite pole of classical friendship theory—two "souls" that "mingle and blend with each other so completely that they efface the seam that joined them, and cannot find it again."[21] But we would do well to hesitate before leaping from this doubly negative assessment to a negative verdict on the case in point. For one thing, as Kant commonsensically remarks in *The Metaphysics of Morals,* "friendship thought as attainable in its purity or completeness . . . is the hobby horse of writers of romances." Practically speaking, he contends, "friendship is only an idea." It is "unattainable in practice, although striving for friendship . . . is a duty set by reason, and no ordinary duty but an honorable one."[22] On this less demanding view of friendship ethics, it starts to look desirable as well as merely possible to discount many of the complaints both Emerson and Thoreau made about each other's failings and the failure of their relationship to sustain itself on the level posited by classical friendship theory, from Aristotle to themselves. As Kant suggests, the friend posited by Transcendentalist theory is a fictive figure—and the theorist knows this perfectly well and in his serener moments accepts the ideal as no more than tenuously connected to life as it is experienced. As Thoreau, for example, remarks, "I have an ideal friend in whose place actual persons stand for a season" (*PJ* 3: 98). Or Emerson, in his early journal: "Friendship is something very delicious to my understanding. Yet the friends that occupy my thoughts are not men but certain phantoms clothed in the form & fact & apparel of men by whom they were suggested & to whom they bear a resemblance" (*JMN* 3: 25).

On the downside, such musings might be taken as compensatory meditations for lonely misfits, as when Thoreau confesses to his journal: "Actually I have no friend I am very distant from all actual persons—and yet my experience of friendship is so real and engrossing that I sometimes find myself speaking aloud to the friend I [*sic*]" (*PJ* 3: 58). On the upside, however, they might be taken as testimonials to the felt importance of an ethic that the ostensibly lonely fantast probably lived out in practice with better success than his theoretical musings imply. Such was precisely the view of Thoreau's character held by his friend and early biographer Ellery Channing: "The living, actual friendship and affection which makes time a reality, no one knew better," he insists. Thoreau's discourse on Friendship in *A Week* Channing freakishly describes as a "romancing with his subject playing a strain on his theorbo like the bobolink." In fact, Thoreau stood by those who cared for him "without the slightest abatement, not veering as a weathercock with each shift of a friend's fortune, or like those who bury their early friendships in order to gain room for fresh corpses."[23] Emerson's son Edward, who in early boyhood thought of Thoreau as a second father, even claimed that Thoreau exemplified his own "noble ideal."[24] As to the question of the friendship between his father and Thoreau, Edward does not so much argue the point as take it as a given, despite any bickering between them. So too, albeit in a backhanded way, does the remark I recently quoted from Thoreau's journal about their "nearness and dearness to each other," notwithstanding the ball-and-chain aspect of this tie which he deplores. Emerson for his part seems clearly to have remained very fond of Thoreau, despite various consternations and disappointments; and to have been at least as faithfully committed to Thoreau as Thoreau was to him, notwithstanding Thoreau's prickliness as they grew apart and Emerson's habitual self-protective reserve. One of the last textual tokens of this from Thoreau's lifetime was an 1861 letter Emerson gave Thoreau to take with him on his unsuccessful recuperative journey to the Midwest. A kind of omnibus introduction to Emerson's contacts there, the letter commends Thoreau as "dear and valued by me and all good Americans" (*Corr* 616). By no coincidence, Emerson strikes much the same note at the end of his essay on Thoreau—"his soul was made for the noblest society," and "the country knows not yet, not in the least part, how great a son it has lost" (*CE* 10: 484–485).

This essay has often been chastised, with some justice, as perversely astringent, as evidence of their late-life estrangement, and in particular for its failure to recognize the excellence of Thoreau's best writing, for which a generation or two later he would be canonized.[25] Yet I think you are driven to different conclusions if you read Emerson's address not so much as an intended piece of literary criticism (which it certainly was not); nor even as a document in the actual history of their friendship (much more telling indices of this are the affectionate, posthumous remembrance of Thoreau in Emerson's journal, and his lifelong attempts to promote and defend Thoreau's work); but rather as a document in the same idealizing vein as Emerson's portraits of historic personages in *Representative Men,* and of the fictive friends of Transcendentalist friendship theory. In these texts, as in the essay on "Thoreau," the human gets deliberately assessed in terms of the highest values (as Emerson sees them anyhow) that he or she sought to attain. In Thoreau's case, from Emerson's perspective, these boiled down to such qualities as steadfastness, purity of purpose, and self-command.

For some this seemed—and continues to seem—a chilly package. From Emerson's standpoint, however, it more likely seemed not only to be an idealized portrait of the persona Thoreau had presented to him (to some extent always, but especially since they had grown apart), but also to depict an ideal (as Emerson's journal shows) of compelling if not altogether irresistible personal appeal. With one side of his mind, though not with his whole being, Emerson surely envied the exemplary figure of constancy and self-command he conjures up in "Thoreau."

In his early journal, not long after Emerson had adopted him as a favored mentee, Thoreau declares that "the world has never learned what men can build each other up to be—when both master and pupil work in love" (*PJ* 1: 257). Although love was later tinged with disappointment, not just for Thoreau but for them both, we now see how their long-term symbiosis also helped catalyze at least a more lasting literary result and historical impact than either of them would have thought to claim in life. Meanwhile, the record of their quarter-century-long interpersonal tie—insofar as the wit and evidence exist to read it—bears out the truth of Nietzsche's retort to the paradoxical aphorism attributed to Aristotle on the impossibility of actualizing friendship:[26]

> Only reflect to yourself how various are the feelings, how divided the opinions, even among your closest acquaintances . . . how manifold are the occasions for misunderstanding, for hostility and rupture. . . . When one realizes this, and realizes in addition that all the opinions of one's fellow men . . . are just as necessary and unaccountable as their actions; . . . perhaps one will then get free of that bitterness of feeling with which the sage cried: "Friends, there are no friends!" One will, rather, avow to oneself: yes, there are friends, but it is error and deception regarding yourself that led them to you; and they must have learned how to keep silent in order to remain your friend; for such human relationships almost always depend upon the fact that two or three things are never said or even so much as touched upon. . . . Through knowing ourselves, and regarding our own nature as a moving sphere of moods and opinions, and thus learning to despise ourselves a little, we restore our proper equilibrium with others.

This impresses me as a shrewd and plausible summation of how Emerson and Thoreau came to relate to each other, including what they seem *not* to have said; of both the respectful and the sometimes not-so-respectful silence, distance, and mutual reserve into which they settled in later years. And it is fitting that this fortuitous exegesis should come from an offbeat philosopher who thought of Emerson as a friend though he only knew him through his texts—and for a number of the very reasons that drew Emerson and Thoreau to each other.

Notes

The epigraph is from Thoreau, *PJ* 2: 87.

1. Although Emerson, intriguingly, chides his contemporaries for the opposite fault in his lectures on the New England character—he sees a "voracity for excitement," "rash and sanguine to the verge of insanity" (*LL* 1: 50). This reprimand, however, refers specifically to the vigor of economic-industrial capitalism in which New England had taken the early lead, and may be designed as a wry appeal to a more traditional, ingrained skepticism about the excess that Emerson also wants to celebrate at least in part.

2. *JMN* 11: 482–483 lists thirty-one friends of Fuller, including Nathaniel Hawthorne among others, but (modestly) excludes Emerson himself.

3. Grant A. Wacker, remembrance offered at "A Service Celebrating the Life of William Robert Hutchison," 28 April 2006, Memorial Church, Harvard University.

4. Aristotle 1962, 219, 221 (1156a–57a).

5. Montaigne 1958, 136, 138.

6. In Weil's "Forms of the Implicit Love of God: Friendship"; see Weil 1951, 204.

7. In Blake's *The Marriage of Heaven and Hell,* plate 20; see Blake 1970, 41.

8. Derrida 1997, 8; see also 63–64, 173, 233 *et pass.*

9. Nietzsche 1986, 274 (aphorism 2: 241).

10. See especially Charles Capper's discussion of the Fuller-Emerson relation in *Margaret Fuller: An American Romantic Life. The Public Years* (2007).

11. Buell 2003, 288–334; see 297–312 for discussion of the Emerson-Thoreau relation specifically.

12. Caleb Crain, *American Sympathy: Men, Friendship, and Literature in the New Nation* (2001), provides a consummately intricate reading of this *ménage à quatre,* especially notable for its emphasis on the complicated erotics of friendship—both heteroerotic and homoerotic—that seems to have entered into both Emerson's and Fuller's attraction to each of the three younger persons, all of whom were (at that time) physically very attractive as well as cultivated and elegant in manner.

13. Another, perhaps related, divergence is Emerson's tendency to presume a plurality of friends as against Thoreau's tendency to focus on *the* ideal friend.

14. Booth 1988, 169–224.

15. In "The Old Manse"; see Hawthorne 1972, 31, 30.

16. For Augustine on friendship, see his *Confessions* 4.4–5 (Augustine 1991, 57–58); and see Wadell 1989, 97–104.

17. Harmon Smith (1999, 98) claims that Thoreau had only three adult male intimates: his brother John, Emerson, and Ellery Channing.

18. The contrast between Thoreau's and Emerson's early journals is striking in this

regard, Thoreau's containing several poetic paeans to friendship versus Emerson commenting much more sparsely and stoically on the subject.

19. E. Anthony Rotundo, "Romantic Friendship: Male Intimacy and Middle-Class Youth in the Northern United States, 1800–1900" (1989).

20. Harmon Smith (1999, 109) dates Emerson's disenchantment with Thoreau to the summer of 1847: "T. sometimes appears only as a gen d'arme good to knock down a cockney with, but without that power to cheer & establish, which makes the value of a friend" (*JMN* 10: 106–107). This was before the European trip, often noted as a turning point in reshaping Emerson into what Thoreau took to be a mannered grandee. He writes in 1852: "Emerson is too grand for me. He belongs to the nobility & wears their cloak and manners. . . . I am a commoner" (*PJ* 4: 310). For a more intensive analysis of Thoreau's alienation from Emerson, see Robert Sattelmeyer's indispensable "'When He Became My Enemy': Emerson and Thoreau, 1848–1849" (1989).

21. Cicero 1923, 125, 141; Montaigne 1958, 139.

22. Kant 1996, 585.

23. Channing 1966, 30–32.

24. Emerson 1917, 58; Edward Emerson also cites testimonials of various other local citizens (1917, 77–78), as well as family memories.

25. The best summation of complications of the Emerson-Thoreau relationship from Thoreau's point of view is Robert Sattelmeyer, "Thoreau and Emerson" (1995).

26. Nietzsche 1986, 148 (aphorism 1: 376). Derrida's *The Politics of Friendship* is a kind of extended exegesis/commentary on Aristotle's (apocryphal?) aphorism: see Derrida 1997, 53–55, 177, 222–224, 235–236, 251, 253, 299–300.

TWO

Forgiving the Giver: Emerson, Carlyle, Thoreau

BARBARA PACKER

In book four of *Paradise Lost,* Satan lights upon Mount Niphates and delivers a soliloquy absolving God of all responsibility for the war in Heaven and the bad angels' fall. What he now calls "pride and worse ambition" has prompted his rebellion against a generous Deity:

> What could be less than to afford him praise,
> The easiest recompense, and pay him thanks,
> How due! Yet all his good proved ill in me,
> And wrought but malice: lifted up so high
> I sdeigned subjection, and thought one step higher
> Would set me highest, and in a moment quit
> The debt immense of endless gratitude,
> So burdensome still paying, still to owe.[1]

Satan's position as the highest among the angels was a perennial temptation to rebellion, and God's very generosity came to seem an intolerable burden because it could never be repaid. Satan's speech is full of the language of debt and the resentment it generates: *pay, quit, debt, immense, burdensome, owe.* Because of the disproportion between God's omnipotence and any finite consciousness, debts of gratitude toward him can leave worshippers despairing, resentful, and mutinous. A like sequence of emotions can be observed among human beneficiaries, as Emerson observed in his 1844 essay "Gifts":

> The law of benefits is a difficult channel, which requires careful sailing, or rude boats. It is not the office of a man to receive gifts. How dare you give them? We wish to be self-sustained. We do not quite forgive a giver. The hand that feeds us is in some danger of being bitten. (*CW* 3: 94)

Emerson had clearly looked at gratitude from both sides: that of the bestower trying to steer his craft of gratitude between or over the hidden rocks of the recipient's potential resentment, but also that of the recipient who feels the gift to be demeaning.

Friendship among Transcendentalists involved the emotions of sympathy, fearlessness, and loyalty; it also naturally involved the giving and receiving of gifts. Who gave these gifts? Who received them? What motives prompted the act, and what effect did the exchange have upon the relationship between giver and receiver? A gift can be anything exchanged—an object, such as a book; an offer of financial assistance or employment; the temporary use of something belonging to the giver, such as a room or a piece of land; help with reading, editing, or finding a publisher for a manuscript. Gifts can also be intangible—ideas, inspiration, energy, encouragement, devotion, worship, love. In many traditional societies gift giving is an expected part of social life and is highly ritualized; even among the Transcendentalists the bestowal of gifts could sometimes assume the predictability of ritual. Edward Waldo Emerson recalled that his father always wrote poems to accompany the gifts he gave on New Year's Day to members of his family.[2]

Most gifts, however, possess the element of spontaneity and surprise. The giver would say that he wishes nothing in return for his generosity. For the recipient the situation is more complicated. Gratitude for gifts seems only natural. Yet gratitude is an unstable emotion, tending to dissolve into resentment. The emotions precipitated by gift exchanges can be explosive and their consequences long-lasting. Sometimes the friendship returns after a period of turbulence to the *status quo ante.* At other times the break is permanent, as between Satan and God in Milton. The relationship among generous American Transcendentalists and the transatlantic writer who inspired them both, Thomas Carlyle, allows us to study what happens when friendships founded upon sympathy are subjected to the corrosive effects of generosity and material help.

When Ralph Waldo Emerson stumbled upon essays and reviews in his favorite British periodicals in the late 1820s that were remarkable for their unusual style as much as content, his sense of gratitude to their anonymous author was immediate.[3] An essay entitled "Signs of the Times" confirmed Emerson's own sense that empirical philosophy and hunger for wealth had combined to drive nobility from the world. Still, the anonymous author assured him that "our spiritual maladies are but of Opinion; we are but fettered by chains of our own forging, and which ourselves also can rend asunder"

(*WTC* 27: 80). No doubt the present age is one of faithlessness and despair. Nevertheless, in "Characteristics" there is the hopeful prophecy:

> Deep and sad as is our feeling that we stand yet in the bodeful Night; equally deep, indestructible is our assurance that the Morning also will not fail. Nay, already as we look round, streaks of a dayspring are in the east: it is dawning; when the time shall be fulfilled, it will be day. (*WTC* 28: 37)

In 1832 Emerson began his *Wanderjahr* after resigning his pastorate at Boston's Second Church. Poor health impelled him to travel; curiosity about the world of contemporary letters led him to seek out the authors whose works had attracted him. Naturally, he hoped to meet the "Germanick new-light writer" whose essays had "cheered & instructed" (*JMN* 4:45)[4] him, although he had learned Carlyle's name from a visiting Englishman only two months before he sailed from Boston.[5] At this point he may have considered himself a grateful disciple, but his attitude toward Carlyle already showed signs of becoming proprietary.

> If Carlyle knew what an interest I have in his persistent Goodness, would it not be worth one effort more, one prayer, one meditation? But will he resist the Deluge of bad example in England? One manifestation of goodness in a noble soul brings him in debt to all the beholders that he shall not betray their love & trust which he has awakened.

And he added a maxim he had found in the *Imaginary Conversations:* "'Praise,' said Landor, 'Keeps men good'" (*JMN* 4: 52–53).[6]

In Rome, Emerson was lucky enough to meet a young French socialist, Gustave d'Eichthal, who gave him a letter of introduction to John Stuart Mill in London, asking him to direct the American visitor to Carlyle. He gave Emerson another letter to Carlyle himself. Mill told Emerson that Carlyle was in Scotland and wrote to Carlyle telling him to expect a visitor—though not, in his opinion, a very promising one (*CEC* 9–11). Emerson made his way to Edinburgh and then to Craigenputtock, the isolated farmhouse southwest of Glasgow where Carlyle and his wife Jane lived.[7] The breathless journal entry Emerson wrote after he left after his overnight visit there shows how hard it was for even an acolyte to rescue coherent sentences from the torrent of Carlyle's speech. "Coleridge, Allan Cunningham; Hazlitt, Gigman; Walter Scott, Sheriff of Selkirk. *One idea.* 'W. Wordsworth wishes to see W. Scott.' Mud magazine. Sand magazine [.] grave of the last sixpence" (*JMN* 4: 220). In *English Traits* (1854) Emerson would expand upon this telegraphic entry when he recalled the conversation. "He had names of his own for all the matters familiar to his discourse. 'Blackwood's' was the 'sand magazine': 'Fraser's' nearer approach to possibility of life was the 'mud magazine'; a piece of road nearby that marked some failed enterprise was 'the grave of the last sixpence'" (*CW* 5: 7–8). Such "streaming humor, which floated every thing he looked upon" (*CW* 5: 8), seemed to Emerson the natural efflorescence of the energy that coursed through "The State of German Literature" or "Signs of the Times" or "Characteristics."

He had been so eager to read the new book that Carlyle was planning to publish serially in *Fraser's Magazine*—namely, *Sartor Resartus*—that he wrote to Fraser and asked that he send the magazine to him in America. When the first installment arrived he was dismayed. What had happened to Carlyle's frankness and bold address? He wrote to Carlyle urging him to abandon his "grotesque teutonic apocalyptic strain" for a lucid economical one:

> You are dispensing that which is rarest, namely, the simplest truths—truths which lie next to Consciousness & which only the Platos & Goethes perceive. I look for the hour with impatience when the vehicle will be worthy of the spirit when the word will be as simple & so resistless as the thought, & in short when your words will be one with things. (*CEC* 99)

We see in this letter the outlines of a pattern that would later be repeated in the Emerson-Thoreau relationship. The disciple receives inspiration from his mentor and responds at first with heartfelt gratitude. Along with gratitude comes a sense of entitlement. The disciple believes that he now has a clearer sense of the mentor's truest self than the mentor does, and the disciple proceeds to chastise him for wavering from it.

Carlyle took the criticism good-naturedly: "With regard to the style and so forth, what you call your 'saucy' objections are not only most intelligible to me, but welcome" (*CEC* 103).[8] And he thanked Emerson warmly for the gifts he had sent—a copy of Sampson Reed's *Observations on the Growth of the Mind* and a volume of Daniel Webster's speeches:

> Some two weeks ago I received your kind gift from Fraser. To say that it was welcome would be saying little: is it not as a voice of affectionate remembrance, coming from beyond Ocean waters, first decisively announcing for me that a whole New Continent *exists,* that I too have part and lot there!

And in a letter of 12 August 1834, Carlyle quoted from *Wilhelm Meister:* "Not till we can think that here and there one is thinking of us, one is loving us, does this waste Earth become a peopled Garden" (*CEC* 101). He sent four copies of a "stitched Pamphlet" made up of the complete *Sartor Re-*

sartus installments from *Fraser's Magazine,* and urged Emerson to keep one and find fit readers for the other three.

The small gift of four pamphlets was eventually to yield Carlyle very large returns, though at first it occasioned only chagrin for both parties. Emerson gave one of the pamphlets to the woman who would soon become his second wife, Lydia Jackson of Plymouth. She showed her copy to a young Harvard graduate, a Carlyle enthusiast named Le Baron Russell. Russell wanted his own copy of *Sartor* so much that he consulted the Boston publisher James Munroe about publishing the work in book form, offering to gather subscriptions. When he easily gathered one hundred fifty subscriptions Monroe decided to bring the book out as a commercial venture in an edition of five hundred copies. By the time Emerson got wind of Russell's plan it was too late to forestall his act of what Slater calls "benevolent piracy" (*CEC* 17): he had to content himself with writing a few anonymous paragraphs as a preface to the book.

By 8 April 1836, Emerson was able to send Carlyle a copy of Monroe's edition of *Sartor Resartus,* its first appearance in book form anywhere in the world. He added to the packet a copy of William Ellery Channing's recent booklet *Slavery* (1835), as a gift from its author.[9] Unfortunately the packet had been mailed by mistake at the letter rate; when it arrived in England, Carlyle was asked to pay the hefty sum of five pounds eighteen shillings for its delivery. Understandably, he refused. He sent John Stuart Mill a comic account of the affair.

> The foreign Packet charged £5..18..0 presented itself the day after your Note. By a Letter that come along with it, I learned that it was—what think you? A pamphlet of Dr Channing's on Slavery (or some such thing), and the American edition of *Teufelsdröckh!* Instantaneous rejection to the dead letter office was inevitable. (*LTJWC* 8: 350)

The next day his brother tried to bargain the postal authorities down. They were willing to let him have the packet for ten shillings, but Carlyle authorized him to offer no more than three-and-six. "So *Teuflk* lies dormant, very singularly again, waiting his new destinies; never to be liberated by *me.* I cannot but laugh at the whole matter, it looks so confused and absurd."[10] Nevertheless some bargain must have been struck by 1 June, for by then Carlyle had the book in his hands. He noted in his journal: "Edition of Teufelsdröckh, very prettily printed, from Boston.... How curious, almost pathetic! But one need not dwell on it" (*LTJWC* 8: 350 n. 3).

Emerson was embarrassed to learn of the trouble his gift had caused, particularly since the edition itself had been something of an accident and had earned Carlyle no royalties. When Carlyle sent him a copy of *The French Revolution* Emerson sought ways of making amends, first by importing finished copies to sell, then by arranging an American edition of the book for his friend's benefit. As he explained it in a letter to his childhood friend William Henry Furness:

> Carlyle sent me sometime since a copy of his History. I dully plotted how to get some twenty copies over, that he might be benefitted, but two days ago somebody [said] you might have made \$500 for the man out of Sartor. So today I went to Boston to see the booksellers & have told them maugre James Monroe's Proposals that I am going to publish this book for the Author's benefit and they may offer me the best terms they will. (27 April 1837)

Little & Co. brought out their edition of *The French Revolution* on 25 December 1837. On 30 July 1838 Emerson was able to send Carlyle the first installment of the edition's profits—a bill of exchange for 50 pounds sterling (242 American dollars). Needless to say, this transatlantic gift was considerably more welcome to Carlyle than the postage-due packet containing *Sartor* and Channing's antislavery tract. In September 1838, he wrote in sincere gratitude: "We ought to say, May the Heavens give us thankful hearts! For in truth there are blessings which do, like sun-gleams in wild weather, make this rough life beautiful with rainbows here and there" (*CEC* 193). Thereafter Emerson took upon himself the task of becoming Carlyle's unpaid literary agent in the new world. This service eventually netted Carlyle over six hundred and fifty pounds—a remarkable sum in an age when most British authors had their works pirated in the United States.[11]

Before 1837 the flow of benefits across the Atlantic had been strictly one-way. Emerson's decision to become Carlyle's American agent meant that tangible thanks were returning from America to England. There were other motives at play, however, as Emerson's own account of his sudden conversion to shrewdness makes clear. Like a rustic who has suddenly learned to mind the main chance, this ex-pastor and lyceum lecturer found himself in Boston driving a hard bargain with several booksellers to secure the best terms for his friend's latest work. To his surprise he discovered that he rather enjoyed the business dealings and was good at them. And he clearly also enjoyed the shift in power that his new role created. On 2 November 1837 he wrote to Carlyle describing the bargain he has made to print *The French Revolution.* After estimating the profits he hopes to realize he writes: "Then, if so good a book can have a tolerable sale . . . I shall sustain with great glee the new relation of being your banker and attorney" (*CEC* 170). In another letter (9 February 1838), speaking of the profits Carlyle can expect to realize on each copy of *The French Revolution* sold, he promises: "you may be assured I shall on this occasion summon to the bargain all the Yankee in my constitution & multiply & divide like a lion" (*CEC* 176). Power has shifted from London to Concord; Emerson is now a benefactor rather than a mere disciple. Any discomfort that Carlyle may have felt with this reversal was dissipated by periodic infusions of dollars which nicely converted into pounds sterling.

This lucrative relationship came to an end shortly after Emerson made his second visit to England, in 1847–1848. Although Emerson preferred to stay in hotels rather than in private houses when he was on a lecture tour, Carlyle insisted upon inviting his American benefactor to his residence at Cheyne Row. The visit was not a success. Carlyle quickly became impatient with his guest's hunger for conversation; his wife Jane looked forward to her husband's inevitable explosion of wrath. Emerson left no written account of the blowup, but he did describe it a short time later to George Searle Phillips, the director of the Mechanics' Institution at Huddersfield, who had invited him to lecture there:

> Carlyle, he said, had grown impatient of opposition, especially when talking of Cromwell. I differed from him, he added, in his estimate of Cromwell's character, & he rose like a great Norse giant from his chair—and, drawing a line with his finger across the table, said, with terrible fierceness: Then, sir, there is a line of separation between you and me as wide as that, & as deep as the pit.[12]

After leaving Carlyle's house Emerson largely avoided him during his return visits to London, though they did take a trip to Stonehenge together in July 1848, when the thought of Emerson's imminent departure helped Carlyle endure his presence with nothing worse than irritation. Before they parted he gave Emerson his own copy of Wood's *Athenae Oxoniensis,* a seventeenth-century biographical dictionary of noted Oxford graduates. Emerson reported that reading it gave him a "lotophagous pleasure" (*CEC* 504). By December Carlyle even expressed something like regret for his behavior when Emerson was his guest. He wrote that he and Jane had admired "your pacific virtues, of gentle and noble tolerance, often sorely tried in this place! Forgive my ferocities." Of course he also had requests to make. He wanted Emerson's help with a financial transaction involving a United States bank, and he forwarded a special request from his wife concerning the Indian meal they were trying to use as a substitute for potatoes, which the potato blight had rendered largely unobtainable. Jane Carlyle wanted to know how to get the bitter or musty taste out of Indian meal; no cooking method they tried seemed to work (*CEC* 443–445). After researching the matter and discovering that corn shipped to England usually tasted bitter because it was kiln-dried at a very high temperature to retard spoilage, Emerson decided to try the experiment of sending them a barrel of his own naturally dried corn by steamship instead of sailing ship, so that kiln-drying would not be necessary. He promised Carlyle that Lidian would send her own recipes "for johnny-cake, mush, and hominy" (*CEC* 450).[13] In the early months of 1849 a barrel full of dried Indian corn and a small bag of ground cornmeal reached Cheyne Row. The Carlyles tried the cornmeal at once and were delighted with it. Thomas wrote to say that the American cornmeal formed "a new epoch for us all in the Maize department: we find the grain *sweet,* among the sweetest, with a touch even of the taste of *nuts* in it; and profess with contrition that properly we have never tasted Indian Corn before" (*CEC* 451). Carlyle hastened to share his newfound appreciation of American maize with his countrymen in an article on "Indian Meal" for the May 1849 number of *Fraser's.*[14] Englishmen disdained maize; Carlyle strove to set them right and in so doing find an alternate source of food for the poor during the potato blight. As he told Emerson:

> There is no doubt to me, now that I taste the real grain, but all Europe will henceforth have to relie [*sic*] more and more upon your western vallies and this article. How beautiful to think of lean tough Yankee settlers, tough as gutta-percha, with most *occult* unsubduable fire in their belly, steering over the Western Mountains, to annihilate the jungle, and bring bacon and corn out of it for the Posterity of Adam! (*CEC* 452)

Not all gifts arriving from America that year would prove so easily digestible as Emerson's cornmeal. On the last day of June 1849, Carlyle left London to make his own tour of famine-ridden Ireland in hopes of looking "face to face upon the ruin and wretchedness that is prevalent there." Ireland's ruin seemed to him the natural outcome of the policies the British government had been pursuing there. It was a test case of all that was wrong with the modern world, and particularly with laissez-faire economics. As he explained in a letter to Lord Clarendon: "Ireland with its raging controversies and hungry necessities already painfully represents itself to me as a country scourged by angry gods,—painful to see and hear. Yet it demands to be seen and heard; is one of the notablest spots in the whole world just now" (*LTJWC* 24: 104). As he traveled round the island, "tattered wretchedness" confronted him everywhere; people looked like walking skeletons, beggars pleaded "*Lave* a penny for the love of God!" (*LTJWC* 24: 113). He took some unlikely reading matter with him on this trip: Henry David Thoreau's first book, *A Week on the Concord and Merrimack Rivers,* published in Boston on 30 May 1849 by James Munroe & Co. The editor of Thoreau's book, Carl Hovde, notes that Emerson helped Thoreau send out seventy-five copies of *Week* to potential reviewers and to literary figures in England and America. When Carlyle wrote to Emerson on 13 August 1849 to thank him for a second barrel of Indian corn (which this time included a sack of "popped corn"), he appended a postcript: "I got Thoreau's Book; and meant well to read it, but have not yet succeeded, tho' it went with me thro' all Ireland: tell him so, please. Too Jean-Paulish, I found it hitherto" (*CEC* 457).[15] He apparently tried again, for on 18 September he wrote letters to his brother John and wife Jane mentioning the book, which he called a "*galimathias*" (a mixture, a medley) and "a very fantastic yet not quite worthless Book" (*LTJWC* 24: 239, 241).

It's easy to see why Thoreau wanted to send his book to a man who had been his model and inspiration. He lectured on Carlyle at the Concord Lyceum on 4 February 1846, seven months after he had moved to Walden Pond. The next year *Graham's American Magazine* published a two-part article by Thoreau entitled "Thomas Carlyle and His Works."[16] Thoreau's passionate tribute makes clear what Carlyle's work meant to him at the beginning of his own independent career as a writer (*EE* 405). To read Carlyle's works with real understanding, he argues, requires sorest need: "Only he who has had the good fortune to read them in the nick of time, in the most perceptive and recipient season of life, can give any account of them." What chiefly attracts Thoreau to Carlyle is his uncanny ability to suffuse written language with the energy of speech. That emphasis was already apparent in the recorded title of Thoreau's 1846 lecture for the Concord Lyceum, "Writings & style of Thomas Carlysle" (*EE* 406):

> His style is eminently colloquial—and no wonder it is strange to meet with in a book. It is not literary or classical; it has not the music of poetry, nor the pomp of philosophy, but the rhythms and cadences of conversation endlessly repeated. It resounds with emphatic, natural, lively, stirring tones, muttering, rattling, exploding, like shells and shot, and with like execution. (*EE* 226)

Emerson liked the style of Carlyle's early essays. Thoreau argues instead that his later style is "the richest prose style we know of" and that it constitutes his distinct contribution to English literature. "Posterity will have reason to thank him for emancipating the language, in some measure, from the fetters which a merely conservative, aimless, and pedantic literary class had imposed upon it, and setting it an example of greater freedom and naturalness" (*EE* 232–233).

Carlyle was pleased to receive this intelligent tribute, so different from the gush of some American admirers, and told Emerson how much pleasure he had gotten from the "admiring greathearted manner" of Thoreau's piece. "In plain prose, I like Mr. Thoreau very well; and hope yet to hear good and better news of him:—only let him not 'turn to foolishness'; which seems to me to be terribly easy, at present, both in New England and Old!" By a "turn to foolishness" Carlyle appears to mean a lapse into the idiom of the sentimental reformer whose cant perverts language and sends society "staggering down to Gehenna" (*CEC* 422).[17] *A Week on the Concord and Merrimack Rivers* is certainly free of cant and shows little interest in reform, sentimental or otherwise. But its slowly eddying prose must have seemed disappointing after the vigor of Thoreau's critical essay. It must have formed an odd contrast to the ruined landscape and desperate beggars Carlyle could see from the windows of his Irish trains. In the end even gratitude for Thoreau's earlier tribute could not propel Carlyle through the *Week*'s seven days.

He was not alone in finding *A Week on the Concord and Merrimack Rivers* hard to read. In 1849 Thoreau wrote bitterly in his journal about an unnamed "friend" who praised his book while it was being written and criticized it now that it was finished.

> The fruit of partiality is enmity.
>
> I had a friend, I wrote a book, I asked my friend's criticism, I never got but praise for what was good in it;—my friend became estranged from me and then I got blame for all that was bad, & so I got at last the criticism which I wanted. (*PJ* 3: 18)[18]

"Partiality" has two related meanings, one more obviously pejorative than the other. The word can refer to an unfair favoring of one side in a dispute; in can also refer to an innocent fondness for a particular person or thing. Emerson had certainly been partial to Thoreau in the years when he encouraged the younger man's writing. He invited Thoreau to live in his house in the early 1840s; he published Thoreau's early essays and poems in

The Dial. Thoreau was grateful for these benefactions and for Emerson's interest in him and yet he felt, like Milton's Satan, that his debt was greater than he could repay. In "The Departure," which John Ronan calls "the most revealing commentary" on Thoreau's happy early months in the Emerson house in 1843 and his increasingly anxious stay there, a "stranger" at first finds welcome in a strange landscape:

> In this roadstead I have ridden
> In this covert I have hidden
> Friendly thoughts were cliffs to me
> And I hid beneath their lea.

His hosts treat him with Oriental hospitality; they "Shook the olive, stripped the vine / And expressed the strengthening wine." Even when the stranger begins to feel that he has outstayed his welcome he lingers in hopes of repaying their kindness, but his lingering only increases his guilt:

> And still the more the stranger waited
> The less his argosy was freighted,
> And still the more he stayed
> The less his debt was paid.[19]

In 1849, after Emerson had for many years tried without success to find a publisher for *A Week on the Concord and Merrimack Rivers* and had finally urged Thoreau to publish it at his own risk, Thoreau began to see another side of obligation. He now learned that when a protégé does not satisfy the expectations of his mentor, partiality can turn to subtle enmity.[20]

Emerson himself would soon discover what it felt like to get a blow from a friend—this time the same friend who had greeted his English visit with hostility. When Carlyle wrote to thank Emerson for his gifts of Indian corn, he also reported on his recent Irish trip. The sight of Ireland's misery and England's inability to relieve it had convinced him that freedom for the masses was a foolish dream. He had a novel suggestion to his Irish hosts about what to do with the masses of starving Irishmen:

> "*Blacklead* those 2 million idle beggars," I sometimes advised, "and sell them to Brazil as Niggers,—perhaps Parliament, on sweet constraint, will allow you to advance them to be Niggers!——In fact, the Emancipation Societies should send over a deputation or two to look at these immortal Irish 'Free men,' the *ne-plus-ultra* of their class: it would perhaps moderate the windpipe of much eloquence one hears on that subject!" (*CEC* 456)

Carlyle could hardly have forgotten that some of the eloquence on the subject of emancipation had been Emerson's. In 1844 Emerson had sent him, with some diffidence, his "Address Delivered in Concord on the Anniversary of the Emancipation of the Negroes in the British West Indies, August 1, 1844." Carlyle acknowledged its receipt with the curtest of replies: "I have read your Slavery Address" (*CEC* 367).[21] In truth, even Emerson's restrained rejoicing over the emancipation of West Indian slaves seemed silly to Carlyle. He was now sure that what the mass of men needed was not freedom but discipline, discipline imposed by the superior few upon the miserable millions. Carlyle wrote to an English correspondent in April 1849 that he considered Irish paupers to be "reduced to the condition of *slaves,* of Servants vitally needing some Master wiser than they" (*LTJWC* 24: 27). The British who had freed the West Indian slaves were going in exactly the wrong direction, turning productive slaves into lazy paupers. Sugar production had dropped dramatically. The planters and refinery owners were without workmen, the islands were sinking into economic ruin, and the British laborer had to pay outrageous prices for sugar to sweeten his tea. That, at any rate, was the contention advanced by the notorious article Carlyle published in the December 1849 issue of *Fraser's Magazine:* "Occasional Discourse on the Negro Question."

Emerson was by this time used to Carlyle's ranting, and if he took the "Occasional Discourse" as a squib against his "Emancipation in the British West Indies" he does not appear to have said so. In any case his attention was preoccupied during the spring of 1850 by events taking place in the United States. The conflict set off by California's application to join the Union as a free state paralyzed the Congress and had southern firebrands threatening secession. Yet there were signs of hope in the country as well. That the desperados of the California goldfields had drawn up a state constitution outlawing slavery was itself a heartening development; even more surprising was President Zachary Taylor's support of their application for admission to the Union. Taylor, though a southerner, a Mexican War hero, and a slaveholder, argued for California's right to enter the Union as a free state. So far from agreeing with Carlyle that the world was sunk in misery from which only dictatorship could rescue it, Emerson saw hopeful signs that the moral law was reasserting itself in history. Carlyle's recent writings seemed to him merely an example of wonderful rhetorical skill deployed for unworthy purposes. Emerson wrote in his journal: "'Tis curious, the magnificence of his genius, & the poverty of his aims. He draws his weapons from the skies, to fight the cause of some wretched English property or monopoly or prejudice or whim" (*JMN* 11: 227).[22]

Carlyle's "Occasional Discourse" was bad enough, but there was worse to come. Early in 1850 he sent Emerson "The Present Time," the first of his *Latter-Day Pamphlets.* Although the pamphlet contained an approving allusion to Emerson in a discussion of the French revolutionary leader Lamartine—"whom a wise Yankee friend of mine discerned to be properly 'the first stump-orator in the world'" (*LDP* 11)—this small compliment is quickly overtaken by the anger that bursts forth from Carlyle when he undertakes to attack democracy, the real target of his pamphlet. "What *is* Democracy; this huge inevitable Product of the Destinies, which is everywhere the portion of our Europe in these latter days? There lies the question for us. Whence comes it, this universal big black Democracy; whither tends it; what is the meaning of it?" (*LDP* 14). Reformers point to the United States as proof that democracy can succeed; Carlyle ridicules the idea. He argues that American prosperity and domestic tranquility both depend upon an endless supply of cheap land. What Americans call their "government" he dismisses with a sneer as "Anarchy *plus* a street-constable" (*LDP* 27). Nor does he stop there. Carlyle repeats the question he had asked Emerson at Stonehenge:

> What great thought, what great noble thing that one could worship, or loyally admire, has yet been produced there? None: The American cousins have yet done none of these things. "What have they done?" growls Smelfungus. "They have doubled their population every twenty years. They have begotten, with a rapidity beyond recorded example, Eighteen Millions of the greatest *bores* ever seen in this world before,—that, hitherto, is their feat in History!" (*LDP* 28)

This famous insult apparently originated in a conversation with Monckton Milnes late in 1848. Carlyle was ridiculing the English reformer Cobden, whose admiration for the United States earned him the nickname in Parliament of "member for America." K. J. Fielding in his study of Carlyle's pamphlet puts it this way: "The original force of the gibe was as a knockdown answer to America's greatest admirer, who never ceased recommending democracy because it worked across the Atlantic."[23] But "The Present Time" makes no mention of Cobden, and Emerson could hardly be blamed for assuming that Carlyle's words referred both to him and to the many friends for whom he had provided letters of introduction.[24] When Carlyle wrote on 19 July 1850 to hint that he might wish to find an American publisher for the now completed *Latter-Day Pamphlets,* Emerson blandly praised the "sturdy tone" of the "wonderful pamphlets" and their "vivid daguerrotype of the times" (5 August 1850). He did not offer to find an American publisher for the book (*CEC* 461–463).

When Carlyle received this letter in Scotland, where he had gone to visit his mother, he fumed to Jane: "Here comes Emerson's Letter too. An unsatisfactory Letter; promising me no result at all from my sore labours" (*LTJWC* 25: 186). A few days later she wrote to inform him that a pamphlet had arrived at Cheyne Row "addressed in the writing of Emerson." It was entitled *Perforations in the Latter-Day Pamphlets by one of the 'Eighteen Millions of Bores'* (*LTJWC* 25: 188). Its author was Elizur Wright, a Boston newspaper publisher whose *Daily Chronotype* Emerson admired for its independence and its firm antislavery stance.[25] However angry he was with Emerson, Carlyle was growing increasingly desperate, as his letter of 14 November 1850 to Emerson makes clear. Sam Ward, one of Emerson's closest friends, had visited London without calling at Cheyne Row, though he sent Carlyle a letter from Emerson to Mazzini with a polite request that Carlyle forward it.[26] Carlyle complained to Emerson that he felt "punished" by not being called upon by Ward. As for those eighteen million bores, why, there are just as many in England; and they are never to be confused with the eighteen *thousand* true noble-men in America to whom he sends his love. He tries to nudge Emerson toward his usual editorial role with a plangent adieu:

> Oh my Friend, have tolerance for me, have sympathy with me; you know not quite (I imagine) what a burden mine is, or perhaps you would find this duty, wh[h] [*sic*] you always do, a little easier done! Be happy, be busy beside your still waters, and think kindly of me here. (*CEC* 463–466)[27]

Emerson ignored the letter. In fact, he did not write to Carlyle for over a year and a half, and then, in July 1851, only after Carlyle pleaded "to have a missive from Boston again" (*CEC* 469). Emerson's lengthening silences distressed Carlyle, who wrote in 1855:

> You know not in the least, I perceive, nor can be made to understand at all, how indispensable your Letters are to me. How you are, and have for a long time been, the one of all the sons of Adam who, I felt, completely understood what I was saying; and answered with a truly human voice,—inexpressibly consolatory to a poor man, in his lonesome pilgrimage towards the evening of the day. (*CEC* 50)

Carlyle made one last gift in honor of his American friend, bequeathing to Harvard University all the books he had used in writing *Oliver Crom-*

well's Letters and Speeches and *Frederick the Great.* Emerson was moved by the bequest. He wrote: "It is very amiable & noble in you to have kept this surprise for us in your older days. Did you mean to show us that you could not be old, but immortally young? & having kept us all murmuring at your Satires and sharp homilies, will now melt us with this manly & heart-warming embrace?" (*CEC* 563–564).

What did the Transcendentalists and their friends learn from their gift-giving experiences? That it is dangerous both to give and to receive. To be put under obligation even to our dearest friends can come to seem an intolerable burden, one to be repaid with insults, slaps, or worse. The legal historian William Ian Miller tells the story of Egil and Einar, two medieval Icelandic poets and warriors who became good friends. When Einar, the younger man, was given a splendid shield adorned with gold and jewels by a Norwegian in whose honor he had composed a poem, he hastened to visit Egil. Since Egil was not at home Einar departed, leaving the shield behind as a gift. When he returned home and discovered this gift, Egil was far from being pleased with his friend's generosity; indeed, he ordered his servants to saddle his horse, vowing to find Einar and kill him. Fortunately, Einar had already gotten too far away. Disgruntled, Egil took the only honorable course remaining to him: he returned home and composed a poem in Einar's honor. Why was Egil so angry? According to Miller:

> Gifts are obligation-creating, more viscerally so than contracts. It was precisely the obligation to make a return that annoyed Egil. By giving someone something you unilaterally bound that person to make repayment. You made the recipient your debtor, thereby constraining him, until repayment was made, to make petty shows of gratitude and deference.[28]

The giver of a gift usurps the power of God to give what the recipient cannot repay, and like God he earns the thanklessness of his beneficiaries, if only because the pain of continuing to owe gratitude is greater than the pleasure conferred by the gift. The deepest scars in friendship may be the ones inflicted by generosity.

Notes

1. Milton 1968, 611. The lines are *Paradise Lost* 4.46–53.

2. In the notes he wrote on "Gifts" in the Centenary Edition of his father's works, Edward W. Emerson wrote: "In the family the old-time New England custom of New Year's presents was never supplanted by the modern Christmas-tree. To his last days, when his grandchildren were around him, Mr. Emerson gave New Year's morning to

this ceremony, and obeyed the rule of writing a poem to be read before each present was opened." And he added an important comment: "As far as time and taste allowed him, he selected his presents for his family, but, even from them, it was a little hard for him to receive" (*CW* 3: 323–324).

3. In his journal Emerson suggests that this sort of benefactor is the one we like best: "We like the company of him whose manners or unconscious talk set[s] our own minds in action & we take occasions of rich opinions from him as we take apples off a tree without any thanks" (*JMN* 5: 385).

4. This journal entry, dated 1 October [1832], is a response to Carlyle's review of the Corn Law Rhymes in the July 1832 number of the *Edinburgh Review.* It occurs on p. 62 of Emerson's manuscript Journal Q.

5. *CEC* 4. Ralph L. Rusk discovered that Emerson learned Carlyle's name from an English Unitarian clergyman named Brown, who preached the afternoon sermon at Emerson's church on 21 October 1832, and then came to dinner at the Emersons' house (Rusk 1949, 165). Charles Emerson wrote that at dinner, Brown "told about Coleridge (who is an opium eater) & about Carlisle the author of the Characteristics article—a German bred scholar . . . Waldo has been of late very much a reader of translations from the German—Schiller & Goethe—& the articles on German literature written by Carlisle in the English magazines" (von Frank 1994, 75).

6. The journal entry is dated 19 October [1832]. Emerson recalls this sentiment after returning to America, in the first letter he ever wrote to Carlyle. See the letter of 14 May 1834: "Like somebody in Wilhelm Meister, I said, this person has come under obligations to me & to all whom he has enlightened" (*CEC* 97).

7. Mill knew only Carlyle's address, not how to find his residence. According to Joseph Slater, Emerson learned the precise location of Craigenputtock from the secretary of the University of Edinburgh while he was sight-seeing with a young Scotsman named Alexander Ireland, who would later help arrange Emerson's 1847–1848 lecture tour of England; see *CEC* 10.

8. *CEC* 103. Carlyle claimed that besides Emerson's letter he had received only one "intelligent response" to *Sartor*—from an anonymous correspondent later identified as an Irish priest named O'Shea; see *CEC* 103 n. 8.

9. Emerson wrote: "I send you also with Dr. Channing's regards & good wishes a copy of his little work, lately published, on our great local question of Slavery" (*CEC* 142).

10. Carlyle to John Stuart Mill [?late May 1836] in *LTJWC* 8: 350, and see n. 3.

11. Joseph Slater has painstakingly reconstructed the story of this transatlantic publishing arrangement in the section of his introduction titled "Bibliopoly"; see *CEC* 16–29.

12. Phillips, who wrote under the pen name January Searle, included this anecdote in his pamphlet *Emerson, His Life & Writings* (London: Holyoake, 1855), 47; quoted by Slater, *CEC* 35–36. Emerson left Carlyle's house on 29 October 1847 to take the train for Liverpool. He lectured at Huddersfield (between Manchester and Leeds) on 17 and 18 December. See von Frank 1994, 219, 223.

13. Emerson wrote: "For the Indian corn,—I have been to see Dr. Charles T. Jackson (my wife's brother . . .) who tells me that the reason your meal is bitter, is, that all the corn sent to you from us is kiln dried here, usually at a heat of 300 degrees, which effectually kills the starch or diastase, (?), which would otherwise become sugar. The drying is thought necessary to prevent the corn from becoming musty in the contin-

gency of a long voyage. He says, if it should go in the steamer, it would arrive sound without previous drying." The *Oxford English Dictionary* defines "diastase" as "a nitrogenous ferment formed in a seed or bud (e.g. in barley or potatoes) during germination, and having the property of converting starch into sugar."

14. The article "Indian Meal" appeared in *Fraser's Magazine* 39 (May 1849), 561–563; see *CEC* 452 n. 2.

15. However painful these injunctions must have been to hear about, Thoreau appears to have taken them to heart. The "Baker Farm" chapter of *Walden* can be seen both as an imitation of Carlyle's Irish journeying and as a reply to his criticisms of *A Week on the Concord and Merrimack Rivers.* If the *Week* was "too Jean-Paulish"—too fantastic, too literary—"Baker Farm" would be a blunt, plainspoken attempt to confront intractable poverty. Thoreau does not try to impose order on the family of the Irishman John Fields, but he does try to urge his own economies upon them—simple clothing, water, and hoe-cakes baked over an open fire. He signally fails to interest them in asceticism. Thoreau concludes the chapter with this rueful meditation on his failure to persuade Fields to change his ways of living: "With his horizon all his own, yet he a poor man, born to be poor, with his inherited Irish poverty or poor life, his Adam's grandmother and boggy ways, not to rise in the world, he nor his posterity, till their wading webbed bog-trotting feet get *talaria* to their heels" (*Wa* 209).

16. Joseph J. Moldenhauer reports that Thoreau lectured on Carlyle before the Concord Lyceum on 4 February 1846. That summer he asked Horace Greeley to help him place an essay on Carlyle. Greeley persuaded George R. Graham, editor of *Graham's American Monthly Magazine,* to accept it. It appeared as a two-part article in the March and April 1847 numbers of the magazine. See the "Textual Notes," *EE* 405–409.

17. In another sentence from this passage, Carlyle urges Thoreau (through Emerson): "whatever else he do or forbear, teach us to look Facts honestly in the face, and to beware (with a kind of shudder) or smearing *them* over with our despicable and damnable palaver . . ."

18. For an extended discussion of this passage, see Sattelmeyer 1989.

19. Ronan discusses Thoreau's complex relation to Emerson in "Thoreau's Declaration of Independence from Emerson in *Walden*" (2006); his discussion of "The Departure" occurs on pp. 9–10. For the text of "The Departure," see Thoreau 2001, 594–595.

20. Harmon Smith says of Emerson's changing attitude toward Thoreau, after his return from England: "Emerson's disappointment in Thoreau expressed itself in a subtle change in his manner toward him that Emerson himself was probably unaware of but that Thoreau felt keenly. More and more, a note of condescension crept into Emerson's tone when he was referring to him." See Smith 1999, 131–132.

21. The full sentence reads: "I have read your Slavery Address; this morning the first half-sheet, in proof, of the Essays has come: perfectly correct, and right good reading." The "Essays" referred to here are *Essays: Second Series.*

22. And he added: "He is no idealist in opinions. He is a protectionist in Political Economy, aristocrat in politics, epicure in diet, goes for slavery, murder, money, punishment by death, & all the pretty abominations, tempering them with epigrams."

23. According to Milnes, Carlyle said: "Cobden is an inspired bagman who believes in a calico millenium. J.C. is always praising America to me. I sd. to him, 'What have the Amer[ican]s done but beget with unexampled rapidity 20 million of the greatest bores on the face of the earth?" Cobden began his career as a commercial traveler and then became part owner of a successful firm of calico printers. He en-

tered political life as an opponent of the Corn Laws and when elected to Parliament advocated free trade and universal disarmament. "J. C." may be John Carlyle, Thomas's brother, for whose prose translation of Dante's *Inferno* Emerson was then attempting to find an American publisher. See Fielding 1996, 55; and *CEC* 442 n. 1.

24. Emerson alludes to "The Present Time" in a letter of 12 May 1850, urging Alexander Ireland to visit the United States. "Mr. Lawrence, I see, tells you once a month, in London, that 'we are a great nation,' and my dear Carlyle tells you that we are a very dull one, but nature never disappoints, and our square miles and the amounts of human labour here are incontestable & will interest all your taste, intelligence, & humanity." Abbot Lawrence was American minister to England from 1849 to 1852 (*CL* 7: 253). At this point Emerson sounds amused rather than annoyed. It was quite another matter when Carlyle suggested that he sponsor the American publication of a text that had insulted all eighteen million of his countrymen.

25. Fielding describes Wright's pamphlet as "no worse than offensively jocular" toward Carlyle, whom it calls "our poor, innocent, philanthropic friend" (1996, 56). Carlyle never read the pamphlet himself, apparently endorsing his wife's stated desire to put it on the fire. Fielding thinks Jane Carlyle may have been mistaken in her identification of the handwriting, but that seems unlikely, given the length of the correspondence between the two men. Emerson praises Wright and the "little Chronotype" in the same letter to Samuel Gray Ward in which he congratulates Ward for the "fine vengeance" of failing to visit Carlyle when he was in London; see *CL* 4: 236–237. It seems more likely that Wright's "Perforations" was Emerson's way of letting Carlyle know what he thought of "The Present Time" without having to say it in his own words.

26. The letter of 9 October 1850 contained Emerson's request to Mazzini for any light he could shed on the last six years of Margaret Fuller's life. Mazzini did not reply, and Emerson wrote to him again on 29 July 1851. See *CL* 4: 232, 255, and 8: 284 (see n. 59). According to Carlyle in a letter of 7 May 1852, Mazzini did write a letter about Margaret, but Emerson never received it; see *CEC* 478.

27. *CEC* 463–466. Carlyle understood very well what the trouble was: "What 'business' it was that deprived me of a call from Mr Ward, or of the possibility of calling on him, I know very well,—and Elizur Wright, the little dog, and others know!" (here p. 463).

28. Miller, *Humiliation and Other Essays on Honor, Social Discomfort, and Violence* (1993), 15–17.

PART TWO

Emerson's "Friendship"

THREE

"In the Golden Hour of Friendship": Transcendentalism and Utopian Desire

DAVID M. ROBINSON

Emerson was not at first drawn to friendship as a philosophical problem, but he eventually found it inescapable. Friendship was intertwined so tightly with his emotional experience, and his sense of the fulfilled life, that it came to demand a philosophical accounting of him. This accounting came principally in his 1841 essay "Friendship," although friendship, love, grief, loneliness, and solitude also play key roles in "Self-Reliance," "Love," and "Experience," and in later essays such as "Nominalist and Realist" and "Society and Solitude." Emerson's considerations of the culture of the soul, the experience of spiritual elation and elevation, the responsibilities of democratic citizenship, and the ethical conduct of life inevitably illumined the importance of friendship. These concerns were in turn illumined by that strange, wild, compelling, and exhilarating drive toward companionship and affection. "The moment we indulge our affections," Emerson wrote, "the earth is metamorphosed: there is no winter, and no night: all tragedies, all ennuis vanish,—all duties even; nothing fills the proceeding eternity but the forms all radiant of beloved persons" (*CW* 2: 114).

For Emerson the importance of friendship as a philosophical subject emerged only gradually through the 1830s, but the appearance of Bronson Alcott in the guise of the Orphic Poet in *Nature* was an early indication that visionary enlightenment was not wholly disconnected from the shared enthusiasms of friendship. Nor should it be forgotten that Emerson completed his first book under the shock of the loss of his younger brother and closest male companion, Charles.[1] As Emerson quite purposefully collected a network of friends in Concord and Boston in the late 1830s, his explicit consideration of a theory of friendship accelerated, spurred by two important forces.

The first arose out of the utopian talk of community, cooperation, and human solidarity that came under the label of Associationism or Fourierism, and led to the Brook Farm experiment. Emerson refused to join the group, but not without some soul-searching, and the presence of so many of his friends, acquaintances, and allies there certainly created a pull on his attention and spurred him to deeper thinking about the possibilities of human community and social discourse. The famous conviviality of Brook Farm, the undercurrent of escapade that seems to have coursed through the group's early years, furthered the commune's claims and appeal.[2]

An even more significant advocate of friendship was Margaret Fuller. Among the Transcendentalists it was Fuller who placed friendship at the center of her philosophy, pressing that issue both philosophically and emotionally on Emerson. We can, in fact, best understand Fuller's innovative and pioneering theorizing of feminism and women's rights to be essentially an outgrowth of her concern with friendship. In a journal entry recollecting the headiest days of the Transcendentalist movement, Emerson wrote that it was in many ways a movement of Margaret's friends: "Margaret with her radiant genius and fiery heart was perhaps the real centre that drew so many & so various individuals to a seeming union" (*JMN* 16: 22).

It was the socially constructed inequality between men and women that made true friendships difficult or impossible, Fuller believed. Such inequality was not only a barrier to friendships between men and women, it also distorted men's relationships with men and women's with women. Fuller contended, as I have argued elsewhere, that the philosophy of self-culture that grounded Transcendentalist discourse implied and demanded an equality between men and women. Her *Woman in the Nineteenth Century* reclaims the possibilities of friendship as the heart of the quest for spiritual learning, just living, and the growth of the soul—all of which are essential aspirations of Transcendentalism.[3]

Emerson met Fuller in 1836, and initially claimed that he was not impressed. But Fuller insisted on friendship and proved to Emerson that she could be a stimulating and challenging companion, and that he needed such stimulations and challenges. Bringing him not only her own energy, originality, wit, boldness, and immense learning, Fuller also brought a group of lively younger friends to Emerson, with the apparent mission of luring him out of himself—not allowing him to settle into the reserve and decorum to which he at times inclined. By 1839 she had engineered a small utopian experiment of her own, in which she and Emerson were the senior members of a group of five that included Caroline Sturgis, Anna Barker, and Samuel Gray Ward—bright, articulate, artistic, and charming young individuals. "Margaret, wherever she came, fused people into society, & glowing company was the result," Emerson recalled of her (*JMN* 11: 449). As soon as "The American Scholar" and "The Divinity School Address" had thrust Emerson into public view as the presumed leader of an avant-garde movement, he also found himself surrounded by engaging protégés who were eager to know him and each other better.

The aim of this group—an aim that Fuller cultivated—seems to have been to establish a circle that was purely open in its communication, spontaneous, thoroughly honest, and free of convention. That there were erotic undercurrents among them is clear enough from the correspondence, and there have been several quite different readings of the group dynamic. It was, in fact, the engagement of Barker and Ward that broke the party up, shocking Fuller profoundly, and bruising her friendship with Emerson. Ward and Barker were married on Ward's birthday, 3 October 1840—a date which, as Robert Hudspeth has written, "Fuller noted each succeeding year" (Fuller 2001, 5). The interconnections and undercurrents among the group are fascinating. Fuller had perhaps been in love with Ward. She had perhaps also been in love with Barker. Fuller's relationship with Emerson was emotionally intense—some readers consider them to have been "in love"—and also filled with stress and conflict. Emerson's letters to Caroline Sturgis, Fuller's closest female friend, are unusually warm and intimate, and Kathleen Lawrence has recently described Sturgis as Emerson's "soul-mate and feminine counterpart" (Lawrence 2005, 38). Emerson and Ward seem powerfully drawn to each other, and Caleb Crain has recently argued that Emerson wrote "Friendship" with Samuel Ward principally in mind.[4] Irresistible though these speculations may be, the more significant point is that Fuller—and implicitly, Emerson—had hoped that the circle would remain as it was: a unified community of souls attempting to redefine friendship and experimenting in a new form of dialogue and intimacy.

The fate of this experiment is one of the more important catalysts for Emerson's essay on "Friendship." While it is technically an "early" Emerson work, part of the first collection of *Essays* that distilled his annual lecture series of the 1830s, the essay rehearses a pattern of thinking that we might associate more closely with Emerson's somewhat later philosophical reorientation, of which "Experience" is the signature essay. In this reorientation, Emerson called into question several of the premises of his earlier work, reconsidering his affirmations of human enlightenment and benevolence, and qualifying his advocacy of the self-reliant individual. One of the causes of this reorientation was Emerson's disillusionment with the seeming certitude produced by, on the one hand, rationalistic idealism, and on the other, visionary or mystical experience. His pursuit of such certitude gradually became secondary to the more complex and demanding goal of ethical discipline and pragmatic effort in the service of broader social justice. If we regard "Friendship" as one of the earlier signs of a shift in Emerson's thinking, one which he self-consciously dramatizes in the structure of the essay itself, then we can also conclude that the collapse of the small but intensely engaged circle of friends that Fuller brought together was one of the initiating events in Emerson's disillusionment. There was clearly something experimental and utopian about this group's aspirations—an implicit but working assumption among them, that the constrictive barriers which had defined friendship in the past were being overcome. In the same way that the Brook Farmers believed that they were reinventing work and community, Fuller—and to varying degrees those she had gathered around her—felt that they were redefining intimate friendship and love as something that was mutually shared among a group rather than restricted to a couple.

When Samuel Ward and Anna Barker announced their engagement, it was as if they had betrayed the larger project of friendship and its potentially revolutionary aspirations. This was an acute emotional blow to Fuller, who not only lost her close connections with Ward and Barker, but also found her relationship with Emerson diminished, because she no longer had the emotional access to him that the larger group of friends provided. Emerson's essay on "Friendship" suggests that, stoic though he seems about it in his letters and journals, the collapse of the group was significant to him as well, teaching him the limits of such utopian aspirations, while simultaneously reinforcing the power and the immense value of human affection and mutual sympathy. Insofar as Emerson, Fuller, and their friends were attempting (in the words of the Orphic Poet in Emerson's *Nature*) to "build" their "own world," they found that they were unable to do so. Ward and Barker retreated into the convention of marriage, thereby abdicating their central role in this newly emerging group friendship.

"Friendship" is therefore rooted in a utopian social experiment, though of an unusual kind. While the essay's representations of life and its images and language are couched in terms of interpersonal relationships, these issues point toward a larger vision of human mutuality and interdependent support, with profound consequences for the conception of family relations, community building, democratic dialogue, participatory citizenship, and just public policy. "Friendship" suggests ways of considering transpersonal goals that have significant promise for cooperative human association in a broad arena of activities. For Emerson, Fuller, and most of the Transcendentalists, a renewed and expanded conception of friendship represented an important dimension of the utopian energy of the 1830s and 1840s. Emerson's theoretical investigation of friendship must be seen in this light, as a moment in which his long engagement with self-culture also yielded an ethical inquiry into right expectations and just conduct among friends, and a re-imagining of the power of friendship to reformulate the social dimensions of experience.

The paradoxical heart of the essay on "Friendship" is Emerson's refusal, on ethical and pragmatic grounds, to accept the very theory of human relationships that he shows logically to be the inexorable law of the human condition. Though unobserved, as far as I have seen, in the ocean of Emerson scholarship, criticism, and commentary, Emerson enacts in this essay a quite extraordinary repudiation of his own philosophy. He first describes the desire of one individual for another as an unchosen or fated condition, the initial promise of which is by nature impossible to fulfill. By this logic, friendship is always already doomed to fail. But Emerson then simply dismisses this iron law of existence as a recognition "not to be indulged," and describes human relationships not as the product of determinism or fate, but of the careful nurture of creative sympathies, and of a discipline that requires both deep perception and unyielding commitment.

Emerson's opening observations on friendship focus on the riddle that "we have a great deal more kindness than is ever spoken" (*CW* 2: 113). Such veiled and unspoken kindness, he suggests, tempers the callousness that we see everywhere around us. "Maugre all the selfishness that chills like east winds the world, the whole human family is bathed with an element of love like a fine ether" (*CW* 2: 113). This assertion of an implicit sympathy and compassion intimates the possibility of a social world that might be transformed through compassion and benevolence, of an alternate social reality that lurks in daily events and ordinary interactions.

> How many persons we meet in houses, whom we scarcely speak to, whom yet we honor, and who honor us! How many we see in the street, or sit with in church, whom, though silently, we warmly rejoice to be with! Read the language of these wandering eye-beams. The heart knoweth. (*CW* 2: 113)

"The heart knoweth," perhaps—but it does not speak, does not act. We rejoice in others, but we rejoice in silence. The problem of friendship—not only of the personal and intimate relations of individuals, but of the social world of which friendship is the sign or emblem—is to overcome this barrier of silence and paralysis, of balked intimacy. Men and women are prisoners of a kind of reserve. They are capable of much greater affection than they actually show. By asserting the pervasive though secret presence of kindness, Emerson subtly indicts the human failure to enact it.

"Friendship" is in this sense a characteristically Emersonian essay: it calls its readers to claim the full measure of their potential. Emerson goes on to suggest the values and benefits of what he calls the "indulgence of this human affection." The practice of friendship provides "exhilaration" and emotional uplift; it enhances "our intellectual and active powers" (Emerson mentions its positive impact on the difficult task of writing); it stimulates our powers of conversation and imagination. Perhaps most importantly it makes "a young world for me again" (*CW* 2: 113–114). "The moment we indulge our affections," he enthuses, "the earth is metamorphosed: there is no winter, and no night: all tragedies, all ennuis vanish,—all duties even" (*CW* 2: 114). The world is renewed, and we in it are rejuvenated. While we ordinarily associate Emersonian moments of new insight and psychic renewal with inner epiphanies or ecstasies in the natural world, here he makes it clear that conversation, social interaction, and all the practices of friendship are themselves modes of self-culture and spiritual growth.

The praise of friendship thus echoes the words of the Orphic Poet in *Nature,* who promised an "influx of spirit" that would also bring "a correspondent revolution in things" (*CW* 1: 45). That "influx of spirit" has friendship as one of its sources. Such moments of renewal promise that dramatic transformations of self and society are a small step away. But how can we take that step? Emerson answers this question as a man emerging from sleep and dream. "I awoke this morning with devout thanksgiving for my friends, the old and the new." It is not insignificant that the relation of the value of friendship comes to him in dreams, recovered from some buried place in the subconscious. Only in the revelation that we sometimes achieve through the recovery of a dream can he justly estimate the power of the human bond. "Shall I not call God the Beautiful, who daily showeth himself so to me in his gifts?" While we may at first be captured by the word "Beautiful" in this exclamation, the operative word is actually the last one, "gifts." We do not, Emerson implies, "make" friends. We receive them, if we are fortunate. Such gifts compel our gratitude, but always remind us that the creative power of friendship is in some respects beyond us. Thus the renewal that friendship seems to promise is, like other forms of enlightenment, sometimes mysteriously inaccessible. "My friends have come to me unsought," Emerson admits. "The great God gave them to me" (*CW* 2: 115). Flattering as it may at first be to think that a friend considered you a gift from God, it would in the long run be more assuring to feel that you were sought out by your friend, that you were the object of your friend's desire and hope.

But as Emerson portrays it, friendship is the manifestation of "the divine affinity of virtue with itself" (*CW* 2: 115). We are drawn to another by a shared quality or nature that transcends both of us as individuals. Here the key word is "affinity," and Emerson uses it strategically to invoke Goethe's *Elective Affinities,* a book that had a powerful impact among those in the Transcendentalist circle.[5] Goethe had made the bold analogy between the material affinities that generate the chemical bond and the passions that underlie the romantic and erotic bonds of men and women. Some four months after Emerson published "Friendship" in his first volume of *Essays,* Margaret Fuller published her important essay "Goethe" in *The Dial,* which included a ringing defense of *Elective Affinities.* Noting that the book had been "assailed with . . . a storm of indignation . . . on the score of gross immorality," Fuller instead found the book "a work especially what is called moral in its outward effect, and religious even to piety in its spirit." She responded to the book's "unspeakable pathos," to the "saintly sweetness" of the character Ottilia, and to "a sadness" as of an "irresistible fatality brooding over the whole." "Not even in Shakespeare," she declared, "have I so felt the organizing power of genius" (Fuller 1841, 31–33). Emerson's "Friendship," at least in its first movement, partakes of this mood of "irresistible fatality" that Fuller ascribes to Goethe, but Emerson seems to substitute a stoical resignation to fate for the pathos that Fuller found in Goethe. While grateful for the gifts of friendship that he is given, Emerson is nevertheless resigned to their transience. "Will these too separate themselves from me again, or some of them? I know not; but I fear it not, for my relation to them is so pure, that we hold by simple affinity" (*CW* 2: 115). Since he has had no role in creating the friendships, he can have no role in sustaining them. Friendships are a product of nature or of God, not something created by men and women. He can only believe that "the same affinity will exert its energy on whomsoever is noble as these men and women, wherever I may be" (*CW* 2: 115). Particular friendships may not endure, Emerson seems to say, but new friendships will surely replace them. This is, at best, coldly comforting, because it actually undermines the value of any specific friendship.

The most disturbing implication of this view of friendship is the recognition that it is less specific men and women that we love, than something which is in one sense much more than they are, but in another sense much less. "In strictness," Emerson observes, "the soul does not respect men as it respects itself" (*CW* 2: 116). The elective affinities are in this sense an expression of the soul's narcissism, what Emerson earlier termed "the divine affinity of virtue with itself" (*CW* 2: 115). We do not, that is to say, love another person; our soul responds to its own likeness as it is mirrored in another. Emerson does not propound this doctrine eagerly or with relish. It must be admitted, he says, "in strictness." This level of candor requires a disciplined intellectual honesty and rhetorical courage, he feels. It costs something to recognize the difficult truth that the soul loves only itself, as he shows with a telling and sharp-edged analogy: "Friendship, like the immortality of the soul, is too good to be believed" (*CW* 2: 116).

This realization of the finally illusory nature of friendship lies behind Emerson's depiction of the tragedy of the self-conscious lover's admission of his lover's, or his own, unworthiness: "The lover, beholding his maiden, half knows that she is not verily that which he worships; and in the golden hour of friendship, we are surprised with shades of suspicion and unbelief" (*CW* 2: 116). The "lover" fears that he is not in love with his maiden, but with his idea of her, or his idea of the perfect maiden. His love is in this sense dishonest or untruthful, and thus a betrayal of his beloved. It is also a damaging form of self-delusion that condemns the lover to perpetual disappointment. The idiom of Emerson's description of the lover's disappointment is consciously ornate—"beholding," "maiden," "verily," "golden hour." It borrows from the artificial and overcharged language of romance precisely because Emerson intends it to deflate such fictions. We can get nowhere in understanding love until we dispose of such fantasies, he believes. Understanding that he has perhaps injured or offended many of his readers who cherish such sentimental ideals of friendship and love, he faces them directly with a searching question. "Shall I not be as real as the things I see?" he challenges. "If I am, I shall not fear to know them for what they are" (*CW* 2: 116). He has prepared us to come to terms with the fact that this phenomenon that we call friendship or love, seen plainly, is less a mutual than a solitary undertaking. "The soul environs itself with friends, that it may enter into a grander self-acquaintance or solitude" (*CW* 2: 116–117). This is indeed hard doctrine.

The brief letter that Emerson then offers as a model of a lover's "true sentiment" for "each new candidate for his love" (*CW* 2: 117) is an attempt to articulate this agonizing recognition of the impossibility of a complete human bond. As Jeffrey Steele has observed, "a fundamental instability characterizes Emerson's view of friendship, for it is nearly impossible to reconcile an idealized model of individual being with an appreciation for human fallibility" (1999, 122). This letter, drawn from a February 1840 entry in Emerson's journal (*JMN* 7: 337), seems to be a kind of "Dear John" letter, but one that is addressed to the whole of humanity.[6] The letter's author tells his friend that he (or she) is not sure of her (or him): the writer is not sure of the friend's "capacity," and is unsure that he can match the friend's mood. Similarly, he does "not presume in thee a perfect intelligence of me." This lack of consonant moods and of assured knowledge of each other makes friendship a "delicious torment"—never steady, never consummated, never sure. Emerson closes, in the spirit of this uncertainty: "Thine ever, or never" (*CW* 2: 117). The emphasis, it seems, falls on the "never." From the perspective of purely philosophical logic, this should be the end of the essay. Emerson has tried friendship and found it wanting by showing the unbridgeable gap between each pair of individuals, what he would articulate a few years later in "Experience" as the "innavigable sea" that "washes with silent waves between us and the things that we aim at and converse with" (*CW* 3: 29).

But the essay does not end here. With a sweep of his hand, Emerson declares that "these uneasy pleasures and fine pains," the sort of "delicious torment" that he referred to in the letter, "are for curiosity, and not for life." They are theories that cannot, or should not, actually be practiced. They are a form of decadent, wasteful, ultimately egotistical amusement. "They are not to be indulged," he commands (*CW* 2: 117).

It is at this point that Emerson begins to describe what we might think of as an entirely new way of conceiving our stance toward friendship, by opposing the category of "life" to that of "curiosity" or (we could say) philosophy. Emerson seems to recognize that his logically consistent account of the impossibility of the human bond has not devalued friendship, but rather unmasked the inadequacy of a rational, sequentially ordered, philosophical approach to friendship. Such philosophy does not directly engage our human experience or our hopes. Its effect is "to weave cobweb, and not cloth." It yields us "a texture of wine and dreams, instead of the tough fibre of the human heart" (*CW* 2: 117).

As we follow Emerson's counter-movement against his own philosophical thinking—his repudiation of that attitude of withdrawn reserve which Fuller sometimes accused him of, and which he sometimes ruefully admitted—we note that he returns, with new intensity, to the emphasis on "affection" with which he began the essay.[7] Men and women are in a state of perpetual incompletion, ever searching for the friend who can make them whole. This desire had been explained away by Emerson in the first movement of the essay as a door that inevitably led nowhere. What Emerson seems to discover—and the essay "Friendship" is the narrative of this discovery—is that friendships "are not glass threads and frostwork, but the solidest thing we know" (*CW* 2: 118–119). However true it might be that two souls can never completely merge, this is useless information—the stuff of idle "curiosity," of "wine and dreams." Even worse, such insights are corrosive of desire itself, starving the spirit and undermining the richness and depth of our experience.

In the second movement of the essay, Emerson attempts to reground the concept of friendship on the foundations of choice, will, and disciplined effort. Having turned away from his earlier conception of fated or elected friendship, calling it something "for curiosity, and not for life" (*CW* 2: 117), he amplifies that reversal by arguing that all philosophy, when measured by the standard of sustaining us through life, is ultimately folly. "For now, after so many ages of experience, what do we know of nature, or of ourselves? Not one step has man taken toward the solution of the problem of his destiny. In one condemnation of folly stand the whole universe of men" (*CW* 2: 119). This radical dismissal of philosophy is somewhat surprising, and Emerson's emphatic language is intended to underline the chasm between theory and right practice in the conduct of life. When we come to this recognition of our futility as thinkers, what is left for us? Only the hope of friendship, and the promise that it holds of a cooperative, mutually supportive, and just society. The promise of human relationships thus displaces the futility of detached efforts at philosophy as a guide to living.

Friendship may perhaps in some respects resemble a gift or a mystery of nature, as Emerson had earlier argued. But it is also, he now insists, a created thing—something which must be cultivated, nurtured, and maintained. He describes it as "the nut itself whereof all nature and all thought is but the husk and shell" (*CW* 2: 119), suggesting in this metaphor that friendship is both the seed of life's potential fulfillment, and the sustenance of its development. The cultivation that it requires is intelligent and patient effort, and a self-effacing acceptance of the "solemnity" (*CW* 2: 119) and laws of friendship, which Emerson then details.

The task of building a friendship begins with a commitment to truth, sincerity, and openness. "A friend is a person with whom I may be sincere," Emerson observes. "Before him, I may think aloud" (*CW* 2: 119). In this conception of friendship neither flattery nor concealment have a place, and he portrays the dynamics of such a relationship as naked openness to another:

> I am arrived at last in the presence of a man so real and equal, that I may drop even those undermost garments of dissimulation, courtesy, and second thought, which men never put off, and may deal with him with the simplicity and wholeness, with which one chemical atom meets another. (*CW* 2: 119)

In this erotically charged description of disrobing and bonding, Emerson returns to his earlier theory of affinity and destiny, but he describes this meeting of friends as the fruit of efforts to resist and overcome the formalities of courteous evasion and dissimulation that limit conventional friendships. "Every man alone is sincere," he argues. "At the entrance of a second person, hypocrisy begins" (*CW* 2: 119). The form of friendship that he envisions would carry that original sincerity forward into social interchange.

Emerson's embrace of "truth" and "sincerity" as crucial laws of friendship should be recognized as a critique of formalized friendship, with its ritual performances of false emotion and its calculated flatteries. Emerson hopes to save friendship from its most visible and vociferous advocates, who would script it into an illusory dance, and thus render it essentially empty. Friendship must not decay into manners. "To most of us," he argues, "society shows not its face and eye, but its side and back. To stand in true relations with men in a false age, is worth a fit of insanity, is it not?" (*CW* 2: 120). As Thoreau will later write in *Walden*: "I have never yet met a man who was quite awake. How could I have looked him in the face?" (*Wa* 90).

Under this category of "truth," Emerson included those aspects of friendship that are most dramatic, bracing, even edgy and confrontational. Friendship is in part a tearing down of barriers, a stripping away of coverings and disguises, and such efforts require both determination and courage. They also assume an equality of strength and confidence that may not always exist between two friends. A relationship that is based on truth alone is a brotherhood or sisterhood, or perhaps a marriage, of titans—or it is one that fails to acknowledge, with probably disastrous results, the needs and vulnerabilities of one or both partners. It is in this light that Emerson modifies his requirement that friendships be grounded in naked truth, with a complementary insistence that they constantly nurture "tenderness" (*CW* 2: 120).

Such tenderness, he explains, must be an active form of affection that expresses itself in engaged, purposeful concern for the welfare of a friend. "I wish that friendship should have feet, as well as eyes and eloquence. It must plant itself on the ground, before it vaults over the moon" (*CW* 2: 120). The imperative for such grounded, pragmatic affection arises from the understanding that need, frailty, and misfortune are the elements that test and temper any relationship, and ultimately give it its lasting worth. "I hate the prostitution of the name of friendship to signify modish and worldly alliances," Emerson declares. Friendship is too valuable to be used for idle and self-gratifying amusement; it does not center on "frivolous display . . . rides in a curricle, and dinners at the best taverns" (*CW* 2: 121). The call of friendship is instead the call "to dignify to each other the daily needs and offices of man's life," and to remain "alert and inventive," never deteriorating into "something usual and settled" (*CW* 2: 121).

This need to prevent a relationship from going stale and lifeless is perhaps the greatest challenge for Emerson's reformulated concept of friendship. In "Circles," Emerson described the cultivation of the self as the unending work of pushing beyond one's limits, and drawing a new circle of attainment.[8] To maintain this continual newness in "Friendship," Emerson counsels "a long probation" in which the friendship can grow and ripen. "Respect so far the holy laws of this fellowship as not to prejudice its perfect flower by your impatience for its opening. We must be our own, before we can be another's" (*CW* 2: 124). To hasten the achievement of the frankness and commitment that friendship requires is to thwart its fulfillment. The patience and reserve required for this "long probation" entail a level of caution in our mode of interactions with a friend, what Emerson calls a "religious treatment" or a "reverence" (*CW* 2: 123) that acknowledges another's originality and distinctiveness. Such reverence demands restraint, a cautious avoidance of trivialities and excessive familiarities.

> Why go to his house, or know his mother and brother and sisters? Why be visited by him at your own? Are these things material to our covenant? Leave

> this touching and clawing. Let him be to me a spirit. A message, a thought, a sincerity, a glance from him, I want, but not news, nor pottage. (*CW* 2: 123)

So much, alas, for the dinner party or the soirée in the performance of friendship. If we feel Emerson's prickly self returning here, it is instructive to remember that the broader context of these mildly irritable remarks is a discussion of the imperative of preserving the freshness and vitality of friendship—something too precious to be dealt with casually. Both stiff formalities and excessive familiarities are the enemies of high friendship; one threatens it with decorum, and the other with a casual disrespect. Friendship must be sustained through a very fine balance of deference and intimacy.

Emerson admits, finally, that such hopes as he has for friendship are difficult to attain, and that "friends, such as we desire, are dreams and fables" (*CW* 2: 125). But the assertion of the utopian nature of friendship as the essay closes is not, I believe, a sign of failure, but perhaps its most significant achievement. It was, as I suggested earlier, the dissolution of Fuller's and Emerson's utopian circle of friends that conditioned Emerson's essay and prompted his disavowal of an individualistic and idealistic philosophy of friendship in the essay's first movement. He has now regained a surer footing in his contention that friendship is not the product of philosophy, but of effort and affection. It is the one resource left to us after philosophy fails.

So his essay ends in a hope and a pursuit, in the same embrace of transition and process that we find in most of his key works, early and late. If we can think of the initiation of a friendship, or the deepening of one, as the drawing of a new circle, then we can see "Friendship" as a companion piece to "Circles," which is Emerson's most sustained exploration of the life of transition and perpetual renewal. The price of the pursuit is a certain austerity, a forfeiture of a familiar and appealingly comfortable form of companionship for a more difficult but more sustaining relationship of shared aspiration and mutual growth. "Our impotence betrays us into rash and foolish alliances which no God attends," he warns. "By persisting in your path, though you forfeit the little, you gain the great." The "great" that we pursue is, he reminds us, worthy of our commitment and our patience.

> You demonstrate yourself, so as to put yourself out of the reach of false relations, and you draw to you the first-born of the world,—those rare pilgrims whereof only one or two wander in nature at once, and before whom the vulgar great, show as spectres and shadows merely. (*CW* 2: 125)

The reading of "Friendship" and its contexts that I have offered can be amplified and supported if we consider the essay in relation to the work of two influential critical works of the past decade, Stanley Cavell's *Conditions Handsome and Unhandsome* and Christina Zwarg's *Feminist Conversations.* Cavell's articulation of Emerson's "aversive" thinking as the wellspring of a strikingly modern and ethically vital body of work was the key to his rehabilitation of Emerson as a philosopher—not only deepening our sense of Emerson's importance, but expanding our sense of the range and responsibilities of what we call "philosophy." Cavell took seemingly negative and generally unphilosophical qualities in Emerson—his spontaneity, his sudden shifts in focus, voice, and tone, his inclination toward metaphor and embedded narrative in his essays—to be positive qualities which are lacking in much current philosophy. Cavell's recovery of Emerson as a philosopher was thus also an implicit critique of business as usual in contemporary philosophy.

Cavell describes Emerson's "aversive thinking" as a thinking that exhibits a "particular disdain for official culture" (1990, 50), drawing his term from a sentence in "Self-Reliance": "The virtue in most request is conformity. Self-reliance is its aversion" (*CW* 2: 29; Cavell 1990, 37). This stance of "aversion" is not, however, aimed at separation or exclusion. As Cavell describes it, and as we find it in "Friendship," aversive thinking is the basis for the creation and sustaining of productive human relationships. For Cavell, Emerson's "disdain for official culture" embodies an ethic of "perfectionism," an "idea of the self as always to be furthered" (1990, 59). Such a posture demands a resistance to things as we find them, or as they are given to us. The direct relevance of this perfectionist ethic for the theory of friendship is made clear when Cavell describes aversive thinking in its relation to society and its norms and claims: "Since aversion is a continual turning away from society, it is thereby a continual turning *toward* it" (1990, 59). The statement seems self-contradictory or paradoxical until we recognize Cavell's playful use of the dimensions of the word "society." In the first instance we avert ourselves from a society characterized by conformity and its manifestations as judgmental moralism, politically apathetic self-involvement, and empty consumerism. It is this form of society that threatens death to the "self always to be furthered," by replacing the desire to renew our experience and reinvent our relations to the world with a regulated and standardized apportionment of identity. If we avert ourselves from this form of society, however, we simultaneously embrace another form of society—society as friendship, as the company of those whom we respect, desire, and cherish. Friendship is thus the alternative to conformity. As Cavell writes, "the friend (discovered or constructed) represents the standpoint of perfection" (1990, 59).

The liberating alternative that friendship represents expands our potentialities, aiding in the quest for betterment that is the calling of each individual. Although Cavell's language for explicating Emerson is distinctive, and quite different from the language and terminology that grounds Emerson, it should be apparent that the aversive thinking and perfectionist ethic that Cavell describes bears an important congruence with the discourse on "self-culture" which was vital to Emerson and Fuller.[9] Both sought a revitalized concept of friendship, cut free from the superficial and insincere pieties that bound the term to convention. Friendship was an important component in the movement toward a formation of a just society. Cavell emphasizes the political value of friendship when he describes perfectionism as the "effort to escape the mediocrity or leveling, say vulgarity, of equal existence, for oneself and perhaps for a select circle of like-minded others" (1990, 56). "Equal existence," as Cavell means it here, is not democracy, but democracy's aversion, conformist sameness.

Cavell's exploration of the connection between friendship and the ethic of "perfectionism" also calls our attention to the work of Christina Zwarg, whose *Feminist Conversations* traces the complex negotiation between Fuller and Emerson over the possibilities, personal and political, of a reconception of friendship. Zwarg's critical stance is clearly more historical than Cavell's, and one of her most crucial scholarly insights has been to expand our sense of what "Fourierism" meant to the Transcendentalists in the 1840s. In a literal sense, Fourierism connoted the theories and writings of the French utopian theorist Charles Fourier, and their transmission to American readers through the work of Albert Brisbane, Fourier's key American disciple. In the 1840s and 1850s these theories had a significant impact in America, generating a wave of communal experiments, including the Brook Farm commune in which George and Sophia Ripley and others associated with the Transcendentalist movement took part. But as Zwarg explains, the connotations of Fourierism went beyond Brook Farm and other experiments at social perfection. Fourierism also suggested issues that we now associate with gender and are likely to categorize under the heading of feminism. "Marriage," Zwarg writes, was "at the center of Fourier's critique" as an institution that "represented everything that was wrong in the prevailing conception of society." Fourier's aim was to foster and enhance the creative and expansive powers of the individual through a rethinking of social and institutional barriers to self-expression. And in marriage he found an institution that "demeaned women through its patriarchal structure" and "thwarted the desire of both partners to seek a variety of relationships" (Zwarg 1995, 139–140).

Zwarg finds the relationship between Fuller and Emerson that emerged in the late 1830s and early 1840s to be a forward-looking model of friendship. "The components of Fourier's domestic utopia are everywhere evident in Emerson's relationship with Fuller," she argues, and this "change in the conceptualization of human interaction," especially the relationships between men and women, generated the opportunity to rethink friendship—and necessarily therefore, questions of equality, power, and gender roles that we now associate with feminism. The conversations, letters, and in many cases the published works of Fuller and Emerson were, Zwarg contends, "a type of philosophical engagement with feminism *before the letter*" (1995, 4). This form of conversation was vital to both of them as they contemplated nineteenth-century American social norms and restrictions.

The creative energy of their friendship grew from "the equality between them and their shared intellectual concern," a convergence that is "often inhibited by the traditional marriage bond" (Zwarg 1995, 39). "Conversation" and "dialogue" are Zwarg's primary terms for describing the achievement and the significance of the Emerson-Fuller friendship, an exchange of ideas and intellectual energy that is utterly dependent on a settled recognition of the equality of the two parties in conversation. "The give-and-take between them resisted the usual hierarchy found in most dialogues between men and women," Zwarg observes, "and seemed preferable for the development of a new model of social interaction" (1995, 47). The equality necessary for constructive dialogue is of course a fundamental principle of democracy, an insight that further confirms the importance of revitalized notions of friendship to the development of democratic politics.

As we have seen, some of the utopian hope and energy was drained away from Emerson, and even more from Fuller, in the collapse of their circle of friends. The failure of Brook Farm would later add to the sense of disillusionment that the 1840s eventually generated among the Transcendentalists. All utopian experiments, of course, remain vulnerable to the skeptical critique of duration and longevity. But it should also be remembered that the fundamental lessons of democratic equality were not lost on Fuller, nor on Emerson, in the years that followed. First in *The Dial,* their joint project in experimental publication, and later in Fuller's growing commitments to feminist advocacy and to a democratic Italy, and in Emerson's growing commitment to abolition in America, the principles of democratic egalitarianism and progressive social change marked the work of these two friends.[10]

Notes

1. For Emerson's relationship with his brother Charles, see Bosco and Myerson 2006, 265–314.

2. For the modern history of Brook Farm, see Delano 2004; for a discussion of the ideology behind the commune, see Francis 1997.

3. See Robinson 1982b.

4. See Crain 2001, 177–237. For a range of views on the complex friendship of Emerson and Fuller, and the dynamics of Fuller's circle of friends, see Strauch 1968; Capper 1992, 282–289; Zwarg 1995; Steele 1999; von Mehren 1994, 104–114, 125–136; and Constantinesco 2008, 220–227.

5. For Goethe's influence on Fuller, see Pochmann 1957, 440–447, 760–768; Durning 1969; Allen 1979, 45–65, 88–90; and Capper 1992, 127–132, 171–175.

6. While Emerson seems to address the world, it is also true, as Caleb Crain has argued (2001, 198–227), that the letter, and much of the essay "Friendship," has its roots in Emerson's experience with the circle of Fuller's friends in 1839 and 1840. The letter and the essay also played a role in Emerson's developing friendship with Thoreau. See Robinson 2004, 60–72; Rossi 2008, 269–277; and Constantinesco 2008, 229–231.

7. See Fuller's letter to Emerson dated 29 September 1840, in Fuller 1983, 2: 350–353; and Emerson's letters to Fuller of 22 and 24 October 1840, in *CL* 2: 159–161.

8. For critical assessments of "Circles," see Bloom 1976, 53–64; Cox 1975; Packer 1982, 14–19; Van Leer 1986, 106–114; and Robinson 1993, 24–29.

9. For further discussion of Emerson's concept of self-culture, see Robinson 1982a; and Lysaker 2008.

10. On Fuller's experience in Italy see Reynolds 1988; von Mehren 1994, 252–351; Capper 2007; and the edition of Fuller's dispatches to the *New-York Tribune,* edited by Reynolds and Belasco Smith (Fuller 1991). On Emerson's developing political identity, see Gougeon 1990; Robinson 1993, 80–88, 124–133; and Garvey 2001.

FOUR

Emerson and Skepticism: A Reading of "Friendship"

RUSSELL B. GOODMAN

Recent conversations with friends and students about Emerson's essay on friendship lead me to suspect that at least some of you will find Emerson's views so strange or radical as not to be about friendship at all. Others will be struck by his anticipations of Nietzsche, whose name I introduce here because like Nietzsche, who read him carefully, Emerson is a genealogist and refashioner of morals. When Emerson criticizes our normal friendships by writing that we mostly "descend to meet," he is recording the possibility, indeed with the word "mostly," the actuality, of something better than what normally passes for friendship. If Emerson finds our friendships disappointing, that is because he thinks that friendship is a high, demanding virtue. In its best actualizations, it carries "the world for me," as he puts it, "to new and noble depths, and enlarge[s] the meaning of all my thoughts." It has the capacity to break down the barriers between people, canceling "the thick walls of individual character, relation, age, sex, circumstance." Friendship is thus a great unifier, a servant of what Emerson calls the "Over-Soul" or "Unity" (*CW* 2: 115). But as Emerson says in his essay on "Montaigne: or the Skeptic," "there are doubts." These doubts about friendships are my main subject in the following essay.

My consideration of Emerson's "Friendship" essay is part of a broader project of trying to make sense of Emerson's thought as a whole by delineating *paths of coherence* through it. These paths fall into two kinds: the consistent enunciation of a view or "master-tone" from essay to essay, and the internal linkage among these views.[1] For example, the notion of process or flux finds its way into all of Emerson's essays, and plays a central role in several of his greatest. Process is more than a subject for continuing discussion in various essays, however, for it is internally linked to many of Emerson's most important claims: that we must learn to skate over the surfaces of life, that all ethical forms are "initial," that language is most effectively used for "conveyance" rather than for "homestead," that "all things good are on the highway."

While thinking about these paths of coherence among Emerson's essays, I have at the same time been attending to the ways in which Emerson's individual essays work: to their order, progression, argument, points of view.[2] In this essay, I want to consider "Friendship" in all of these ways: to chart the course of its argument, to delineate its connections with other writings of Emerson's, and to explore the conceptual connections between friendship and such other Emersonian concepts as self-reliance.

I begin not with the "Friendship" essay itself, but with strands of Emerson's discussion of friendship that we find in some of his other essays. In "Spiritual Laws," a companion piece to "Friendship" in the *Essays: First Series,* Emerson describes the way friendships begin. They have nothing to do with effort, worldly accomplishments, or physical beauty, he asserts, but are rather matters of attraction or affinity. When "all is done," Emerson writes,

> a person of related mind, a brother or sister by nature, comes to us so softly and easily, so nearly and intimately, as if it were the blood in our proper veins, that we feel as if some one was gone, instead of another having come: we are utterly relieved and refreshed: it is a sort of joyful solitude. (*CW* 2: 87)

Friendships, like much of the best in life as Emerson sees it, are spontaneous and unforced.

Friendship appears in a rather different context in "The Divinity School Address," where Emerson complains that Christianity has lost the essential friendliness of Jesus' message, so that "the friend of man is made the injurer of man." The language "that describes Christ to Europe and America," Emerson complains,

> is not the style of friendship and enthusiasm to a good and noble heart, but is appropriated and formal,—paints a demigod, as the Orientals or the Greeks would describe Osiris or Apollo. . . . The time is coming when all men will see, that the gift of God to the soul is not a vaunting, overpowering, excluding sanctity, but a sweet, natural goodness, a goodness like thine and mine, and that so invites thine and mine to be and to grow. (*CW* 1: 82–83)

Jesus is the divine friend of divine men and women, Emerson holds. He is a god who is not foreign but right at hand—as close as our friends are to us in our best moments together, when we are invited "to be and to grow." The friendly message of Jesus, Emerson is saying, has been usurped, or as we would now say, hijacked—transformed into a message of fear, alienation, and hostility.

If friendship is central to Emerson's conception of Christianity, it is equally central to his conception of art, specifically to painting. Describing his first experiences with the great paintings of Europe in the essay "Art," Emerson writes that he "fancied the great pictures would be great strangers; some surprising combination of color and form; a foreign wonder." Instead, he found the paintings "familiar and sincere, . . . the plain *you and me* I knew so well,—had left at home in so many conversations" (*CW* 2: 214). He found Raphael's *Transfiguration,* in particular, was "familiar . . . as if one should meet a friend" (*CW* 2: 215).

But Emerson strikes another note here in "Art" that will be crucial to my reading of "Friendship"—for it is a skeptical note. Continuing the argument we have been examining, he takes one of his characteristic dialectical turns, signaled by a new paragraph beginning with the word "yet":

> Yet when we have said all our fine things about the arts, we must end with a frank confession, that the arts, as we know them, are but initial. Our best praise is given to what they aimed at and promised, not to the actual result. He has conceived meanly of the resources of man, who believes that the best age of production is past. The real value of the Iliad, or the Transfiguration, is as signs of power; billows or ripples they are of the stream of tendency; tokens of the everlasting effort to produce. . . . There is higher work for Art than the arts. They are abortive births of an imperfect or vitiated instinct. (*CW* 2: 215)

Emerson's terms for the arts he has experienced are derogatory: they are said to be "abortive births," and to give only a "mean" idea of human resources and creativity. Yet Emerson also asserts their value as "signs of power," as inspirations or reminders of something "aimed at and promised." He turns against the great European painting that he has just praised because of its distance from the ideal, just as he turns from even the best books when he has his own work to do. In a similar manner and for similar reasons, he turns from his friends.

The final essay I wish to cite before considering "Friendship" is "Experience," a complex assessment of human life in the context of the death of Emerson's son Waldo. "Experience" presents what Stanley Cavell has called an "epistemology of moods," according to which life is a succession of different and sometimes irreconcilable perspectives on or appreciations of things (Cavell 2004, 11). In the passage I wish to consider, Emerson considers the different books with which he has had intense relationships:

> Once I took such delight in Montaigne that I thought I should not need any other book; before that, in Shakespeare; then in Plutarch; then in Plotinus; at one time in Bacon; afterwards in Goethe; even in Bettine; but now I turn the pages of either of them languidly, whilst I still cherish their genius. So with pictures; each will bear an emphasis of attention once, which it cannot retain, though we fain would continue to be pleased in that manner. How strongly I have felt of pictures, that when you have seen one well, you must take your leave of it; you shall never see it again. . . . The reason of the pain this discovery causes us (and we make it late in respect to works of art and intellect), is the plaint of tragedy which murmurs from it in regard to persons, to friendship and love. (*CW* 3: 33)

This passage from "Experience" brings friendship into alignment with a tragic theme in Emerson's thought that is often overlooked. Although we may still "cherish the genius" of the books and people we are no longer in touch with, Emerson is saying that we lose something too—and that this loss is painful and inescapable, hence tragic. We must take our leave of pictures, we must take our leave of friends, we must take our leave of books. These things that "you shall never see . . . again" are the flip side—the less-pleasant face—of the surprises and flashing insights that Emerson characteristically seeks and records.

Emerson's idea that our human lives with others are disappointing chimes with Cavell's discussion of lived skepticism in *The Claim of Reason.* Our skepticism about others, Cavell asserts, is not an academic exercise, but as common as the jealousy of Othello, the blindness of Lear, the disappointment we feel with a conversation in which we have not expressed ourselves adequately. Cavell conceives of such lived skepticism not only as being unsure of others (as Othello is of Desdemona), but as rooted in a deep disappointment with even our best cases of knowing—as if, he writes, "we have, or have lost, some picture of what knowing another, or being known by another, would really come to—a harmony, a concord, a union, a transparence, a governance, a power—against which our actual successes at knowing, and being known, are poor things" (Cavell 1979, 440).

Emerson's critique is not directed at our best cases of friendship, whose satisfaction and promise he credits, but at friendships that fail to deliver on their initial promise. When he is in a glum mood about his life with his friends, he will say, as he does in one of the darker moments of the essay to which we will shortly turn: "Friendship, like the immortality of the soul, is too good to be believed" (*CW* 2: 116). Emerson doesn't quite believe in his friends (he neither names nor refers to a particular friend in his essay), but he seeks and for some hours has found friendship. Cavell's work on "skepticism about other minds," centers on the question of our own responsibility—Lear's responsibility, Othello's responsibility—for failing to know others. Emerson's focus is different, not on our failures to acknowledge others but our failures to ask the best of both others and ourselves. I take from Cavell both the idea that skepticism is lived out in our lives with others, and a set of questions: whether skepticism is inescapable and whether it reveals something about our condition; whether it is to be accommodated, yielded to, overcome, or refuted. To put my cards on the table, I think Emerson shows us that a kind of lived skepticism concerning others is a feature of our lives, but that the accomplishments of friendship are too; and that in its powerful effect on us, friendship instills the hope for something better than the best friend we have.

Emerson's essay on "Friendship" begins in an unexpected place: with people "whom we scarcely speak to," or whom we merely "see in the street." We "warmly rejoice to be with" them, Emerson asserts. But what kind of *being with* is this? Emerson seems to be talking about a sense of human community and even love, which we feel even when there is no sign that it is reciprocated. No particular friend or relationship is singled out in Emerson's statement that the "whole human family is bathed with an element of love like a fine ether" (*CW* 2: 113). The tone is sanguine, but the reader is left to wonder where in this picture is the friendship of one person for another.[3]

The second paragraph continues with the idea of a generalized feeling of love and companionship, what Emerson calls "emotions of benevolence and complacency which are felt towards others." There is a hierarchy of such emotions, he now asserts, from "the lowest degree of good will," which seems to be Emerson's subject in these opening paragraphs, to "the highest degree of passionate love" (*CW* 2: 113)—something he never quite manages to discuss in the essay.

In the third paragraph Emerson moves from these somewhat abstract and generalized remarks to a specific type of experience: our anticipation of the arrival in our house of a "commended stranger." One might ask, what is this "stranger" doing in an essay on "Friendship"? The stranger seems to stand for the possibilities of an ideal friendship, a friendship that we seek but do not have. In this way the commended stranger "stands for humanity," as Emerson puts it.

Emerson asserts of the stranger that "He is what we wish" (*CW* 2: 114), implying that we seek the stranger's company because he will give us or inspire in us something we now lack—what Emerson calls in "History" our "unattained but attainable self" (*CW* 2: 5). Continuing his generic story of the arrival of the stranger, Emerson writes that the "house is dusted" and among its residents the stranger's "arrival almost brings fear to the good hearts that would welcome him" (*CW* 2: 113). After all the preparation and anticipation the stranger's visit at first goes very well. We speak better than we are accustomed to, so that "our own kinsfolk and acquaintance . . . feel a lively surprise at our unusual powers." However, as the visit continues, the stranger turns out to be not as commendable as we had supposed, and the friend we had sought something still to be wished for. For the stranger begins "to intrude his partialities, his definitions, his defects, into the conversation," and then:

> it is all over. He has heard the first, the last and the best, he will ever hear from us. . . . Vulgarity, ignorance, misapprehension, are old acquaintances. Now, when he comes, he may get the order, the dress, and the dinner,—but the throbbing of the heart, and the communications of the soul, no more. (*CW* 2: 114)

What does this have to say about friendship? Not much, it might seem. There is no friend here, but mostly vulgar "old acquaintances" who don't show us the best of themselves and who do not elicit the best in us. It is this normal condition that we had hoped to escape and for a while did escape with the commended stranger. The stranger awakens our always present desire for "the throbbing of the heart and the communications of the soul," for a humanity of the future. But he also disappoints us.

Emerson's little drama is a paradigm of lived skepticism in the following sense: it shows that our doubts about friendship are justified by the course of our experience. The stranger's arrival excites us with the hope of genius—his and ours—and he seems for some moments to be the ideal we seek. Emerson generalizes the point in "Experience" not just to commended strangers but to our friends. Our friends, he writes, "appear to us as representatives of certain ideas" (*CW* 3: 251), but there is "an optical illusion" about them. Each turns out to have boundaries that are never passed, so that what seemed spontaneous and lively "in the year, in the lifetime . . . turns out to be a certain uniform tune which the revolving barrel of the music-box must play" (*CW* 3: 249). Emerson's "Friendship" essay is a meditation or set of variations on this theme of hope and disappointment in our lives with others. His initial drama includes several moods: the "throbbing heart" of anticipation and the "fear" of the meeting with the stranger, the expansive elation in the beginnings of conversation when our own powers surprise those who know us, the mood of disappointment and resignation as we return from elated conversation to become once again the "dumb devil" who greets tedious old acquaintances. If, as Emerson says in "Experience," our life is "a train of moods like a string of beads" each showing "only what lies in its focus," then Emerson's friendship essay records the moods of our lives with others.

Let us return now to the course of Emerson's essay. As if beginning afresh, Emerson moves in paragraphs four and five to a discussion of the pleasures and advantages of friendship, which he now describes as "an encounter of two, in a thought, in a feeling" (*CW* 2: 114). Yet amidst this praise for the overcoming of the boundaries between individuals comes the suggestion that those boundaries remain: "I chide society, I embrace solitude, and yet I am not so ungrateful as not to see the wise, the lovely, and the noble-minded as from time to time they pass my gate." This is an image of friendship, or perhaps just admiration, at a distance, and recalls the opening paragraph's cool pleasure in the people to whom one does not speak.

The sixth paragraph returns to the impending visit of a stranger, but now (as if in a new key) in the first-person singular rather than the first-person plural. "A new person is to me a great event," Emerson confesses, "and hinders me from sleep." Again he strikes a skeptical note: "I have often had fine fancies about persons which have given me delicious hours; but the joy ends in the day: it yields no fruit" (*CW* 2: 115). Here it is not a disappointment with our criteria as such that is at issue, but a disappointment that reasonable criteria of friendship—which have been met in our best moments with our friends—are not met by this new visitor. Emerson oscillates between an appreciation of and skepticism about his friend: "I must feel pride in my friend's accomplishments as if they were mine," he states; but also: "We overestimate the conscience of our friend" (*CW* 2: 115). Do we idolize our friends and they us, or do we accurately read each other's reality and promise?

Emerson begins the lengthy seventh paragraph with a series of skeptical observations and conclusions about belief and knowledge: "Friendship, like the immortality of the soul, is too good to be believed. The lover, beholding his maiden, half knows that she is not verily that which he worships; and in the golden hour of friendship, we are surprised with shades of suspicion and unbelief" (*CW* 2: 116). In Emerson's other essays, surprises bring joy and expansion, a new and fuller perspective on life. Here, however, we are surprised to find that our friend is more limited than we thought, that we project virtues onto her that are not really there. Rather than an underlying, living unity, Emerson now holds up "an Egyptian skull at our banquet"—"an infinite remoteness" between persons.

From that remoteness Emerson turns to himself, to the self-reliant thought that a "man who stands united with his thought conceives magnificently of himself." Even if I do not fully feel my own wealth, he adds, "I cannot choose but rely on my own poverty, more than on your wealth." The friend, he continues, is not "Being," not "my soul," but only "a picture or effigy." And this brings Emerson to a thought that he elaborates throughout the essay: that our friends are for us to grow with and use, rather than components of a stable, unchanging relationship. The soul "puts forth friends," he writes, "as the tree puts forth leaves, and presently, by the germination of new buds, extrudes the old leaf" (*CW* 2: 116). Our friends, the metaphor says, are forms of our growth, but they are not essential to us: they are replaced by our growth into new friendships.

The soul's growth, as Emerson sees it, is an alternation between states of society and solitude, each of which induces the opposite. "The soul environs itself with friends," he continues,

> that it may enter into a grander self-acquaintance or solitude; and it goes alone, for a season, that it may exalt its conversation or society. This method betrays itself along the whole history of our personal relations. The instinct of affection revives the hope of union with our mates, and the returning sense of insulation recalls us from the chase. Thus every man passes his life in the search after friendship. (*CW* 2: 117)

Emerson's "instinct of affection" takes the form of a sample letter he writes to each new candidate for his friendship. The letter is couched in terms of certainty and doubt: the letter-writer is not "sure" of his friend, cannot "presume in thee a perfect intelligence of me," but acknowledges that the desire for knowledge of and by the friend is "a delicious torment."

If Emerson turns against an easy acceptance of what passes for friendship, he also begins to turn against skepticism about friendship at the beginning of the ninth paragraph, a turn that is again announced by the word "yet": "Yet these uneasy pleasures and fine pains are for curiosity and not for life. They are not to be indulged." Life, Emerson is saying, offers us possibilities, glimpses, and hours of something better, and our doubts and disappointments should not deflect us from pursuing and appreciating them. We should not aim at "a swift and petty benefit" from our friends, but have the patience to allow them to be themselves. But after this pragmatic counsel of patience, the paragraph gravitates away from the possibilities of friendship back to a dire portrayal of society:

> Almost all people descend to meet. All association must be a compromise, and, what is worst, the very flower and aroma of the flower of each of the beautiful natures disappears as they approach each other. What a perpetual disappointment is actual society, even of the virtuous and gifted! (*CW* 2: 117)

But as if paragraph nine introduces a theme that is then taken up more strongly in paragraphs eleven and twelve, Emerson now turns toward the claim that ideal friendship is also "real"—something that is found, however impermanently, in our experience. "I do not wish to treat friendships daintily," Emerson states, "but with roughest courage. When [friendships] are real, they are not glass threads or frostwork, but the solidest thing we know" (*CW* 2: 118–119). Skepticism recedes as Emerson advances the epistemological claim that we know our friends, at least as well as anything else we know. Reprising themes of his opening paragraph, he speaks of the "sweet sincerity of joy and peace, which I draw from this alliance with my brother's soul. . . . Happy is the house that shelters a friend!"

Midway in the immense thirteenth paragraph, Emerson develops a conceptual analysis of friendship, as composed of Truth or Sincerity on the one hand, and Tenderness on the other (*CW* 2: 120). Sincerity is a noble virtue, a "luxury," he states, "allowed, like diadems and authority, only to the highest rank, *that* being permitted to speak truth, as having none above it to court or conform unto" (*CW* 2: 119). Sincerity resembles the straight talk and honest judgments of the "nonchalant boys, . . . sure of their dinner" in "Self-Reliance," who "would disdain as much as a lord to do or say aught to conciliate one" (*CW* 2: 29).

In "Self-Reliance," Emerson writes: "we are afraid of truth, afraid of fortune, afraid of death, and afraid of each other" (*CW* 2: 43). In the "Friendship" essay this fear is depicted as insincerity: "We parry and fend the approach of our fellow man by compliments, by gossip, by amusements, by affairs" (*CW* 2: 119). For their part, our fellow men and women avoid the little we have to say or give by requiring that we humor *them:* each person, Emerson complains, "has some fame, some talent, some whim of religion or philanthropy in his head that is not to be questioned, and which spoils all conversation with him" (*CW* 2: 120).

With a real friend, in contrast, one may be perfectly sincere, as one is with oneself. The friend is thus "a sort of paradox in nature," Emerson argues, because although (a) "every man alone is sincere," and (b) "at the entrance of a second person, hypocrisy begins," yet (c) the true friend is an other with whom I may be as sincere as I am with myself. Emerson gives this paradox a metaphysical slant, and recalls the "idealism" that runs as a leitmotiv through his writing, as he ends the paragraph. He states:

> I who alone am, I who see nothing in nature whose existence I can affirm with equal evidence to my own, behold now the semblance of my being in all its height, variety and curiosity, reiterated in a foreign form; so that a friend may well be reckoned the masterpiece of nature. (*CW* 2: 120)

This is one of many moments in Emerson's texts where, along with his confrontation of an essential self, he also finds an other—sometimes in nature, sometimes in the words of a poet, and sometimes, as here, in a friend. The setting of the encounter with the ideal friend is one of pleasure and spectacle. As Emerson puts it in one of his seemingly throwaway lines: "My friend gives me entertainment without requiring any stipulation on my part" (*CW* 2: 120).

Emerson has distinguished two elements of friendship: sincerity and tenderness. In paragraph fourteen, he addresses tenderness, beginning with the tender anxiety we feel in the face of another person to whom we are drawn: "we can scarce believe that so much character can subsist in another as to draw us by love." But he undercuts this tenderness when he states: "I . . . tender myself least to him to whom I am the most devoted" (*CW* 2: 120). The lesson seems to be: devotion yes, tenderness not so much. Emerson's critique (but not abandonment) of tenderness relies on the previous paragraph's discussion of sincerity and self-reliance. An excess of tenderness or a false idea of tenderness—humoring someone, or following someone's stipulations—is the death of friendship, precisely because it conflicts with following one's own path.

Emerson thus sketches a reformed tenderness, blending "the municipal virtues of justice, punctuality, fidelity and pity" with a dose of the extraordinary or new. Friendship is to "dignify to each other the daily needs and offices" of our lives, but it should avoid degenerating into "something usual and settled." Friends "should be alert and inventive" (*CW* 2: 121).[4]

In paragraphs fifteen and sixteen Emerson discusses numbers: can more than two persons achieve the high conversation that is the form friendship often takes? What he calls the "law of one to one" is essential for "conversation," and conversation is "the practice and consummation of friendship." The presence of two people is necessary for friendship, but not sufficient, for conversation is a matter of "affinity," not of will. A man reputed to be a great conversationalist, Emerson explains, does not therefore necessarily have "a word [for] his cousin or uncle" (*CW* 2: 122).

The argument begun in paragraph thirteen concerning truth, tenderness, and the encounter with one's majestic "semblance" is interwoven with themes of distance, reception, patience, and self-reliance. Emerson rewrites a lesson of "The Divinity School Address," where he advises the graduates not to be "too anxious to visit periodically all families and each family in your parish," but to make their occasional visits count: "when you meet one of these men or women, be to them a divine man; . . . let their timid aspirations find in you a friend; let their trampled instincts be genially tempted out in your atmosphere" (*CW* 1: 90). Now in "Friendship" Emerson writes that we should not "desecrate noble and beautiful souls by intruding on them." The friend is great enough to be revered, but reverence requires distance. "Treat your friend as a spectacle," Emerson advises. "Of course he has merits that are not yours, and that you cannot honor, if you must needs hold him close to your person. Stand aside; give those merits room; let them mount and expand" (*CW* 2: 123). The closeness of friendship requires a certain distance. This closeness is not physical: "You shall not come nearer a man by getting into his house." It is a matter not of will but of what Emerson calls "the uprise of nature in us to the same degree it is in them: then shall we meet as water with water" (*CW* 2: 123–124).

Emerson writes in "Self-Reliance": "do your work and I shall know you" (*CW* 2: 32). The condition of being known is that you do your own work. Friends have more than just knowledge of each other, for they constitute a unity. All this is being said in "Friendship" when Emerson writes: "There must be very two, before there can be very one. Let it be an alliance of two large formidable natures, mutually beheld, mutually feared, before yet they recognize the deep identity which beneath these disparities unites them" (*CW* 2: 123).

In "The Divinity School Address" Emerson contrasts the friendly message of Jesus with the fearful message of the church. Yet here in "Friendship," the friend should inspire awe and even fear: fear of what? Not of divine punishment as from a wrathful god, clearly, but of condescension as she rises to new heights.[5] Friends are equals who spur each other to greater efforts, and greater deeds. Readers of Nietzsche will find anticipations of *Thus Spoke Zarathustra*'s chapter "On the Friend" in the passage from "Friendship" just quoted, and in Emerson's continuation, which goes as follows:

> That great defying eye, that scornful beauty of his mien and action, do not pique yourself on reducing, but rather fortify and enhance. . . . Guard him as thy counterpart. Let him be to thee forever a sort of beautiful enemy, untameable, devoutly revered, and not a trivial conveniency to be soon outgrown and cast aside. (*CW* 2: 123–124)

We turn from the friend who no longer drives us toward our good, but not from the friend with whom we still beautifully contend. We should thus want to enhance and preserve the friend as a "beautiful enemy": only as such will a friend remain worthy of being with us "forever."

In a remarkably similar passage in *Zarathustra*, Nietzsche writes:

> In a friend one should still honor the enemy. Can you go close to your friend without going over to him?
> In a friend one should have one's best enemy. You should be closest to him with your heart when you resist him. . . .
> Are you pure air and solitude and bread and medicine for your friend?
> . . .
> Are you a slave? Then you cannot be a friend. Are you a tyrant? Then you cannot have friends. (Nietzsche 1982, 168–169)[6]

Nietzsche's tyrant corresponds to Emerson's overly tender or solicitous "friend," who wants us to humor him. We who humor him are his slaves. Friends for both Nietzsche and Emerson preserve and enhance both their own freedom and power and that of their friend. As Emerson puts it in the last sentence of his essay, friendship "treats its object as a god, that it may deify both."

Emerson's essay progresses from a diffuse friendship at a distance, to our disappointments with our friends, to the reality of friendship in our lives and its promise of something better than any friendship we have yet achieved. The essay concludes with the repeated warning that much of what we accept as friendship is not the real thing. The concluding tone is set in paragraph twenty-two, which opens in a slightly world-weary fashion: "The higher the style we demand of friendship, of course the less easy to establish it with flesh and blood. We walk alone in the world. Friends, such as we desire, are dreams and fables" (*CW* 2: 125).

In our impatience for companionship, Emerson goes on to say, we settle for friendship of a lower type: for "rash and foolish alliances," "false relations," and "leagues of friendship with cheap persons" (*CW* 2: 125). Reprising the themes of affinity and patience, he counsels his readers not to reach for others who do not belong to them by nature, but to persist in their own paths. Not by will, but only by the attraction of their character will they be able to "draw" to themselves "the first-born of the world."

Echoing earlier passages about the virtue of domestic poverty versus the allure of foreign wealth, Emerson now states:

> We go to Europe, or we pursue persons, or we read books in the instinctive faith that these will call it out and *reveal us to ourselves*. Beggars all. The persons are such as we; the Europe, an old faded garment of dead persons; the books, their ghosts. Let us drop this idolatry. Let us give over this mendicancy. Let us even bid our dearest friends farewell, and defy them, saying, "Who are you? Unhand me: I will be dependent no more." (*CW* 2: 125–126, my stress)

We beg, when we should look at home for what we need. Those from whom we beg are also beggars. Emerson calls our begging practice "idolatry." We mistake another beggar for a god. Idols are made of stone, whereas divinity lies in the power of thought and transition—as found in, for instance, the conversations and confrontations of great friends.

In the essay's penultimate paragraph, Emerson confesses that in his "languid moods" he fails to follow the advice he has given. He occupies himself with "foreign objects" rather than his own development, and settles for the "household joy" and "warm sympathies" that constitute so much of what ordinarily passes for friendship. Yet he also testifies to his turnings from such friendships, a policy of aversion that runs parallel to the relation to books he recommends in "The American Scholar." For while books are a great part of the scholar's education, their true purpose is to inspire the scholar's own thought. This is why "books are for the scholar's idle times" (*CW* 1: 57). It is not that when you are reading you are not doing anything, but that reading is secondary to your own life. As with books, so with friends:

> I do then with my friends as I do with my books. I would have them where I can find them, but I seldom use them. . . . I cannot afford to speak much with my friend. If he is great, he makes me so great that I cannot descend to converse. In the great days, presentiments hover before me in the firmament. . . . Then, though I prize my friends, I cannot afford to talk with them and study their visions, lest I lose my own. (*CW* 2: 126)

As the "Friendship" essay comes to its end, the themes of self-reliance and an extreme if benign separation from others come to the fore. Emerson ends the penultimate paragraph with the thought that he will meet with his friends "as though we met not, and part as though we parted not." He returns to the idea of friendship at a distance in the essay's final paragraph: "It has seemed to me lately more possible than I knew, to carry a friendship greatly on one side, without due correspondence on the other." But he immediately undercuts the alleged advantages or virtues of such a friendship when he states: "Yet these things may hardly be said without a sort of treachery to the relation. The essence of friendship is entireness, a total magnanimity and trust" (*CW* 2: 127). Where does this leave us?

Looking back on the "Friendship" essay, we can see that Emerson offers a range of experiences that constitute friendship: great struggles and great alliances between beautiful enemies, conversational brilliance and expansion, a joyful solitude (as if someone has departed rather than arrived), a generalized benevolence toward people in the street to whom one does not speak, the warm sympathies and household joy one shares with a familiar friend, the disappointment of a friend outgrown. But what our best friendships give us, Emerson holds, is a sense of our own power and prospects.

If I were to register any criticism of Emerson's essay it would be for something he leaves out, namely the death of a friend. No doubt I am particularly sensitive to the issue, as I have lost a dear friend in the past year. It is not as if Emerson knew nothing of such loss, for by the time he published *Nature* in 1836, he had lost his wife Ellen and his younger brother, Charles. Indeed, he brings up the subject of a friend's death in the plaintive and somewhat abrupt end to the first chapter of *Nature.* After praising nature for her comforts, and recording an ecstatic experience "in snow puddles, at twilight," Emerson ends the chapter as follows:

> Nature always wears the colors of the spirit. To a man laboring under a calamity, the heat of his own fire hath sadness in it. Then, there is a kind of contempt of the landscape felt by him who has just lost by death a dear friend. The sky is less grand as it shuts down over less worth in the population. (*CW* 1: 10–11)

Here the world as a whole loses significance: we are in the domain of what Wittgenstein calls the "world" of "the unhappy man" (1963, 72).

There is another form the loss of a friend takes in our lives, in which it is not the world as a whole that loses its worth or significance, but a part of oneself that is threatened. Emerson sets us in the right direction for appreciating this point when he writes in "Spiritual Laws": "That mood into which a friend can bring us is his dominion over us" (*CW* 2: 84). The word "dominion" means control or lordship, and also the lands or domains of a lord. Putting these senses together we can understand Emerson as saying that our friend allows us to live in a domain that we enter only in the mood into which he can bring us. Now when the friend dies, the mood into which he can bring us, the domain in which we lived together under his authority, dies with him. I think of this as a diminution of the self, a loss of that part of us that shows itself only with this friend (James 1983, 280–282). Emerson suggests a different view in "Experience" when he considers the loss of his child and finds, to his surprise and dismay, not a loss of self but a self still intact, though it is unable to absorb or process the events of its life.

Emerson's skepticism about friendship is part of his critique of the lower forms that human life mostly takes. His account of friendship shows an intense focus on moral perfection—on our unattained but attainable self, alone and with others—but an equally intense awareness of what he calls "the plaint of tragedy" that sounds throughout our lives "in regard to persons, to friendship and love."

Notes

1. Emerson uses the term in "Culture" (*CW* 6: 72, where it is written "master-tones"), but I am following Cavell's adaptation of the term in understanding it to name main themes of his work (Cavell 2004, 117).

2. See "Emerson's Mystical Empiricism" (Goodman 1997a) and "Paths of Coherence in Emerson's Philosophy: The Case of 'Nominalist and Realist'" (Goodman 2009).

3. In Aristotle's *Nicomachean Ethics,* reciprocity is a necessary condition for friendship.

4. This blend of the daily and the inventive matches nicely with Cavell's descriptions of "remarriage comedy" in *Pursuits of Happiness* (1981).

5. Cf. Emerson's statement that "virtue is Height" (*CW* 2: 40).

6. Nietzsche reread Emerson's essays during the summer before he composed *Thus Spoke Zarathustra*. See Walter Kaufmann's introduction to *The Gay Science* (Nietzsche 1974) and my "Moral Perfectionism and Democracy in Emerson and Nietzsche" (Goodman 1997b).

FIVE

On the Faces of Emersonian "Friendship"

JOHN T. LYSAKER

> We strangely stand on,—souls do,—on the very edges of their own spheres, leaning tiptoe towards & into the adjoining sphere.
>
> EMERSON

By invoking the figure of the friend we enter a terse if not adverse context. From the vantage point of canonical social science and its altruism-egoism binary, friendship reduces to a series of modest self-sacrifices in the interest of long-term dividends. Friendship also bears a kind of social pressure apparent to those who wonder where all the good times went. Given the dispersion of unified communities and the sheer estrangement of large-scale society, friendship, like intimacy, must address our need for companionship and recognition, even as the pace of contemporary social life eats up the shared time friendship requires. In fact, the demands of workplace and home, to the degree that computers and cell phones haven't elided that distinction, often leave us with friendships that offer, at best, what Emerson terms a "short and confounding pleasure" (*CW* 2: 123). Mostly, however, we share entertainments that serve less to entwine than to keep us at arm's length. Of course, we might cushion our lives with liaisons that further our careers, but that would only, as Emerson says, prostitute "the name of friendship to signify modish and worldly alliances" (*CW* 2: 121).

I note these social contexts because they set what is to come at a distance, and give it a certain urgency. In order to better receive those thoughts, however, I must also recall another context, namely, self-culture, which I regard as a central issue of Emerson's texts. Self-culture seeks an eloquent life that manifests the character that we have found ourselves able and willing to live out. Not that eloquence entails self-mastery. Given the breadth of our "quoting" nature and its ongoing metamorphoses, we manifest more than possibilities found and affirmed. Second, in a manner that confounds analysis, the life we aim to cultivate is given pre-reflectively in variously mooded events of native and ecstatic genius. The former is tied to temperament, a determinate affinity for certain worldly engagements (e.g., knowing, doing, or saying) and thus for certain corners of the world (e.g., commerce or reform). Ecstatic genius involves similar disclosures and alliances, though these exceed native dictates, and thereby prove to be incalculable.

This twofold genius is the wellspring for an eloquent life. It focuses our ongoing conversation with things, and allows us to meet ourselves, coming and going amid the world. But genius is not self-executing. Instead, its pre-reflective launches must be translated into practical power, and this requires a series of reflective acts. Some reflective acts are negative, such as aversion to conformity and apology; others are positive, such as abandonment to the ventures our genius proffers. And some among the latter are creative in their own right, e.g., prospecting possible futures for what is dawning upon us. Self-culture is thus a raveling and unraveling braid of pre-reflective and reflective events.

Though purposive and thus teleological, self-culture never concludes. We are ever subject to motion and rest, living under a law of metamorphosis. Self-culture is thus an interminable affair; there will always be a chance that our genius will call us to undo who we have been. And so, from where I read and think: "The primary question that distinguishes like a Day of Judgment between men is: Are they still advancing? Or are the seals set to their character and they now making a merchandise simply of that which they can do?" (*EL* 3: 235).

On my reading, friendship marks a principal site of Emersonian self-culture, a turnstile that might advance us in ways that elude the ledgers of capital and the calculus of hedonism. In fact, Emersonian friendship has the power to facilitate spectacular encounters. Everything hinges, of course, on addressing and receiving our friends appropriately, and Emerson's "Friendship" pursues this matter, albeit in a puzzling manner that both celebrates and despairs of friendship. In fact, if read as a synchronous assemblage of propositions, the essay is riddled with contradiction: for instance, friends make the sweetness of life but do not exist. The contradiction also seems performative when Emerson confesses in paragraph seven: "I cannot deny it, O friend, that the vast shadow of the Phenomenal includes thee also" (*CW* 2: 116).[1] Now, one expects an Emersonian to observe any given essay's contradictions, if only in preparation for a more nuanced reading. But here I find the essay's internal tensions to be phenomenological. Friendships ebb and flow—initial enthusiasm, then disappointment, and hopefully, later renewal. I thus find a kind of mimesis in Emerson's essay whose acuity less defines friendship than unfolds the task it entails and the prospects that await those who assume it.

Let us begin with the first six paragraphs, which are flush with promise and focused by an unabashed confession: "A new person is to me a great event" (*CW* 2: 115). Several observations provoke the remark. First, reciprocal interest and affection is a source of great pleasure. "What is so pleasant," Emerson writes, "as these jets of affection which make a young world for me again?" (*CW* 2: 114). But pleasure is not the half of it. A friend evidences a possibility rarely apparent, which in turn unveils a life yet to be lived. As Emerson tells Margaret Fuller: "Yet every assurance that magnanimity walks & works around us we need: it is the best of all external experiences, we pray toward it as to the holy city" (*CL* 2: 344).[2] Moreover, with the onset of friendship "our intellectual and active powers increase with our affection," and so a friend not only awakens life, but also what we have to bring to its rushes. In fact, an early letter suggests that without friends our inspirations tend to fizzle. "A thousand smart things I have to say which born in silence die in silence for lack of his ear" (*CL* 1: 224). Or, in words that Emerson recorded in Topical Notebook XO: "'Thou learnest no secret,' says Hafiz, 'until thou knowest friendship, since to the unsound no heavenly knowledge comes in'" (*TN* 2: 224). In other words, friends ignite us, bringing us face to face with powers we otherwise might not have had.

But why should a friend have this power? In the presence of one we admire, we want to shine. Recalling how he tried to dazzle his wife, Alice, Calvin Trillin says: "But I never stopped trying to match that [first] evening—not just trying to entertain her but trying to impress her. Decades later—after we had been married for more than thirty-five years, after our girls were grown—I still wanted to impress her."[3] It isn't simply that we wish to win favor. Rather, her judgment matters, and deeply, for it is also our judgment—we praise what we esteem. So when those we admire are impressed, they are so within this mutual understanding, and they become a kind of conscience to us that gazes out of other eyes.

Set within this scene of mutual recognition, friendship finds a core that binds, whether the friends are apart or new persons come aboard. Thus Emerson asks, "Will these too separate themselves from me again, or some of them?" And he continues,

> I know not, but I fear it not; for my relation to them is so pure, that we hold by simple affinity, and the Genius of my life being thus social, the same affinity will exert its energy on whomsoever is as noble as these men and women, wherever I may be. (*CW* 2: 115)

Such an appreciation draws Emerson toward what Aristotle regards as a friendship of ηθος, what we might translate as "character," though in a way that underscores its orientation toward the good life, hence the term's cognate, ηθικος, or ethics. Whereas friendships of use and pleasure share temporary ends or satisfactions, ethical friendships share a vision of flourishing, thereby convening characters that are structured by tradition and habit to pursue their mutual good. As Emerson says toward the essay's end: "In the last analysis, love is only the reflection of a man's own worthiness from other men. Men have sometimes exchanged names with their friends, as if they would signify that in their friend each loved his own soul" (*CW* 2: 125). This is a remarkable thought. Love for a friend acknowledges his worthiness (i.e., nobility) and tends to his flourishing insofar as he is noble. For example, we may help another develop talents, overcome vices, or explore new vistas. Such acknowledgments do not simply respect nobility, however, but are themselves noble—they address a worthy peer in a worthy manner. Now, if the befriended is truly noble, he will return the favor, thus perpetuating a mimetic praxis that eventuates in characters analogous to one another, and to the point that a friendship rewards itself. As Emerson says: "The only reward of virtue is virtue: the only way to have a friend is to be a friend" (*CW* 2: 124).[4]

In presenting friendship's reward via ethos, Emerson actualizes an early insistence, contra those he calls the "Hobbists," that we genuinely "promote the very good fortune of my friend" (*JMN* 3: 25). In an ethical friendship, we seek another's flourishing because we hold that virtue should be rewarded, and our own virtuous response is that reward. Such a response is neither altruistic nor egoistic, however. First, friends aren't setting their own interests aside in tending to one another. Seeing one another flourish is precisely their reciprocal interest. But this is not a matter of egoism. Friendship rewards virtue with virtue because that is what being noble means, not because it furthers one's strategic goals. And if one proves only to be out for one's own well-being, one will prove other than noble and will thus not merit the love of a friend.

I note the ethical cast of Emersonian friendship for three reasons. First, it makes plain how distant this kind of friendship is from prevailing conceptions. Unlike those of pleasure and use, ethical friendships set terms that do not admit of compartmentalization. Instead, they claim us at every point along the circumference of our being, and by way of ends which they both articulate and actualize. Second, such terms dramatically present the initial promise of friendship: of another self, and should the fever spread, of something approaching an actualized humanity, a concrete universal. As Emerson says to Caroline Sturgis: "a true and *native* friend is only the extension of our own being and perceiving into other skies and societies, there learning wisdom, there discerning spirits, and attracting our own for us, as truly as we had done hitherto in our strait enclosure" (*CL* 2: 326). No wonder, then, that Emerson finds in friendship not only the power to please and stir, but also to cheer and sustain. "Let the soul be assured that somewhere in the universe it should rejoin its friend, and it would be content and cheerful alone for a thousand years" (*CW* 2: 114).[5] Third, I find the remainder of Emerson's essay to be a lesson in this ethos, and thus we need to know the rigors of its commerce if we expect to gauge the character it requires.

After six paragraphs, Emerson's essay leaves us flush with the presence of newly found friends. We forget, however, that no one ever remains so new; their event subsides. And in that ebb, their promise tarnishes until in the "golden hour of friendship, we are surprised by suspicion and unbelief," and are eventually forced to acknowledge that friendship, "like the immortality of the soul is too good to be believed" (*CW* 2: 116). This is the despair of paragraph seven (*CW* 2: 116–117), fueled by the observation: "I cannot make your consciousness tantamount to mine." In the knowledge that we are distinct, in what Emerson elsewhere terms our "fall," enthusiasms wane, and the weave of an actualized humanity begins to fray at the fingers of a thought that "all persons underlie the same condition of infinite remoteness." This thought troubles us because it undermines the reliability of whatever stimulus and recognition a friend provides. Are we regarding them rightly? Will they read us well? It also evidences how ethical friendships admit of qualitative distances: "Thou hast come to me lately, and already thou are seizing thy cloak and hat." In other words, even our friends may prove like the "commended stranger," introduced in paragraph three, whose approach brings out our best but whose arrival, replete with partialities, disappoints and draws us into less venturesome orbits.

Now, Emerson doesn't suggest that our desire for friendship halts at this fault line. Rather, it casts our longing within a continual movement between solitude and a communion that pleases but flickers in the "vast shadow of the Phenomenal." In its first seven paragraphs, then, the "Friendship" essay swings from bursting confidence to dispirited lament.

But the beat goes on. In fact, paragraphs eight to ten make plain that we shouldn't accept the terms on which friendship is but a "delicious torment" (*CW* 2: 117–118). Such "uneasy pleasures and fine pains are for curiosity, not for life." This distinction between curiosity and life forecasts the move that opens Emerson's essay on "Fate," where a question concerning the *Zeitgeist* resolves into one concerning the conduct of life. That is, in "Friendship" as in "Fate," Emerson retreats from speculation into action and the life that is conducted there, as if speculation leads us astray.

To my mind, we are at a principal pivot, one where a turn in how to think the friend begins to teach us how to be a friend. First, we are chastised in paragraph eight: "We seek our friend not sacredly, but with an adulterate passion which would appropriate him to ourselves." I take this to say that the divergences of the friend, her so-called partialities, shouldn't be read as cracks in the character of our friendship. Or said otherwise, ethical friendship, in seeking another self, should seek enlargement and not agreement. As Emerson will say later, trapped in masculine metaphorics:

> Let him not cease an instant to be himself. The only joy I have in his being mine, is that the *not mine is mine*. I hate, where I looked for a manly furtherance, or at least a manly resistance, to find a mush of concession. Better be a nettle in the side of your friend than his echo. (*CW* 2: 122–123)

Or, in the words of paragraph nine: "I ought to be equal to every relation." This line adds provocation to paragraph eight's chastisement, one that indicates an open conversation where paragraph seven found a fissure.

One certainly could read this third set of paragraphs as a retraction of paragraph seven. But note how paragraph ten begins: "Our impatience is thus sharply rebuked," i.e., in its initial hopes and despair, which the essay has now proved to be overhasty. I find this language instructive. It suggests less a conceptual error than one of conduct; namely, it is sheer impatience to expect that the actualization of our ethos could be coincident with a friend's arrival. Emerson's point is not simply negative here, however; it sets patience within the constellation of virtues that make up ethical friendship. "Respect the *naturlangsamkeit,*" Emerson stresses—the "natural slowness"—"which hardens the ruby in a million years," and "let us approach the friend with an audacious trust in the truth of his heart" (*CW* 2: 118).

But why patience? (We will return to trust.) I think the answer lies in appreciating Emerson's reasons for redirecting our inquiry toward "life" and away from "curiosity"—reasons that are given concisely at the close of "Experience," where he declares: "I know that the world I converse with in the city and in the farms, is not the world *I think*. I observe that difference, and shall observe it" (*CW* 3: 48). Curiosity moves in the world of the "I think," but that is not the realm of life, the realm where I converse, a realm wherein I might think the friend phenomenal, but nevertheless address her or him (as Emerson twice does in paragraph seven). Among friends, therefore, we should proceed in observance of that difference, which is to say, we should return again and again to those scenes in which life is conducted, and strive to prove equal to what is found there—such as the fact that we address another as friend, or have been hailed as one. Perhaps we might conclude, then, as Emerson does in his "Wide World" journal: "Friendship is [the] practical triumph over all forms of malignant philosophy" (*JMN* 2: 193).

Of course, "Friendship" does not end here, though in some ways it begins here—or rather, and this is the point, it begins *again*. Emerson renews his undertaking by turning to identify, almost by way of philosophical definition, some of friendship's essential traits, as if only where life is conducted could we begin to assay the demands of friendship. This discussion, which runs from paragraph eleven through paragraph thirteen, is striking in several ways (*CW* 2: 118–121). First, as if to remind us of the stakes, Emerson explicitly eschews consideration of friendship's social benefits. Second, one has to wonder whether the proposed "elements that go into the composition of friendship," namely sincerity and tenderness, aren't offered as a test of sorts. (I say this given Emerson's previous resistance to "curiosity.") Not that they are offered ironically. Rather, I take it that the previous discussion should prepare us to receive these elements in a particular way, more as friendly maxims than as components of a categorical definition—aids to being and having friends, not criteria for identifying the real McCoy. In other words, I read these elements under the aegis of Emerson's own observation that a "friend is a sane man who exercises not my ingenuity but me."[6]

Other provocations also grace these paragraphs, and one arrives in the last: friendship "should never fall into something usual and settled, but should be alert and inventive, and add rhyme and reason to what was drudgery." I find it helpful to read this through the opening poem's suggestion that in the worth of a friend, "The mill-round of our fate appears / A sun path . . ." (lines 15–16). These thoughts come together in what they avoid, i.e., foolish repetitions, even consistencies; but also in what they affirm, namely, the unexpected and its occlusion, or a "sun path," which is of course a matter of dawns and twilights, midnights and noons. Friendship is thus not merely seasoned by invention, but is kept lively. Moreover, if we are to be "equal to every relation," particularly among our friends, we must be patient and alert, poised to "detect and watch that gleam of light which flashes across his mind," to transpose a line from "Self-Reliance" (*CW* 2: 27). I recall the line from paragraph nine because being "equal to every relation" means being able to rise to every occasion—and that may prove surprising, even strange, if the soul in fact becomes as "Self-Reliance" claims. Moreover, in ethical friendships "the Genius of my life" proves social, that is, the ethical affinity of friends can "exert its energy on whomsoever is as noble as these men and women" (*CW* 2: 115), and so we must remain alert for such exertions, uncertain of the quarter from which they will seize us. When they do arrive, however, we must seize them. Thus Emerson later commands, with reference to the friend: "Worship his superiorities: wish him not less by a thought, but hoard and tell them all. Guard him as thy counterpart" (*CW* 2: 124).

If friendship is to prove such a lively affair, it must be sincere, which is to say, more or less naked. Emerson writes, being just that with his readers:

> Before him, I may think aloud. I am arrived at last in the presence of a man so real and equal, that I may drop even those undermost garments of dissimulation, courtesy, and second thought, which men never put off, and may deal with him with the simplicity and wholeness, with which one chemical atom meets another. (*CW* 2: 119)

This exuberance recalls me to the figure of genius, to disclosures that overwhelm us and form the vantage point from which other thoughts receive instruction. In allowing our genius to be social—by taking on the sallies of another, by risking our own in their presence—we are exposed, possibly embarrassed. I stress this because these images say more than that we should always be frank with our friends—which is fair enough; sincerity may require that. But we should not think this reduces to telling friends and colleagues how much we dislike their prose. The charge instead, drawing on the opening poem's penultimate line, is to broach contact in the "fountains of my hidden life," which is a charge to be true to what unfolds, risky as that may be. And this helps us to think Emerson's earlier claim that friendship requires a total trust. At the point of genius, we must be willing to revel in involuntary combustions, and that requires a trust that exceeds the reach and performativity of inductive foresight.

It is apparent that the ethos of Emersonian friendship leans toward and into an *agon,* though one that is less concerned with disputation than with daemonic bursts. I was thus cheered by Emerson's later command to receive the friend in ways that subvert the taxonomic force of the category: "Let him be to thee forever a sort of beautiful enemy, untamable, devoutly revered, and not a trivial conveniency to be soon outgrown and cast aside" (*CW* 2: 124). If, in our love, we are open to a friend's noble bearing such that it might become our own (and I take it that such openness is part of the ethos of Emersonian friendship), then she might suddenly arrive as the enemy of our past selves and (like any aspect of genius) call us down paths we had not expected to travel. I appreciate this rhetorical inversion of "friend" and "enemy," because it keeps us alert to the potential strangeness with which our friends might reward our virtue, and to how those who are not yet our friends might prove to be so. Said otherwise, if the ethos of Emersonian friendship requires us to be "equal to every relation," its claim extends us beyond any circle of extant friends and into an open regard for the full breadth of our conversations.[7]

We have wandered into the essay's final bursts, but before we leave Emerson's exercise in definition, one more element bears notice—and precisely as an element, that is, as a point where atoms meet. If our friendships are to be venturesome, they will require what Emerson terms "tenderness."

> The end of friendship is a commerce the most strict and homely that can be joined. . . . It is for aid and comfort through all the relations and passages of life and death. It is fit for serene days, and graceful gifts, and country rambles, but also for rough roads and hard fare, shipwreck, poverty, and persecution. (*CW* 2: 121)

This is a hardy companionship, as loyal as it is tender, and it observes two insights already apparent in an early journal entry. "It is good for a man to feel that he is cared for, that anxious eyes are cast upon the course of his fortunes as they are tossed on Time's waters. He will not distrust the faculties that another does not distrust" (*JMN* 2: 198–199). Ethical friendships sustain because, as we have seen, the high regard of one that we find noble is itself ennobling, and so tenderness not only tends to wounds, but to the future as well. Tenderness also buoys the lover. "Every man who aspires to high things is more or less suspicious and suspected of being more exquisitely self-loving. The best way to parry this charge, is to be deeply interested in another's welfare" (*JMN* 3: 198–199). The only way to have a friend is to be one, you may recall—and this we do, in part, by proactively tending to each other.

Thus far my effort has been to argue that "Friendship" assays an ethos that eschews self-preservation in favor of far-flung ventures of self and other. But how often is that possible—and for how long? This is the precise question that opens the essay's final section, paragraphs fourteen to twenty-four (*CW* 2: 121–127): "Friendship may be said to require natures so rare and costly . . . that its satisfaction can very seldom be assured." I find this wording to be precise. Given its demands and elemental character, friendship's terms are rarely satisfied, and we, in striving to meet them, rarely meet with satisfaction. Because this observation concerns assurances, I do not hear the despair of paragraph seven being repeated, but rather a kind of humility before a daunting task. I also say this because paragraphs fourteen to sixteen thicken the terms that friendship must satisfy. For instance, a "rare mean betwixt likeness and unlikeness" must meet, for in its absence folk "will never suspect the latent powers in each." And while Emerson does not limit friendship to two, he does suggest that the naked, daemonic conversation that consummates it is a two-person affair, and a fleeting one at that. It is an "evanescent relation—no more." Moreover: "My friends have come to me unsought" (*CW* 2: 115). Said otherwise, some measure of luck lies behind profound meetings, friendship being the "uprise of nature in us to the same degree it is in them." In still other words, we cannot manufacture friendships through sheer dint of will: "We talk of choosing our friends, but friends are self-elected" (*CW* 2: 123).

Emerson's feel for the fragility of friendship is particularly refined at this point. Thoroughly amicable relations are born of accidental beginnings and their consummations do not linger. This is not what truly keys this final section, however. Rather, it is Emerson's response in paragraph seventeen: "Friendship demands a religious treatment. . . . Reverence is a great part" (*CW* 2: 123). Deep in friendship's rising, Emerson again invokes a sort of bearing or comportment—similar to what Heidegger, rendering *praxis* in Greek, terms a *Haltung*—a determinate orientation toward what we undergo and how we undergo it. In this case of friendship, Emerson's favored regard has phantasmic implications.

> Treat your friend as spectacle. Of course he has merits that are not yours, and that you cannot honor, if you must needs hold him close to your person. Stand aside; give those merits room; let them mount and expand. . . . To a great heart he will still be a stranger in a thousand particulars, that he may come near in the holiest ground. (*CW* 2: 123)

Here Emerson adds to the patience he enjoins in paragraph ten. He acknowledges that love for the friend draws us near enough to discover divergences, even traits that we cannot praise (though not because they are vicious, but simply because they are too like or unlike what fuels our fire). But rather than have them threaten our satisfactions, he steps aside to better witness, enjoy, and even tend to the friend's unfolding. Without this reserve, delicious torments await us and breaches open where extraordinary sights might otherwise have been. Or, one suffocates: "All human pleasures have their dregs & even Friendship itself hath bitter lees," writes Emerson. "Who is he that thought he might clasp his friend in embraces so tight, in daily intercourse so familiar that they two should be one?" (*JMN* 2: 227). Not that the language of "spectacle" implies that one should turn one's friend into an entertainment (in the current sense of what it is to "entertain"). Rather, in leaving room for their abundance, the "spectacle" of the friend will also prove a "spectacle" for our visions—"something that aids the intellectual sight," as Webster's tells us in 1828. Said more directly, finding space for another's particular bursts facilitates his or her enlargement as well as our own.[8]

Patience, alertness, sincerity, humility, tenderness, and worship, these are some of the terms of the ethos convening Emersonian friendship, terms offered to keep us close—though not too close—to hidden fountains that sometimes jet into one another, mixing like and unlike and thus remaking each. This ethos thus affirms what earlier provoked despair, namely, the difference and departures that make up friendship.

> Seest though not, O brother, that thus we part only to meet again on a higher platform, and only because we are more our own? A friend is Janus-faced: he looks to the past and the future. He is the child of all my foregoing hours, the prophet of those to come, and the harbinger of a greater friend. (*CW* 2: 126)

This passage thrills us because a Janus-faced friend is a figure of ebb and flow, one whose departure may later (and knowingly) return to an enlarged "I" and "we." What once seemed strange may return in the glare of genius, fixing us with insight, provocation, and prospect. It also thrills because it suggests that in each instance we should receive the friend like the "commended stranger" introduced in paragraph three. A reverent regard receives the friend as a "stranger in a thousand particulars" (*CW* 2: 123) and yet as commended by "foregoing hours." In order to be equal to his arrival we must eschew, therefore, what is usual and settled, and remain alert to the possibility that one of these thousand strange particulars may prove the prophet of future hours.[9]

At such points, friendship and self-culture meet in what is really a double consciousness, wherein we side with our emerging selves against the inertia of our foregoing hours, alert to the prophecy of one another and loyal to our prospects. But because this is friendship, we owe the same to our companions, and thus must side with their emerging selves as well, come what may. In *Conduct of Life,* Emerson celebrates self-culture because it unlocks us from our "mastertones," which I read as native genius or temperament (*CW* 6: 72). It even "succors us against ourselves" so that we might develop a catholicity that reaches beyond our normal ken. But then, this is precisely what the friend effects if we reverently approach and tend to his spectacle. Ethical friendships are practices of enlargement—each friend is the harbinger of a better one, one whose character more eloquently articulates the affirmations that convene and bind them. A friend thus not only helps us stay true to ourselves, but to venture and travel wider than we might otherwise have dared, our reach no less lengthened than strengthened by their conduct.[10] And again—this centripetal event is two-fold, perhaps even manifold. We owe it to our friends to be as eloquently noble as possible, and to reward their virtue with our own. And presuming complacency is a vice, something akin to hubris, as if we had completely come into our own, then we owe our friends a life of proactive self-culture, one capable of proving a prophet of hours to come. From the perspective of self-culture, then, we can speak of friends as Emerson speaks of history's great figures: "within the limits of human education and agency, we may say, great men exist that there may be greater men" (*CW* 4: 20).

We have traveled some distance with Emerson, welcoming the address of his essay in the hopes of clarifying friendship by way of themes, performances, and certain prospects. In much of what he offers, a kind, humble restraint has proven a key virtue, and one I have tried to observe at various points. Like all activities that would be virtues, however, it admits of excesses, and Emerson's own essay, at least toward its close, sways and falls in the direction of what I would term impersonality, following his usage in the essay "Love."

> But this dream of love, though beautiful, is only one scene in our play. In this procession of the soul from within outward, it enlarges its circles ever. . . . Neighborhood, size, numbers, habits, persons, lose by degrees their power over us. . . . Thus even love, which is the deification of persons, must become more impersonal every day. (*CW* 2: 107)

If the fountains of hidden lives commence in an upsurge of nature, we will eventually prove sublime as vaster relations arrive within and as our spectacle. But how far might friends follow out their expansions and credibly remain friends? This worry is not lost on Emerson, who sees quite well that the "higher style we demand of friendship, of course the less easy to establish it with flesh and blood" (*CW* 2: 125). But how well does he negotiate this expanding gulf?

In the essay's penultimate paragraph, Emerson announces: "I do then with my friends as I do with my books. I would have them where I can find them, but I seldom use them. We must have society on our own terms, and admit or exclude it on the slightest cause" (*CW* 2: 126).[11] This line clashes with the promise of paragraph thirteen, which insists that friendship is "fit for serene days, and graceful gifts . . . but also for rough roads and hard fare, shipwreck, poverty, and persecution" (*CW* 2: 121). The deep conflict between this passage and his later analogy is that books, while they may in various ways impoverish us, cannot also suffer a poverty that we ought to remedy. But then, "tenderness" is precisely one of Emerson's own terms, and thus the inconvenience of another's malady shouldn't offer him sufficient cause for exclusion. Nevertheless, he also confesses that:

> I cannot afford to speak much with my friend. If he is great, he makes me so great that I cannot descend to converse. . . . It would indeed give me a certain household joy to quit this lofty seeking . . . and come down to warm sympathies with you; but then I know well that I shall mourn always the vanishing of my gods. (*CW* 2: 126)

The dissonance rises between the denigrating "household" joys and Emerson's earlier affirmative statement that the "end of friendship is a commerce the most strict and homely that can be joined." "Homely" says much—namely, that the demands of friendship are sometimes unattractive, but no less that they pertain to where we live. And so, to return to Emerson: "we cannot forgive the poet if he spins his thread too fine, and does not substantiate his romance by the municipal virtues of justice, punctuality, fidelity, and pity" (*CW* 2: 121).[12]

At stake here is more an issue of tone and bearing than categorical missteps—but it is the same in friendship, where our manner alone can easily misalign orbits. For example, if we do not visit one another, I may come to wonder whether my concrete presence is more burdensome than welcome. And my unease would only intensify if I were to overhear this declaration:

> So I will owe to my friends this evanescent intercourse. I will receive from them not what they have, but what they are. They shall give me that which properly they cannot give, but which emanates from them. But they shall not hold me by any relation less subtle and pure. We will meet as though we met not, and part as though we parted not. (*CW* 2: 126)

But a love for what emanates from me is barely a love for me. In fact, such a love may prove equal parts contempt if what I *have* in addition to my emanation is simply homely. In the least, it seems to limit the interchange of friends to times of convenience. My concern therefore lies less with Emerson's odd belief that friends do not need to often meet, than with those moments when his feel for the friend wanes monological.[13]

Perhaps what I resist is simply the consummation of Emersonian friendship. Paragraph twenty-one insists: "We walk alone in the world. Friends, such as we desire, are dreams and fables" (*CW* 2: 125). Would not the voice of a solitary walker produce a monologue? But the point of Emersonian friendship, in its movement past the despair of paragraph seven, has been—while never denying the irreplaceably singular nature of the self—to lead and encourage one to venture outward and find oneself reflected in the character and love of another, hence the claim: "A friend, therefore, is a paradox in nature" (*CW* 2: 120). Moreover, Emersonian friendship is prophetically *en route*. What we desire in such a friend, therefore, is very much someone who keeps open the dream of a better future. In fact, noble friends should provide, by example (and even fabulistically), steps toward that horizon, as Socrates does for Crito. As Emerson notes in his *Platonia:* "Crito bribed the jailor, but Socrates would not go out by treachery. Whatever inconvenience ensue, nothing is to be preferred before Justice. These things I hear like pipes & drums whose sound makes me deaf to everything you say" (*JMN* 10: 483).

And yet, Emerson seems to be dismissing precisely any anxiety over this impersonality when he says: "It is foolish to be afraid of making our ties too spiritual, as if we could lose any genuine love," adding in the essay's final paragraph: "But the great will see that true love cannot be unrequited" (*CW*

2: 125, 127). But from where are such assurances made? An early line holds a partial answer. "The laws of friendship are austere and eternal, of one web with laws of nature and morals" (*CW* 2: 117). A second occurs in his essay, "Compensation": "All things are moral. That soul which within us is a sentiment, outside of us is a law. We feel its inspiration; out there in history we can see its fatal strength. A perfect equity adjusts its balance in all parts of life" (*CW* 2: 60). I am drawn back to "Compensation" because only that degree of strength—the kind wielded by divine, invisible hands—could assure us that love does not dissipate in its own evanescence.

This invocation of the doctrine of compensation here may seem invasive, but paragraph eleven of "Friendship" already announces what I am only now marking. There, Emerson terms friendship a "sacred relation which is a kind of absolute" compared to which "nothing is so divine." And look at how paragraph ten grounds its trust of the friend: "Love, which is the essence of God, is not for levity, but for the total worth of man . . . let us approach our friend with an audacious trust in the truth of his heart, in the breadth, impossible to be overturned, of his foundations" (*CW* 2: 118). And as he tells George Adams Sampson: "But never do I despair that by truth we shall merit truth; by resolute searching for truth ourselves we shall deserve & obtain wisdom from others. If not now, yet in God's time & the souls [*sic*], which is ages & ages" (*CL* 1: 378). A theological suture thus binds the ethos of Emersonian friendship, from its foundations to its most audacious trust. And the weave of a theodicy holds together "flesh and blood" at points where others, say those who write in the wake of divine decomposition, find only traces of a foregone great event.

Because I find myself writing in just that aftermath, I would pull back from the theological heights and depths that frame Emersonian friendship. My problem is not simply incredulity in the face of his doctrine of compensation; nor do I think the doctrine calls for too much one-to-one time with the divine. I take Emerson at his word when he professes a "sublime hope . . . that elsewhere, in other regions of universal power, souls are now acting, enduring, and daring, which can love us and which we can love" (*CW* 2: 125). But his idea of compensation does lead him to imagine friendship's consummation in terms that leave little room for "flesh and blood": "We may congratulate ourselves that the period of nonage, of follies, of blunders, and of shame, is passed in solitude, and when we are finished men, we shall grasp heroic hands in heroic hands" (*CW* 2: 125). To my ear, this sensibility offers real friendship few prospects. First, mortal life will have few friends if "nonage" names (as the essay "Circles" suggests) a state into which we fall again and again. Second, if friendship, in its provocations and tenderness, is essential to the ongoing task of coming into one's own, then gratefulness for solitude prior to maturity is a self-undermining disposition. Third, if folly and blunders are to be borne in solitude, what is the role of tenderness in Emersonian friendship? Wedded to the eternal, heroic hands will neither need nor have cause to expect tenderness, particularly if we are obliged to bear infirmities in silence.[14]

If what I foresee is right, I will remain in the homely and strict commerce of paragraph thirteen: one that is rich in loyalty, sincerity, patience, alertness, and humility. Poised for the arrival of commended strangers who might prove beautiful enemies in the sociality of genius, I will do without guaranteed compensations. Instead, I will address my friends, without melancholy, in the spirit and letter that Emerson offers Margaret Fuller in 1839:

> Let us in the one golden hour allowed us to be great & true, be shined upon by the sun & moon, & feel in our pulse circulations from the heart of nature. We shall be more content to be superseded some day, if we have once been clean & permeable channels. I should indeed be happy tonight to be excited by your eloquence & sympathy up to the point of vision,—and what more can friendship avail? (*CL* 2: 246).

And remaining so poised, and expecting no more, I think I will better observe the difference between the world I think and the one in which we converse, which itself should help me tend to my companions along rough roads, or simply in delight.

Notes

The epigraph is from Emerson, *JMN* 9: 228.

1. This line echoes a dictum which Montaigne attributes to Aristotle, and Emerson records: "O my friends, there is no friend" (*JMN* 6: 161).

2. Consider also this more convoluted missive: "Especially if any one show me a stroke of courage, a piece of inventive wit, a trait of character, or a pure delight in character when shown by others, always must I be that man's or that woman's debtor as one who has discovered to me among the perishing men somewhat more clean & incorruptible than the eternal light of these midnight stars" (*CL* 2: 341).

3. Trillin 2006 in *The New Yorker*, "Alice, Off the Page."

4. One meets with this thought again in a letter of 1853: "I suppose the only secret that gives us power over social nature, as over all nature, is, worth; is to deserve" (*CL* 4: 365).

5. An aligned thought occurs in an early journal entry: "Now if surely I knew there was a mind somewhere thinking & willing that is a repository of these sentiments, . . . and in that future I am to meet this mind in connexions of the most cheerful & close fellowship should not I be glad?" (*JMN* 3: 274).

6. After decades of meta-poetics, it should be unsurprising that we can read this essay as the address of a friend, particularly given Emerson's three references to letter-writing throughout the essay, and the suggestion elsewhere that he writes to unknown friends: "Happy is he who looks only into his work to know if it will succeed, never into the times or the public opinion; and who writes from the love of imparting certain thoughts & not from the necessity of sale—who writes always to *the unknown friend*" (*JMN* 10: 315; cf. *CW* 2: 113, 117, 124).

7. "Character" suggests that being equal to the ongoing occasion of friendship is a joy unto itself: "I know nothing which life has to offer so satisfying as the profound good understanding, which can subsist, after much exchange of good offices, between two virtuous men, each of whom is sure of himself, and sure of his friend. It is a happiness which postpones all other gratifications, and makes politics, and commerce, and churches, cheap" (*CW* 3: 64). Given where we are in "Friendship," I take "sure of himself, and sure of his friend" to mean that friends are sure of themselves and each other as "friends," which means, they are confident that each will be equal to the occasion of whatever arises. The point is not that they are certain of what one another will bring to any occasion. At this stage of friendship, that expectation has been set aside.

8. It is worth noting that Margaret Fuller reproached Emerson for not facilitating her unfolding, for not "offering me the clue of the labyrinth of my own being" (Fuller 1983, 2: 341). But perhaps she sought too much, as if another could unlock us. We will return to this in note 14, below.

9. A degree of alertness is all the more important given the flighty nature of genius, social or otherwise: "It is full of mysteries, it is full of fate. Our daemons or genii have obviously more to do with it than the measure-loving intellect, and what most of all fascinates me in my friend is not permanently in him, but comes & goes, a light that plays about his head, but does not always dip so low as into his eyes" (*CL* 8: 12–13).

10. In "The Transcendentalist," Emerson is rhapsodic about the power of friends (or genuine sociality) to call us toward a better self, though he also notes that friendship sometimes makes mere sociality a burden: "To behold the beauty of another character, which inspires a new interest in our own; to behold beauty lodged in a human being, with such vivacity of apprehension, that I am instantly forced to inquire if I am not deformity itself; to behold in another the expression of a love so high that it assures itself,—assures itself also to me against every possible casualty except my unworthiness;—these are degrees on the scale of human happiness, to which they have ascended; and it is a fidelity to this sentiment which has made common association distasteful to them" (*CW* 1: 208).

11. The association is predictable given Emerson's regard for books: "The truth is all works of literature are Janus faced and look to the future and to the past. . . . There never was an original writer. Each is a link in an endless chain. To receive and impart are the talents of the poet and he ought to possess both in equal degrees. . . . This is but the nature of man, universal receiving to the end of universal giving" (*EL* 1: 284).

12. In *Nature,* Emerson treats the friend less as a book and more as an incipient thought which, once ours, best survives *as* a thought in the wake of the friend's disappearance from our lives. More precisely, he suggests that the friend who initially was

able to "outgo our ideal" of humanity, eventually becomes an "object of thought" that is "converted in the mind into solid and sweet wisdom," which Emerson takes as a "sign to us that his office is closing" (*CW* 1: 29). One finds a similar thought in "Experience": "Our friends early appear to us as representatives of certain ideas, which they never pass or exceed" (*CW* 2: 33).

13. So too when I read Emerson writing to Caroline Sturgis: "Present, you shall be present only as an angel might be, & absent you shall not be absent from me" (*CL* 2: 334).

14. I am thus finding a theological fault behind Emerson's notorious lack of warmth, which he describes as a lack of tenderness in a letter to Margaret Fuller: "Can one be glad of an affection which he knows not how to return? I am. Humbly grateful for every expression of tenderness—which makes the day sweet and inspires unlimited hopes. I say this not to you only, but to the four persons who seemed to offer me love at the same time and draw to me & draw me to them. Yet I did not deceive myself with thinking that the old bars would suddenly fall. No, I knew that if I would cherish my dear romance, I must treat it gently, forbear it long,—worship, not use it,—and so at last by piety I might be tempered & annealed to bear contact & conversation as well mixed natures should" (*CL* 2: 351). My charge is that Emerson's piety—what I see as his steadfast belief that true friends will return to one another—eventually undermines contact and conversation, leaving him detached from those conversations that consummate friendship. Thus, even if Fuller sought too much from Emerson (see note 8, above), one can nevertheless find in Emerson's own reckoning with friendship an insufficient tenderness.

PART THREE

Thoreau's Divergent Melodies

SIX

"In Dreams Awake": Loss, Transcendental Friendship, and Elegy

WILLIAM ROSSI

For Joel

> Friendship, like the immortality of the soul, is too good to be believed.
>
> EMERSON

The broad outlines of Henry Thoreau's complicated relationship with Ralph Waldo Emerson are well known. Embraced as a protégé following his graduation from Harvard College in 1837 and admitted to the circle of radical thinkers and young seekers who had gathered around Emerson, Thoreau benefited enormously, throughout the first decade of their friendship, from the older man's encouragement, material assistance, professional advice, and rising stature as a writer and philosopher. In the seven-year period between April 1841, when he first moved into the Emerson house, and July 1848, when Emerson returned from an eight-month lecture tour in Britain, Thoreau passed more time with Emerson—under his roof or under his sponsorship—than with his own family. Thoreau was more invested in the friendship "for the simple reason that Emerson was the inspiration of his early years" (Sattelmeyer 1995, 26).[1] But after a serious falling out in autumn 1848, apparently exacerbated by Emerson's belated criticism of Thoreau's first book, *A Week on the Concord and Merrimack Rivers* (1849), the relationship never regained its former intimacy.[2] Wounded and proud, his literary career on indefinite hold after the commercial failure of *A Week,* Thoreau seemed to Emerson to be wasting his time on nature studies, wandering the fields and forests like some deluded wood god.[3] For his part, Thoreau began to feel that "Emerson is too grand for me[.] He belongs to the nobility & wears their cloak & manners—is attracted to Plato not to Socrates" (*PJ* 4: 309). Although they remained on good terms as neighbors and as allies in local and national causes, principally abolition, Thoreau captured both the present and the future of their friendship when he reflected in January 1852, "Simply our paths diverge" (*PJ* 4: 274). In the end, having been Thoreau's neighbor, mentor, friend, and belated critic, Emerson became his most prominent, most influential eulogist. In "Thoreau," published in the *Atlantic Monthly* soon after his friend's death in 1862 and reprinted over and over again in subsequent decades, Emerson saluted Thoreau as an "iconoclast in literature" while also fixing, for generations down to the present day, the image of that life as one of "renunciation and withdrawal" (Emerson 2008, 394; Sattelmeyer 1995, 37).

Like children of an acrimonious divorce, modern critics have tended to take sides (more recently Thoreau's), stressing "the disciple's independence at the master's expense" or telling "the Emerson to Thoreau story as a tale of insurgence rather than of continuity" (Buell 2003, 299–300). But even for partisans it has not been easy. In attempting to parse the complicated dynamic between the two authors, commentators have been compelled not only to sort out various tensions in the relationship—tensions arising from the men's fourteen-year age difference, considerable personality quirks, philosophical divergences, and Thoreau's ambiguous role in the Emerson household—but also to reckon with the ideology of friendship they shared. Bronson Alcott captured the significance that Transcendentalists attached to friendship when he described it as "the only religion possible to moderns" in an increasingly secular age (Alcott 1938, 199). Conceived as a speechless bond between "higher" selves, with each person lovingly committed to cultivating the best in the other, transcendental friendship may strike us now as blithely naive and impossibly ideal, "a relationship of mutual recognition so perfect that it could never be fully realized on earth" (Steele 1999, 136). Yet, however otherworldly and interpersonally peculiar, Thoreau's friendship with Emerson clearly proved invaluable for him, fostering a successful apprenticeship and, during the Walden Pond years, his emergence as a writer of extraordinary vision and talent.

At the heart of this friendship dynamic was Emerson's self-invention as a radically unconventional authority figure, one who, as Lawrence Buell puts it, "invites you to kill him off if you don't find him useful." In practice, the "double message" conveyed to disciples, "'I say unto you, be self-reliant,'" made Emerson less a mentor in the usual sense than an "anti-mentor" (Buell 2003, 292, 308). This double bind is nicely illustrated by a well-intentioned, if sharp, piece of advice Emerson reports having given his twenty-four-year-old live-in protégé in September 1841:

> I told H. T. that his freedom is in the form, but he does not disclose new matter. I am very familiar with all his thoughts—they are my own quite originally drest. But if the question be, what new ideas has he thrown into circulation, he has not yet told what that is which he was created to say. (*JMN* 8: 96)

Even as he invites Thoreau to express freely that "which he was created to say," Emerson seems at the same time patronizing, proprietary, and hard to please. Plugged in as he was to the oracle of what were then called the "New Views," Thoreau could hardly help uttering thoughts "familiar" to his mentor. Indeed, given the gratitude Thoreau routinely expresses in his journal of the time, Emerson's impression of having originated Thoreau's ideas may well reflect the younger writer's homage. Yet in Emerson's barely concealed, self-congratulatory pleasure at seeing his own thoughts "quite originally drest," we may glimpse not only the difficulty for a disciple to achieve originality in Emerson's eyes, but also the means by which he might attain a measure of it. Were Thoreau to "disclose" his own "new matter" by extending the master's ideas in a new "form," that is, he might simultaneously pay tribute to them and creatively redouble their "circulation." Indeed, although bound by the terms of transcendental friendship to complement Emerson's thought in learning to say "what he was created to say," Thoreau was equally bound by Emersonian self-reliance to diverge from his mentor.

The inspiration Thoreau derived from this complex relationship, the love and gratitude he felt, and the literary heights to which it carried him are palpably present in the long discourse on friendship in *A Week*'s "Wednesday" chapter. But if, as I will argue, Thoreau's discourse not only represents his complementary engagement with Emersonian thought and writing on the subject of transcendental friendship, but is itself a *performance* of that friendship, we should not wonder that he felt deeply betrayed by Emerson's criticism, whether its tone or substance. "I had a friend, I wrote a book, I asked my friend's criticism, I never got but praise for what was good in it," Thoreau wrote in his journal in early autumn 1849. But "my friend became estranged from me and then I got blame for all that was bad,—& so I got at last the criticism which I wanted" (*PJ* 3: 26).[4]

Yet to better understand Thoreau's stake in the relationship, to see how it shaped his literary emergence and his own conception of friendship in *A*

Week, we must also consider how that relation was complicated by loss and grief—not only his own but his friend's. As Jeffrey Steele has shown, the Transcendentalists' theories of friendship were typically formulated "in response to moments of crisis," including "separation or personal misunderstanding," unrequited feelings, and death. Under the best of circumstances a fragile state, friendship's bliss of mutuality may ultimately and inevitably be destined for dissolution. From this fundamental instability arises "one of the paradoxes of Transcendentalist literary expression: its central subject matter—profound moments of imaginative and spiritual intensity—could only be described in retrospect, from the vantage point of someone who had passed through and remembered the experience" (Steele 1999, 121). Similarly, in moments of intense grief, when the distance between a remembered relation and its present absence seems so final, questions of intimacy and mutuality may become most urgent. Facing the deaths of those we love most, the existential question of how to maintain faith in our closest friendships puts into question the form of one's own survival, with or without the friend, including what Emerson called "the progress of the soul."

The complex layering of grief inherent in transcendental friendship helps account for Thoreau's distinctively elegiac presentation of friendship in "Wednesday," where elegy may be defined as a means of containing or living with as well as of expressing loss.[5] This is not surprising in a book dedicated to memorializing Henry's brother John and the two-week-long boating expedition they had taken in 1839, three years before John's death. But John is not the only materially absent or vaporously present referent of "the Friend." When read as a complementary response both to Emerson's writing and to Emerson's friendship, Thoreau's distinctively elegiac mode of performing transcendental friendship in *A Week* can be seen to represent his furthest divergence from his mentor during the period in which they thought themselves close.[6] Put simply for now, while both men represent friendship as a relation that can never be sustained, Thoreau insists that neither can it be permanently lost.

Grief, Transcendentalism, and Double Consciousness

This essay considers three moments in Thoreau's literary emergence, culminating with a brief analysis of his performance of transcendental friendship in *A Week*. The first centers on a consolatory letter he wrote to Emerson on 11 March 1842, two months after John Thoreau's death from tetanus and six weeks after Waldo Emerson's from scarlatina. Since the previous April, Thoreau had been living upstairs in the Emersons' house, an arrangement originally planned to last twelve months (Richardson 1986, 113). On a typical day, he tended the garden and did chores in the morning, leaving ample time to read, write, and converse (or not) with various visionaries and radicals who visited the Emersons' home. As Ellen Emerson was only two years old when he moved in (Edith was born in November), Thoreau became particularly close to five-year-old Waldo, sharing his father's delight in the boy's precocious questions and innocent witticisms, repairing his toys, making whistles and miniature boats for him, and perhaps taking him out in his boat, then moored on the river just across the village, which he and John had built two years earlier for their excursion up the Concord and Merrimack Rivers.

After a few weeks' absence with his family following John's death on 11 January 1842, when he suffered a severe case of sympathetic lockjaw that replicated all the physical symptoms of John's final agony, Thoreau returned to keep Lydia Emerson company while Emerson fulfilled lecture engagements in New York (Smith 1999, 62). On 11 March, the two-month anniversary of John's death, Thoreau also resumed regular journal-keeping, having recorded only spotty and fragmentary entries in late February and early March. And by late spring, with Emerson's encouragement, he was working on his "Natural History of Massachusetts," subsequently published in *The Dial*, which Emerson was now editing.[7]

Yet, even though he seemed outwardly to be recovering, Thoreau's fragmentary journal for late February and March reveals how deeply he remained grief-stricken, vacillating between extremes of reassurance and despair, passive resignation and anxiety about his own "lingering." On one hand, he was buoyed by the thought that what is truly "good" or "worthy" in our friends can never "depart" ("It does not go and come but we") and that death is only "a transient phenomenon" (*PJ* 1: 369). For if "to live is a condition of continuance and does not mean to be born merely," then there "is no continuance of death" (*PJ* 1: 372). At such times, he felt content to "receive my life as passively as the willow leaf that flutters over the brook, . . . resting quietly in God's palm" (*PJ* 1: 371). On the other hand, sometimes within the same entry, he confessed fearing his own death or reflected poignantly that "when sorrow comes how easy it is to remember pleasure" (*PJ* 1: 400). Over and over again, Thoreau impatiently judged his creative paralysis as a "low and grovelling" state, implicitly comparing himself at one point to the hens he tends ("These long march days setting on and on in the crevice of a hayloft with no active employment") or imploring, more directly, "My life my life—why will ye linger? . . . How often has long delay quenched my aspirations" (*PJ* 1: 382, 392, 371).

If we hear in these passages the wish "to put an end to one's own meaningless existence," as Richard Lebeaux has observed, it is also possible to detect, as Henry Seidel Canby remarked, the desire "to be put to work from the lips of a man convalescing from a great grief" (Lebeaux 1978, 173; Canby 1939, 178–179). In this sense, Thoreau did indeed begin to work through his loss toward a new sense of vocation. As Steven Fink has argued, after years of "grappling in the pages of his journal with the difficulties of remaining aloof, untainted, and unrelated to the world and the public," Thoreau "emerge[d] from this period of grief and isolation with a significantly different attitude toward the world" (Fink 1992, 40, 41).

These journal entries also reveal Thoreau's deep reliance on Emersonian thought, especially in the ways the diarist navigates his sorrow relative to psychic landmarks recently laid out by his mentor. In elaborating on the vision of death as "a transient phenomenon," for example, Thoreau reflects,

> There seem to be two sides to this world presented to us at different times—as we see things in growth or dissolution—in life or death—For seen with the eye of a poet—as God sees them, all are alive and beautiful, but seen with the historical eye, or the eye of the memory, they are dead and offensive. If we see nature as pausing[,] immediately all mortifies and decays—but seen as progressing she is beautiful. (*PJ* 1: 372–373)

If the God-like vision Thoreau attributes to the poet resembles similar claims Emerson had begun to make in December in his Boston lecture series on "The Times," the double vision Thoreau describes here equally recalls Emerson's formulation of "double consciousness" in "The Transcendentalist," another lecture in the series, delivered at the Masonic Temple shortly before Christmas (*CW* 1: 43).[8] There, for the first time, Emerson acknowledged the nagging skepticism that he would explore more fully in "Experience," a self-divided condition between two states of consciousness, namely "the understanding" and "the soul." These two states, he confessed, "really show very little relation to each other, never meet and measure each other: one prevails now, all buzz and din; and the other prevails then, all infinitude and paradise." Thoreau's mournful determination to summon with "the eye of a poet" a vision of nature as "beautiful" when "seen as progressing" follows a similar Transcendentalist logic as Emerson's desire to preserve the predominance of "the soul." In view of the fact that, "with the progress of life, these two lives" of the understanding and the soul "discover no greater disposition to reconcile themselves," Emerson counsels: "Patience, and still patience." Eventually "this petty web we weave will at last be overshot and reticulated with veins of the blue," he declares, and "the moments" of vision and meaning "will characterize the days" (*CW* 1: 213–214).[9] Thoreau's corresponding desire to occlude the "eye of the memory," the "historical eye," is especially pressing in his present condition, because the life of the soul, virtually identical with the life of "nature," is the only guarantor that John's life may persist beyond death.

Anyone struggling to make sense of not one but two sudden deaths might well be expected to hold tight to his idealism. Thoreau held on tightly enough to give his recent biographers the impression that he wished to deny death altogether (Lebeaux 1978, 181; Richardson 1986, 114, 115). Yet his remarkable letter of condolence to Emerson suggests that, in the midst of his own episodic and wildly vacillating recovery, Thoreau was also struggling to rework the binary logic of "double consciousness" in such a way as to acknowledge his actual grief without relinquishing the ideal—in Emersonian terms, the life of the soul. Since its first publication by Franklin Sanborn in 1895, Thoreau's letter to Emerson has often been noted for the cool, elevated consolation it appears to offer. "If we did not know from other information the tragic circumstance occasioning the letter," Sanborn opined, "this epistle would scarcely disclose it" (1895, 352). Indeed, addressed to a man temporarily separated from his family and still overwhelmed by the loss of his son six weeks before, Thoreau's apparently casual observation that death is not only "as common as life" but "beautiful when seen to be a law, and not an accident" seems at best callously abstract. At worst, it suggests that Waldo's death was "beautiful" because somehow fated. "How plain that death is only the phenomenon of the individual or class," Thoreau writes, presumably explicating the beautiful "law": "Nature does not recognize it, she finds her own again under new forms without loss. . . . When we look over the fields we are not saddened because the particular flowers or grasses will wither—for the law of their death is the law of new life" (*Corr* 64). Sanborn believed this letter might have been one source of the stoicism Emerson attributed to Thoreau in his eulogy, a trait Robert Richardson also associates with it (1986, 115). To be sure, the letter is a stiff performance, its personal message of consolation overburdened by literary quotations and half-buried in allusions. A closer reading, however, discloses not only a more nuanced and sympathetic relation to Emerson's grief than has previously been noticed, but also a multilayered representation of Thoreau's own sorrow, apprehended through a kind of double consciousness.

First, as Emerson might have recognized, Thoreau dated his letter on the two-month anniversary of John's death. Stoic acceptance or not, characteristic Transcendentalist dismissal of calendar time notwithstanding, such anniversaries invariably yield their raw moments of death relived, an experience especially to be expected in a case as traumatically witnessed as John's death was. Speaking directly out of a distinctive temporality of grief yet addressing their common bereavement, Thoreau almost certainly writes to console himself as much as to comfort his friend.

Second, situated as a resident in the Emerson household, Thoreau identifies with his friend's grief in another way. His seemingly callous pronouncement that death is part of a lawful natural process, rather than being offered as an abstract truth, arises from a present-tense observation as he looks out on the landscape familiar to both men. "The sun has just burst through the fog, and I hear blue-birds, song-sparrows, larks, and robins down in the meadow." Neither innocent nor simply affirmative, moreover, this observation is shadowed by the memory of a walk the "other day . . . in the woods," when Thoreau found himself "rather denaturalized by late habits" (*Corr* 64). The tentative, perhaps even desperate, character of Thoreau's imaginative effort to maintain the ideal is underlined again at the end of the letter (*Corr* 65), in what can only be called, following Canby, a prayer: "After I have imagined thus much[,] will not the Gods feel under obligation to make me realize something as good?" As Fink notes, this intimation of "a covenant" suggests the intense sense of mission Thoreau associated with prophetic transcendental authorship (1992, 39). Yet this prayer is uttered in a state of uncertainty and desire that is more than vocational. The "something" Thoreau hopes "the Gods" will help him "realize" is presumably an elegiac piece of some sort, perhaps a poem or a book. But as his self-conscious acknowledgment of having "imagined thus much" suggests, his letter to Emerson is itself such a piece. Although only half-realized, it offers a localized pastoral elegy in narrative form, concretely situated in the place of mourning and registering both the instability of an ideal, consoling vision and the hope that it will not soon melt back into a fog of despair.

Finally, although the concept of natural law Thoreau invokes through images of seasonal change may seem conventional enough, this too represents an attempt to update and personalize, not simply to reproduce, elegiac conventions. Good classicist and junior pastoralist though Thoreau was, rather than harking back to an ancient Stoic cosmos ruled by fate or the generalized Nature of pastoral tradition, his references to death as a cyclical metamorphic process and a phenomenon of the individual or species call to mind more contemporary analogues. Like Emerson, Thoreau assumed that natural law and "moral" law were metaphorically equivalent; and, like Emerson, he looked to contemporary science for relevant models (Walls 2003, 42–55, 221–226). The uniformitarian form of natural law presented here was probably inspired by Charles Lyell's *Principles of Geology,* which Thoreau had begun reading eighteen months earlier and would exploit heavily in *A Week* (Sattelmeyer 1988, 227; Walls 1995, 42–44; Rossi 1994). Lyell's theory of incessant, gradual, but nondirectional change, conceived on a Newtonian model of "antagonist forces," contradicted the biological progressionism favored by most of his scientific peers—a theory whose teleology, culminating as it did in the production of humankind, struck Lyell as incipiently and dangerously Lamarckian. In elaborating his counter-theory of cyclical, steady-state change, Lyell went so far as to suggest that, given favorable climatic conditions, extinct genera might reemerge, albeit in new specific forms (Gould 1987, 123).

For all its sublime evocations of deep time, though, Lyell's uniformitarian vision is curiously ahistorical. In a move that Stephen Jay Gould characterized as "the neatest trick of rhetoric . . . in the entire history of science," Lyell conflated his uniformitarian theory with a methodological program that privileged the present as *the* scientific prospect from which to view the past (Gould 1987, 120; Rossi 1994, 278–284). Reading *Principles* in the light of Emerson's *Essays,* Thoreau therefore encountered an empirically rich, authoritative uniformitarianism that did for natural history and geological time what Emerson's essay "History" does for the alterity (the "preposterous There and Then") of human history, dissolving it into moments of timeless present vision (*CW* 2: 7). If Emerson repeated to Thoreau the dismissal of Lyell's book he expressed to Margaret Fuller—that "it was only a catalogue of facts"—so much the better for a mentee whose self-realization depended upon complementing while diverging from his mentor (*CL* 2: 41).

In his consolatory letter to Emerson, then, Thoreau presents this uniformitarian stability and longevity of nature as tranquilly encompassing transient human life.

> Nature is not ruffled by the rudest blast—The hurricane only snaps a few twigs in some nook of the forest. The snow attains its average depth each winter, and the chic-adee lisps the same notes. The old laws prevail in spite of pestilence and famine. No genius or virtue so rare & revolutionary ap-

> pears in town or village, that the pine ceases to exude resin in the wood, or beast or bird lays aside its habits. (*Corr* 64)

Like beasts and birds, young men and little boys do lay aside their lives, of course. But in a steady-state uniformitarian system, "death is only the phenomenon of the individual or class," "the law of their death is the law of new life," and Nature "finds her own again under new forms without loss" (*Corr* 64).

At the same time, in the letter's embedded narrative, this elevated vision of death as "beautiful when seen to be a law" is repeatedly undercut by reminders of the difficulty of sustaining that vision, especially by sharp memories of the beloved dead not yet passed into "new forms without loss." Thus, when recalling his walk "the other day" and reminding his lately "denaturalized" self (and thereby his friend) that the Concord meadow landscape—a landscape embedded with memories of Waldo and John—presents "the same nature that Burns and Wordsworth loved[,] the same life that Shakspeare and Milton lived," Thoreau conveys a two-sided reality (*Corr* 64). The transhistorical, trans-spatial, uniformitarian nature is the same nature that has always carried human sorrow, carried it through the mutability sonnets, and the elegies of dead and living British poets. Yet if sudden natural events ("the rudest blast—The hurricane") are contained within a uniform, lawful system, with death "as common as life" and winter (in a bitter pun) "the pastime of a full quarter of the year," Thoreau's catalogue of naturalized autumnal images of death—"the sallow and cadaverous countenance of vegetation, its painted throes"—likewise carries the vivid, abiding memory of John's corpse and the trauma of witnessing his final agony exactly two months prior (*Corr* 64). Whether intentionally or not, the attempt to sustain a vision above loss, to maintain what Thoreau had called "the eye of the poet" as the eye of God, is here irremediably in tension with, and ever disrupted by, "the historical eye, or the eye of the memory." Situated in a state of double consciousness peculiar to grief, the mourner thus strives to imagine nature as the ideal whole he can recall partaking in yet can no longer confidently expect ever to realize again, even as he must hope to, and even as he offers that hope to his friend.

Incorporating Grief at Walden

It was two and a half years before Thoreau could begin fully to act on the prayer voiced at the end of his consolatory letter to Emerson. In the interim he had modest, if unpaid, success with contributions to *The Dial*, under

Emerson's editorship, including poetry, translations, a review essay, and the literary excursion "A Winter Walk." He published another excursion ("A Walk to Wachusett") and a few pieces in wider venues, but his attempt to crack the New York literary market while living on Staten Island for six months in the home of Emerson's brother, William, came to little, leaving him dispirited and in debt. Little wonder that although his recovery from John's death "was real, if gradual" during this period, it was also "punctuated by periods of lingering depression and self-accusation" (Robinson 2004, 49). Nonetheless, Emerson continued to help create the conditions for Thoreau to say "what he was created to say." This time he did so inadvertently by purchasing fourteen acres of Walden Pond shoreline in September 1844 (Maynard 2004, 60–61).

Soon thereafter, having arranged to squat on Emerson's land and in preparation for drafting *A Week,* Thoreau began transcribing journal passages related to the brothers' excursion into his "Long Book," a notebook he would take to Walden Pond along with two new journal volumes (*PJ* 2: 449–450).[10] His determination to make his first book an elegy is clear from an inscription (eventually the book's first epigraph) he had written onto the notebook's front endpaper:

> Where'er thou sail'st who sailed with me,
> Though now thou climbest loftier mounts
> And fairer rivers dost ascend
> Be thou my muse, my Brother (*PJ* 2: 2–3; *AW* 1)

In appealing to his brother as muse, Thoreau was now associating inspiration with transcendental friendship rather than, as before, with "the Gods." As he adapted a passage originally written six weeks after John's death, "The death of friends will inspire us as much as their lives. If they are great and rich enough they will leave consolation to the mourners as well as money to defray the expenses of their funerals" (*PJ* 2: 38).[11]

A similar but more complex gesture marks another inaugural moment the following summer at Walden as Thoreau again invoked the transcendental friend as muse when he opened a new journal volume. Dated 5 July 1845, the day after he moved to the Pond, the entry begins, famously, "Yesterday I came here to live" (*PJ* 2: 155). As Robert Sattelmeyer observes, this act clearly resonates with Thoreau's "heightened sense of the significance of his experiment" (*PJ* 2: 454). But that elevated awareness involves more than his newfound freedom or an incipient sense of the literary potential of his project. Considering that John Thoreau would have been thirty years old on 5 July, as

Henry (whose own birthday was seven days later) would not have failed to recall, this famous entry also resonates through the grief it contains.[12] Like the inscription at the head of the Long Book, this gesture strives to incorporate John's life as inspiration: the life he would have had and perhaps has still.

As Linck Johnson observes in a comprehensive analysis of the pastoral elegiac mode in *A Week,* in his epigraph Thoreau "echoes Milton's line [in 'Lycidas'], 'Where other groves, and other streams along,' but he depicts a natural paradise rather than a Christian heaven" (1986, 52). But whereas this epigraph locates the brother in a spiritual landscape of "loftier mounts" and "fairer rivers," the 5 July entry on the shore of Walden Pond draws John into "here," the present time and place, an act all the more intimate for being performed so privately. By placing the announcement of his own independence day within an acknowledgment of John's life and loss, Thoreau writes that loss and that life into his experiment and into his own continuing life at the Pond.

The quiet intimacy of this gesture rather strikingly anticipates Thoreau's unusual narrative technique in *A Week:* using the first-person plural pronoun to describe the week-long excursion as a joint experience, though John is never named. Although the book has often been read as the author's means of distancing himself from or displacing his grief, as David Robinson shrewdly observes, the narrator "not only remembers his brother but remembers for his brother, assuming a voice . . . that seems to speak for them both." That voice constitutes a "remarkably unified 'we,' essentially absorbing John's vision into himself, or, in another sense, giving John new life through his own eyes" (2004, 60). Rather than taking the form of a psychic disinvestment in the lost object (on the Freudian model), Thoreau's elegy reconstructs the siblings' past trip as a present narrative act with the deceased brother as a symbolic participant in the survivor's ongoing existence.[13] As an unnamed but active presence in *A Week,* as here on the eve of the book's first drafting, John is neither displaced nor embalmed but rather enlivened through narrative memory: the friend and brother incorporated into our experience of the text as into its making.

Performing Transcendental Friendship in *A Week*

Thoreau completed the second draft of *A Week* in the spring of 1847, before he left Walden (Johnson 1986, 265). By this point, as Robinson notes, "Emerson had replaced John at the center of Thoreau's emotional life" (2004, 64).

Yet the long discourse on friendship in "Wednesday" also indicates how Thoreau carried forward the relationship established with John into his conception of transcendental friendship, especially his relationship with Emerson. As he wistfully reflected in his journal not long after the break with his former mentor, "I was never so near my friend when he was bodily present as when he was absent" (*PJ* 3: 19).[14] Framing his loss in this way, it should be noted, served Transcendentalist literary purposes as much as it did Thoreau's emotional needs. For in developing the discourse on friendship in the uniformitarian elegiac mode of his memorial narrative, Thoreau could place the problematic transience or instability of close relationships in a new light, drawing another circle, as it were, around the phenomenon Emerson had described memorably in his essay "Friendship."

No less than Thoreau's, Emerson's figuring of the dissolution of relationships was shaped by his own mourning, his own several losses. During those times, Emerson's hard-won conviction that the deepest energies of the self-reliant soul participate in a progressive, ultimately benevolent cosmic order or "law" no doubt provided a significant measure of solace. If a friend is left behind or a close relationship abruptly terminated, the sufferer must somehow be enriched, Emerson argued, and his greater being thereby expanded. Looking back on his losses in "Compensation," the speaker views them as part of a "natural history of calamity" that discloses "advertisements of a nature whose law is growth," for the compensatory, progressive law through which we gain friends must also be at work in removing them from our presence (*CW* 2: 72). As this phenomenon is imaged in "Friendship," "the soul puts forth friends as the tree puts forth leaves, and presently by the germination of new buds, extrudes the old leaf" (*CW* 2: 116). Critical opinion remains divided as to how effectively this vision served Emerson as he mourned the devastating loss of his son.[15] But if the melancholy speaker of "Experience" can fathom no compensation, or none yet, Emerson's brutally honest, bewildered description of losing Waldo figures a deciduous process that is eerily reminiscent of the extrusion of friends in "Friendship." "This calamity," he writes, "does not touch me: something which I fancied was a part of me, which could not be torn away without tearing me, nor enlarged without enriching me, falls off from me, and leaves no scar. It was caducous" (*CW* 3: 29).

Although *A Week* deals with issues raised by "Experience," as "Ktaadn, and the Maine Woods" has been shown to do, plumbing that dimension of Thoreau's engagement with Emerson is beyond the scope of this essay.[16]

For the present purpose of exploring Thoreau's complementary divergence, it is enough to note how his experience as Emersonian mentee was foremost in his mind as he expanded his discourse on friendship in "Wednesday." As in March 1842 when he composed his letter of consolation to Emerson, Thoreau was again living in his sponsor's home, having been recalled from Walden Pond in September 1847 to stay with the family while Emerson lectured in Britain. Writing to him in February 1848, mentioning that "Lectures begin to multiply on my desk," including "one on Friendship which is new,"[17] Thoreau addresses his mentor familiarly for the first (and last) time as "Dear Waldo, For I think I have heard that that is your name" (*Corr* 208, 207).

> I believe I never thanked you for your lectures—one and all—which I heard formerly read here in Concord—I *know* I never have—There was some excellent reason each time why I did not—but it will never be too late. I have had that advantage at least, over you in my education. (*Corr* 207)

Given his attitude of indebtedness, combined with a sense of having finally made good on his Emersonian "education,"[18] it is not surprising that, in the phrasings and figures of his digression in "Wednesday," Thoreau prominently displays his debt to Emersonian ideas of friendship. Among the most important is that friendship is a natural phenomenon, one whose evanescence and recurrence is analogized to various forms of polarity, including gravitation, chemical and electrical attraction/repulsion, tidal ebb and flow, systolic and diastolic circulatory pulsing, all analogues abundantly evident during the river journey.[19] Like Emerson, Thoreau characterizes the friend as a collaborator in one's self-culture; and he notes the beneficent effect of anticipating new friendship, as illustrated by Emerson's anecdote of the "commended stranger" (*CW* 2: 113–114). Like Emerson, he has difficulty imagining that the "society" of friends can admit more than two or three; yet, with his mentor, he extols the utopian vision opened up by true friendship, claiming that "all the abuses which are the object of reform . . . are unconsciously amended in the intercourse of Friends" (*AW* 267).

As Robinson asserts, such distinct echoes point to a complex intertextual and interpersonal engagement.

> It is inconceivable that Thoreau would not have read "Friendship," in particular, without a sense of the dynamics of his own relationship with Emerson. . . . [R]eading these commentaries on friendship by two friends side by side reminds us how intertwined such texts were in the actual relationships

> that Emerson, Thoreau, and their circle of friends were attempting to practice. These essays contain quite specific interpersonal signals, translating the daily experience of their own interactions into broader theoretical axioms. (2004, 64, 70)

Indeed, Thoreau's excursive meditation in "Wednesday" bears reading as just such an "interpersonal signal," an exploratory performance of what Emerson had termed the "evanescent intercourse" of friendship (*CW* 2: 126). As the literary embodiment of ideal relations (further stimulated perhaps by his friend's bodily absence), Thoreau's performance strives to imagine the transient, intersubjective relation of transcendental friendship; and in so striving he subtly engages Emerson through *his* "Friendship."

Thus, taking up his mentor's ambivalent observation that "Friends, such as we desire, are dreams and fables" (*CW* 2: 125), Thoreau figures friendship as the epitome of our dreamlike and double relation to the transcendental life, the glimmering presence of which always seems to lie on the verge of actual existence. This is the overarching theme of "Wednesday." Hence the chapter's discovery motif and "questing atmosphere," described by Buell; and hence its exploration of transcendental friendship (Buell 1973, 228). Here, dreaming provides Thoreau a resonant, experiential touchstone for the multi-leveled, shifting state of relations between the friend and his or her ideal, both self and other. Optimally, for instance, we stand toward the true friend, and to transcendental life generally, as in the state now known as lucid dreaming: "Our truest life is when we are in dreams awake" (*AW* 297).[20] At the same time, like the dream, friendship is represented as a state of being that is recurrently formed and dissolved by the powerful undercurrent of human desire. In this, it parallels the "shifting islands" Thoreau mentions earlier in the chapter as holding such an "undefined and mysterious charm" for him. This charm, however, resides not only in the islands' autonomy or insularity as images of the solitary self, as some have argued,[21] but also and primarily in their "shifting." They fascinate, that is, because of the way sedimentary islands are eroded by the same currents that have previously formed them.[22] This omnipresent yet unstable uniformity exhibited in islands, continents, and dreams is likewise exhibited in the phenomenon of friendship. It "takes place . . . because there is such a law, but always without permanent form, though ancient and familiar as the sun and moon, and as sure to come again" (*AW* 261–262).[23] On one hand, "All men are dreaming of it," "dreaming that our Friends are our *Friends,* and that we are our Friends' *Friends*" (*AW* 264, 265). On the other, friendship is a daily "drama, which is always a tragedy" (*AW* 264). This inherent instability serves notice that the narrator's excursive meditation, like the ideal friendship he strains to imagine, will dissolve as well, only to be "remembered [later] like heat lightning in past summers" (*AW* 261).

But long before it dissolves, the narrator's dream of friendship noticeably intensifies, immediately following an interpolated missive from a "true and not despairing Friend" to his Friend. The pivotal placement of this frankly confessional address is all the more striking because it precisely duplicates Emerson's strategy in "Friendship," which features a remarkably tormented letter such as "every man," were he to "record his true sentiment, . . . might write . . . to each new candidate for his love" (*CW* 2: 117). The rhetorical dynamics of that letter epitomize what Caleb Crain has termed the "hierotomy" of Emerson's style, the effect of a compositional method that simultaneously deepens both the abstract and the personal dimensions of his prose. The effort to discern abstract meaning through an intensely personal register, and vice versa, "may even give the reader the feeling of being in a personal relationship with Emerson." Because "the reader must [repeatedly] extend sympathy into the prose to make sense of it," the "character of the friend is the easiest character for the reader to play" (Crain 2001, 227).[24]

If any sensitive reader may be induced to play this role and to experience such high-minded and supercharged intimacy, we can be sure that Thoreau did. Consequently, it is difficult not to read his less formal version as both literary homage and personal response to one of those "quite specific interpersonal signals" detected by Robinson, especially when we recall the kind of reciprocal intimacy Thoreau longed for. Frankly adopting the voice of a "true" and "not despairing" friend, Thoreau's speaker appears to be directly engaging precisely such a *despairing* friend as "Friendship" portrays, when Emerson writes:

> Dear Friend:—
>
> If I was sure of thee, sure of thy capacity, sure to match my mood with thine, I should never think again of trifles, in relation to thy comings and goings. I am not very wise: my moods are quite attainable: and I respect thy genius: it is to me as yet unfathomed; yet dare I not presume in thee a perfect intelligence of me, and so thou art to me a delicious torment.
>
> Thine ever, or never. (*CW* 2: 117)

Thoreau's corresponding imagined epistle reads, in part:

> I never asked thy leave to let me love thee,—I have a right. I love thee not as something private and personal, which is *your own*, but as something universal and worthy of love, *which I have found*. O how I think of you! You are purely good,—you are infinitely good. I can trust you forever. . . .
>
> This is what I would like,—to be as intimate with you as our spirits are intimate,—respecting you as I respect my ideal. Never to profane one another by word or action, even by a thought. Between us, if necessary, let there be no acquaintance.
>
> I have discovered you; how can you be concealed from me? (*AW* 269–270)

In the three sections that follow this counter-message of friendship, "Wednesday" shifts into a mode of intersubjective relation that diverges from, while still engaging, the more solitary Emersonian mode. In this portion of Thoreau's text, transcendental friendship is most palpably performed as a relationship imagined not from the point of view of the solitary soul or lover but interdependently, in concert with the loved other: "The Friend asks no return but that his Friend will religiously accept and wear and not disgrace his apotheosis of him. They cherish each other's hopes. They are kind to each other's dreams" (*AW* 270). Even the enmity that attends the dissolution of friendship is rendered relationally: "Let the Friend know that those faults which he observes in his Friend his own faults attract. There is no rule more invariable than that we are paid for our suspicions by finding what we suspected" (*AW* 277).

As if to demonstrate that the act of sustaining such complementarity requires "an exercise of the purest imagination and the rarest faith" (*AW* 272), the narrator shifts, in the space of a few sentences, from abstract third-person narration into an intimate free direct discourse.

> He never asks for a sign of love, but can distinguish it by the features which it naturally wears. We never need to stand upon ceremony with him with regard to his visits. Wait not till I invite thee, but observe that I am glad to see thee when thou comest. It would be paying too dear for thy visit to ask for it. . . . Let our intercourse be wholly above ourselves, and draw us up to it. (*AW* 272–273)

To say, at this level, that "the language of Friendship is not words but meanings" is to seek its recognition in the reader for and with whom these "meanings" are performed in "an intelligence above language" (*AW* 273). Moments like this, which were written of course to be read in silence, but which also silently voice an intersubjective intimacy, represent the high points of Thoreau's excursive meditation.

Yet even the high points are never without tension, never envisioned as the completion of desire, as "all infinitude and paradise," to recall Emerson's depiction of Transcendentalist sensibility quoted earlier. Thus, if true friendship is "never established as an understood relation" and if in its ideal form that relation is above speech, this absence—of understanding, of speech—also provides the condition for friendship's collapse, as the Merrimack River currents undermine the shifting islands they have formed. As the narrator notes later in the essay, "in human intercourse the tragedy begins, not when there is misunderstanding about words, but when silence is not understood." For "then there can never be an explanation" (*AW* 278). Nowhere is this inherent instability or double-sidedness more succinctly expressed than in the observation that friendship "is a miracle which requires constant proofs. It is an exercise of the purest imagination and the rarest faith" (*AW* 272). That is, the same exercise of imagination and "rarest faith" that is required to live in the miracle of transcendental friendship coexists with a skepticism that requires not just proof but "constant proofs." Consequently, in characterizing friendship as "a drama which is always a tragedy," Thoreau not only prefigures the eventual falling off or descending curve of his essay's meditative trajectory; he also intimates that the "end" of friendship, the crisis, has in fact always been present as an undercurrent or double consciousness, even in the dream of intersubjective attainment.

Whether this prophetic performance of divergence from his mentor and friend consoled Thoreau in the aftermath of their separation is hard to say. Certainly the vivid intimacy he imagined helps account for the severity of pain Thoreau experienced from Emerson's criticism. For in presenting friendship as a shifting relational phenomenon within a steady-state physical and metaphysical system, he had placed a higher faith in relations than in the onward march of an essentially solitary self. Yet that performance may also account for the peculiarly stoic resignation Thoreau tried to maintain. For if, through *A Week*'s reinvention of pastoral elegy, the natural evanescence and dissolution of friendship is acknowledged, its essential continuity and persistence is likewise affirmed: possible neither to sustain nor wholly to lose, our dearest friendships remain "always without permanent form, though ancient and familiar as the sun and moon, and as sure to come again" (*AW* 262).

Notes

I am grateful to Robert Hudspeth, who provided a transcription of Thoreau's manuscript letter of 11 March 1842, and to Karen Ford, Jim Crosswhite, and Lynne Rossi for encouragement and criticism. The epigraph is taken from Emerson, *CW* 2: 126.

1. For the two most extensive treatments of the writers' relationship, see Joel Porte 1966 and Harmon Smith 1999.

2. Sattelmeyer (1989) argues persuasively that the break probably also involved Thoreau's idealized feelings for Emerson's second wife, Lydia Jackson Emerson (whom her husband called "Lidian").

3. "Henry Thoreau is like the woodgod who solicits the wandering poet & draws him into antres vast & desarts idle, & bereaves him of his memory, & leaves him naked, plaiting vines & with twigs in his hand. Very seductive are the first steps from the town to the woods, but the End is want & madness" (*JMN* 10: 344).

4. Thoreau continues, "There is as much hatred as love in the world. Hate is a good critic."

5. The model of elegiac remembrance and mourning I employ in this essay differs from the so-called normative and melancholic models of mourning that typically inform interpretations of elegy and literary studies of mourning. See, most notably, Sacks 1985, Ramazani 1994, and (in the American Transcendentalist context) Steele 2001. Whereas these works derive from a Freudian model that privileges decathexis, my reading follows the recent clinical work of Neimeyer, Attig, and others who have reexamined mourners' efforts to maintain the memory of the dead within a post-traumatic reconstruction of meaning. Although such efforts are commonly enough valued in non-Western cultures, in the West more often than not they have been pathologized as prolonged or "unresolved" grieving in the traditional psychoanalytic model.

For a historical and cultural study of mourning much more extensive than mine, but which also attends to "the profound productivity of mourning," see Luciano 2007. The "pronounced nineteenth-century attention to grief and mourning" in the United States, centered in the feeling body, she argues, "responds to anxiety over the new shape of time by insisting that emotional attachment had its own pace—a slower and essentially nonlinear relation to the value of human existence that defended it against the increasingly rapid pace of progress," offering "if not a way of stopping time, a means of altering the shape and textures of its flow" (Luciano 2007, 4, 2).

6. The performative dimensions of Thoreau's discourse on friendship in *A Week* encompass three different connotations of the term as employed in performance theories: the display of a skill, here the art of literary nonfiction; a self-conscious awareness, implying distance between statement and performing self; and the performance's implicit reference to a tacitly received standard or set of conventions, in this case the ideology of transcendental friendship. See Carlson 1996 and Esterhammer 2000.

7. As Emerson reported to Margaret Fuller, the magazine's former editor, Thoreau was serving as "private secretary to the President of the Dial" (*CL* 3: 47).

8. Besides reading "The Poet" in the series delivered in Boston (2 December 1841–20 January 1842), Providence (10–17 February), and New York (3–14 March), Emerson read an early version of this lecture, then titled "Nature and Powers of the Poet," at the Concord Lyceum on 3 November 1841 (*EL* 3: 341–342, 347).

9. See Robinson 1993, 54–59.

10. For the dating of Thoreau's transcriptions in the Long Book, I follow Johnson 1986, 267–269.

11. As originally written and dated 20 February 1842, the first sentence reads: "The death of friends should inspire us as much as their lives" (*PJ* 1: 369).

12. In *Thoreau's Seasons,* Lebeaux observes that Thoreau made this first entry "on the anniversary of his brother's birth" (1984, 5).

13. See Walter 1996, Attig 1996, and the essays collected in Neimeyer 2001. For a traditional Freudian reading, based on the work of Erich Lindeman, see Lebeaux 1978, 172–204.

14. The editors place this undated entry between 26 May and 11 September 1849.

15. See Packer 1982, 162–179; Cameron 1986; Cavell 2003; and Walls 2003, 148–153.

16. See Robinson 1997, "Thoreau's 'Ktaadn' and the Quest for Experience."

17. Johnson describes Thoreau's never-delivered lecture as an "expanded version of part of the first draft" of the section on friendship, which more than tripled its length from the first manuscript version completed in 1845 (Johnson 1986, 359–369).

18. Thoreau returned from Walden Pond with not one but two book manuscripts, and with two essays ("Thomas Carlyle and His Works" and "Resistance to Civil Government") and the travel narrative "Ktaadn, and the Maine Woods" in print or production.

19. For Emerson's use of polarity as "a model of universal order" and Thoreau's polar figurations of friendship, see Buell 1973, 159–165, 225–230.

20. In the *Oxford English Dictionary Online,* the first instance of this term, meaning "a dream in which the sleeper is aware that he or she is dreaming and is sometimes able to control or influence the course of the dream," occurs in a 1913 article published in the *Proceedings of the Society for Psychical Research.*

21. For a recent example, see Shamir 2006, 219.

22. "The shifting islands! who would not be willing that his house should be undermined by such a foe! The inhabitant of an island can tell what currents formed the land which he cultivates; and his earth is still being created or destroyed. There before his door, perchance, still empties the stream which brought down the material of his farm ages before, and is still bringing it down or washing it away,—the graceful, gentle, robber!" (*AW* 244).

23. Dream experience and transcendental friendship thus manifest, in the psychic sphere, the same uniformitarian law-like processes visible in geological phenomena Thoreau describes, such as eroded cavities or potholes in Amoskeag Falls (*AW* 246–249), as well as the shifting islands.

24. As Crain demonstrates, Emerson most likely wrote this letter, drafted in his journal on 3 February 1840, while thinking of Samuel Gray Ward, to whom he frequently wrote in "a tone of affectionate longing" during this period. See Crain 2001, 215–216.

SEVEN

"Let Him Be to Me a Spirit": Paradoxes of True Friendship in Emerson and Thoreau

ALAN D. HODDER

Verily, not for the sake of the husband is the husband dear but for the sake of the Self (*ātman*) is the husband dear . . . not for the sake of the wife is the wife dear but for the sake of the Self is the wife dear . . . not for the sake of the children are the children dear but for the sake of the Self are the children dear . . . not for the sake of the worlds are the worlds dear but for the sake of the Self are the worlds dear . . . not for the sake of the gods are the gods dear but for the sake of the Self are the gods dear . . .

BṚHADĀRAṆYAKA UPANIṢAD

Whoever has been initiated so far in the mysteries of Love and has viewed all these aspects of the beautiful in due succession, is at last drawing near the final revelation. And now, Socrates, there bursts upon him that wondrous vision which is the very soul of the beauty he has toiled so long for. It is an everlasting loveliness which neither comes nor goes, which neither flowers nor fades, for such beauty is the same on every hand, the same then as now, here as there, this way as that way, the same to every worshiper as it is to every other. . . . And this is the way, the only way, he must approach, or be led toward, the sanctuary of Love. Starting from individual beauties, the quest for the universal beauty must find him ever mounting the heavenly ladder, stepping from rung to rung—that is, from one to two, and from two to every lovely body, from bodily beauty to the beauty of institutions, from institutions to learning, and from learning in general to the special lore that pertains to nothing but the beautiful itself—until at last he comes to know what beauty is.

PLATO

If I love you, what is that to you?

GOETHE

Although ornate epigraphy is no longer the academic fashion it once was, I could not resist reviving it momentarily here, if only to encapsulate the broad tradition of religio-philosophical speculation within which I want to frame Transcendentalist conceptions of love and friendship.[1] Despite their disparate origins, each of the passages cited above verges on a paradox in which everyday notions of love are turned inside out. What the world extols as a romance centering on some beloved enchanting other, philosophy reveals as a romance of the self. In the excerpt from Yajnavalkya's sermon on love, as in the memorable quip from *Wilhelm Meister's Apprenticeship,* love circles perpetually back on the self. In an uncompromisingly monistic system like the Upanishads, this leads to a paradox of identity: the I and the thou are both separate and in some sense the same. Love proves no less circular in Plato, as we see dramatized in this excerpt from Diotima's speech to Socrates in the *Symposium,* which construes love as the means by which the soul re-ascends to her source in the contemplation of the One.[2] In every case, love is not as it would seem. Emerson provides his own version of the paradox in the closing paragraphs of his "Friendship" essay, published in 1841: "In the last analysis, love is only the reflection of a man's own worthiness from other men. Men have sometimes exchanged names with their friends, as if they would signify that in their friend each loved his own soul" (*CW* 2: 125).

For Emerson no less than for Yajnavalkya and Goethe, love is always, ironically enough, an affair of the self; and for Emerson as for Plato, love serves an entirely spiritual purpose. Emerson's own essay "Love," a companion piece to "Friendship," is nothing if not a reprise of Diotima's vision:

> And beholding in many souls the traits of the divine beauty, and separating in each soul that which is divine from the taint which it has contracted in the world, the lover ascends to the highest beauty, to the love and knowledge of the Divinity, by steps on this ladder of created souls. (*CW* 2: 106)

According to the "Ideal theory," as Emerson had blandly introduced it in *Nature,* the point of love and friendship was to summon the Self forth, to draw it out from its transcendental recesses into the wider arena of the world (*CW* 1: 29). Together with a periodic recourse to solitude, communion with others was the means by which the Self processed "from within outward," realizing its unbounded potential, for as he put it in the closing paragraph of "Friendship": "Thou art enlarged by thy own shining" (*CW* 2: 107, 127). Thoreau's version of this paradox, which he formulated at the start of his apocryphal letter to a friend in a long digression on friendship in the "Wednesday" section of *A Week on the Concord and Merrimack Rivers,* may be seen as a kind of amplification of Goethe: "I never asked thy leave to let me love thee,—I have a right. I love thee not as something private and personal, which is *your own,* but as something universal and worthy of love, *which I have found*" (*AW* 269). Various as they may be, each of these conceptions rides on a metaphysical paradox endemic to the tradition of philosophical idealism to which the Transcendentalists more or less subscribed in this (still early) period of the movement. Emerson neatly essentialized it this way in his journal just a few years prior to writing the "Friendship" essay: "A believer in Unity, a seer of Unity, I yet behold two" (*JMN* 5: 337).

Following on these premises, Emerson and, following him, Thoreau both conceived friendship—true friendship, what we will call transcendental friendship—in avowedly spiritual terms as the expression of an exalted and rarefied ideal. "That high office," as Emerson put it in a way that seems almost prescient of the rise, and later the demise, of his actual relationship with Thoreau, "requires great and sublime parts. There must be very two, before there can be very one. Let it be an alliance of two large formidable natures, mutually beheld, mutually feared, before yet they recognize the deep identity which beneath these disparities unites them." Friendship thus consisted of the coming together of two self-sufficient and self-realized souls, two "rare and costly" natures, and it could only result from "a long probation." Eschewing all of the lower modes and motives of friendship—friendship as convenience, as support, as encouragement, as consolation, and so forth—Emerson boldly conceived his highest ideal and then adhered stoically to its implications. "Let him be to me a spirit," he wrote of the true friend—rather than some grasping, envious petitioner. Apparently, neither the practical impossibility of such insistence nor the paradox it engendered was lost on him:

> A friend, therefore, is a sort of paradox in nature. I who alone am, I who see nothing in nature whose existence I can affirm with equal evidence to my own, behold now the semblance of my being in all its height, variety and curiosity, reiterated in a foreign form; so that a friend may well be reckoned the masterpiece of nature. (*CW* 2: 120–123)

But if Emerson's conception of friendship springs from a *metaphysical* paradox—"a seer of Unity, I yet behold two"—it founders finally on a *functional* one, namely, that once the requisite conditions for true friendship had been fully and finally realized, friendship was no longer necessary. It goes without saying, as several critics have pointed out, that this exalted ideal of friendship also placed considerable strain on each writer's actual friendships, particularly between each other.[3]

In what follows, I have two basic objectives: first, I would like to throw into bolder relief than is usually done the religious dimensions of Transcendentalist friendship theory, since without adequate awareness of these dimensions the theory can seem cold-blooded and rather perversely severe; second, I would like to consider and compare Emerson's and Thoreau's somewhat differing responses to the antinomy between actual and ideal friendship, as well as the challenges to real-life relationships posed by their Transcendentalist ideal. Since my interest gravitates to the dramatization of this ideal, my focus will be primarily on the rhetorical representations of friendship in Emerson's essay of 1841, on Thoreau's long digression on the same topic in *A Week on the Concord and Merrimack Rivers,* and on *Walden,* and only secondarily on relevant biographical facts as brought to light in selected letters and journals. I should point out here, however, that I take it as given that Transcendentalist practice did not always, or even mostly, adhere to Transcendentalist theory—that Emerson and Thoreau's actual experience of friendship did not always conform to the austere ideals they had set for themselves. There is much in the biographical record to indicate that each of these writers was a much more unstinting, steadfast, and valued friend than some of the following formulations might suggest. Nevertheless, I do believe that the ideals each espoused had a real bearing on their actual interactions with friends. My argument then, in its most condensed form, is that whereas Emerson allows the paradoxes of true friendship to stand, retreating little from even their most disturbing social implications, Thoreau seeks an experiential resolution to the conflicts between real and ideal friendship in the natural world and the sphere of solitude itself, through a more developed and robust inner life.

Emerson's Ideal Theory

Any attentive reading of Emerson's 1841 essay "Friendship" must first negotiate its rather confusing crosscurrents. At points, the essay oscillates almost dizzyingly between sonorous expressions of praise for the value of friendship, such as now appear on the side of a box of soothing teas on my kitchen shelf (as usual, Emerson has not been faithfully served by the marketing office), while elsewhere its tone is monitory and forbidding. Some of this is no doubt programmatic, an expression in practice of "the systole and diastole of the heart" about which he writes, or what in 1837 he had dubbed "Polarity," the "great principle of Undulation" (*CW* 2: 115; 1: 61). At other points, the sentiments he expresses must certainly reflect feelings with which Emerson actually struggled, as in this passionate apostrophe from the mid-section of the essay:

> What a perpetual disappointment is actual society, even of the virtuous and gifted! After interviews have been compassed with long foresight, we must be tormented presently by baffled blows, by sudden, unseasonable apathies, by epilepsies of wit and of animal spirits, in the heydey of friendship and thought. Our faculties do not play us true, and both parties are relieved by solitude. (*CW* 2: 117–118)

It is difficult to read this passage without detecting some fairly raw, unresolved feeling, so closely does it track Emerson's actual responses to his social interactions during this emotionally fraught period, as we know them from his journals and letters. The "heyday" he refers to here may be an oblique allusion to *Hamlet,* but it probably also conjured up the hectic atmosphere and strange ardors of the previous summer, when Concord had become a gathering place for several of Emerson's most gifted and importunate admirers.[4] On the one hand, there is the seductive allure of such companionship, suggested by the following undisguisedly erotic passage:

> What is so pleasant as these jets of affection which make a young world for me again? What so delicious as a just and firm encounter of two, in a thought, in a feeling? How beautiful, on their approach to this beating heart, the steps and forms of the gifted and true! (*CW* 2: 114)

On the other hand, Emerson recoils from an excess of personal contact:

> Why should we desecrate noble and beautiful souls by intruding on them? Why insist on rash personal relations with your friend? Why go to his house, or know his mother and brother and sisters? Why be visited by him at your own? Are these things material to our covenant? Leave this touching and clawing. (*CW* 2: 123)

When Margaret Fuller and Caroline Sturgis called him to account for "a certain inhospitality of soul" during the previous summer—a lack of willingness, as they put it, to yield to their friendship in "the full & sacred sense"—Emerson conceded "the fact of cold & imperfect intercourse," but disavowed any "deficiency of my affection." To the young Sturgis, he simply wrote, "You give me more joy than I could trust my tongue to tell you" (*CL* 2: 325). In the published essay also, Emerson seems torn between the enticements to love and friendship ministered by his young friends, and a renunciation of them in the interests of privacy, self-protection, and, finally, a quest for self-authenticity.

Part of Emerson's oft-cited aloofness was no doubt personal, the result of temperament and a certain Yankee reserve; but part of it was also a matter of principle and the natural expression of a philosophical orientation that he had been consolidating for close to a decade. "In strictness," he argues here, "the soul does not respect men as it respects itself. In strict science, all persons underlie the same condition of an infinite remoteness" (*CW* 2: 116). However regrettable his own emotional reserve may have been, it was grounded after all in an existential truth. Consequently, after the initial survey of the blandishments of love and friendship, Emerson throws down the philosophical gauntlet: "Shall we fear to cool our love by mining for the metaphysical foundation of this Elysian temple?" he asks rhetorically (*CW* 2: 116). His answer, come what may, is a resounding no: "And I must hazard the production of the bald fact amidst these pleasing reveries, though it should prove an Egyptian skull at our banquet" (*CW* 2: 116). I would not characterize this moment in the essay as an expression of the egotistical sublime, as one might be otherwise tempted to do—some afflatus of the imperial Self reminiscent of "Self-Reliance." It is too rueful, too circumscribed for that: "I cannot choose but rely on my own poverty, more than on your wealth" (*CW* 2: 116). What we have here rather is Emerson's sober acknowledgment of what we might call the burden of the self, the irreducible fact of personal consciousness. The resulting critique of friendship as we know it rested for him on three key supports: Emerson's own experience, his commitment to the "Ideal theory," and an acute psychological analysis, notable at several points in the essay, of the insidious collusion between friendship and desire (*CW* 2: 120–122).

Despite the essay's apparent contradictions and persistent backtracking, Emerson's prevailing religio-philosophical vision here is still recognizably Platonist, in the way this tradition had been mediated to him through the work of the Cambridge Platonists and the mystical readings of Thomas Taylor.[5] As in other essays of the *First Series*—notably "Love," "Self-Reliance," and the "Oversoul"—traces of the Platonic vision are apparent at various points in the essay. But here, in the more explicitly philosophical interlude noted above, it comes fully to the fore:

> I cannot deny it, O friend, that the vast shadow of the Phenomenal includes thee, also, in its pied and painted immensity,—thee, also, compared with whom all else is shadow. Thou art not Being, as Truth is, as Justice is,—thou art not my soul, but a picture and effigy of that. (*CW* 2: 116)

In a letter to Fuller the previous summer, Emerson had referred self-mockingly to his ongoing reading of Plato and the Vedas, and there is nothing in "Friendship" or the lists he kept in his journals to discount this claim (*CL* 2: 320). Earlier in the essay, Emerson alludes to Aristophanes' macabre story of the hermaphroditic origin of love in the *Symposium,* and shortly thereafter he conjures up a vision of love steeped in what can only be described as a kind of Neo-Platonic pantheism:

> My friends have come to me unsought. The great God gave them to me. By oldest right, by the divine affinity of virtue with itself, I find them, or rather, not I, but the Deity in me and in them derides and cancels the thick walls of individual character, relation, age, sex, circumstance, at which he usually connives, and now makes many one. High thanks I owe to you, excellent lovers, who carry out the world for me to new and noble depths, and enlarge the meaning of all my thoughts. (*CW* 2: 115)

However that may be, the overt reference to Plato's doctrine of eternal Ideas in the prior citation will certainly vouch for the essay's Platonic subtext. The burst of philosophizing noted here leads directly to the cryptic Coleridgean letter to a friend that culminates the first movement of the essay. Whatever else one may say about this all-but-incomprehensible little letter, it concludes with a sign-off that neatly epitomizes the paradoxical all-or-nothing character of the conception of friendship—"Thine ever, or never"—that Emerson will develop in the subsequent section of his essay (*CW* 2: 117).

If Emerson still conceived the subject of friendship within the larger scope of Platonic and Neo-Platonic idealism, as he did other essays of the *First Series,* it was an exacting, socially grounded idealism that was quick to affirm the demands of ethics and of science. "The laws of friendship," he now goes on to insist, "are austere and eternal, of one web with the laws of nature and of morals" (*CW* 2: 117). Lofty rhetoric notwithstanding, there will be nothing cheap or easy about the friendship Emerson has in view. This is a hard-worked and dearly bought form of communion, and like the diamond or ruby, it will require much time ("the *naturlangsamkeit*") to refine and perfect (*CW* 2: 118). At this point, Emerson makes it clear that such a vision of friendship requires an approach befitting its solemnity and grandeur, and this he locates above all in religion. "Friendship demands a religious treatment," he writes (*CW* 2: 123)—but by this point in the essay, the shift to a predominantly religious register has already taken place:

> The attractions of this subject are not to be resisted, and I leave, for the time, all account of subordinate social benefit, to speak of that select and sacred relation which is a kind of absolute, and which even leaves the language of love suspicious and common, so much is this purer, and nothing is so much divine. (*CW* 2: 118)

Two elements comprise the friendship he has in view: truth and tenderness. In holding these two standards aloft, he rejects both the usual commodification of friendship and its rampant sentimentalization (*CW* 2: 121). Friendship requires two "rare and costly" natures, the "rare mean betwixt likeness and unlikeness," and "the ability to do without it" (*CW* 2: 121–123). Highest friendship in Emerson's view involves the progressive diminution of actual physical and even verbal contact, until such point as the friend becomes to him little more than the materialization of spirit: "Let him be to me a spirit," he writes. "A message, a thought, a sincerity, a glance from him, I want, but not news, nor pottage. I can get politics, and chat, and neighborly conveniences, from cheaper companions. Should not the society of my friend be to me poetic, pure, universal, and great as nature itself?" (*CW* 2: 123). As we see illustrated here, in keeping with his prevailing Platonism, Emerson's conception of the activity of friendship suggests a kind of spiritual ascent—from conversation involving the physical presence of friends, to a simple exchange of letters, leading finally to a wise, self-contained silence, the pinnacle of transcendental friendship:

> What is so great as friendship, let us carry with what grandeur of spirit we can. Let us be silent,—so we may hear the whisper of the gods. Let us not interfere. Who set you to cast about what you should say to the select souls, or how to say any thing to such? No matter how ingenious, no matter how graceful and bland. There are innumerable degrees of folly and wisdom, and for you to say aught is to be frivolous. Wait, and thy heart shall speak. (*CW* 2: 124)

Silence in this upward spiraling vision is the fulfillment of the actual contact and conversation between friends.

After elevating friendship to such stratospheric levels, Emerson has no choice at this penultimate point in the essay but to grant the obvious:

> The higher the style of friendship, of course the less easy to establish it with flesh and blood. We walk alone in the world. Friends, such as we desire, are

> dreams and fables. But a sublime hope cheers ever the faithful heart, that elsewhere, in other regions of the universal power, souls are now acting, enduring, and daring, which can love us, and which we can love. (*CW* 2: 125)

In view of the thoroughgoing spiritualization of friendship and the notably ascetic character of this passage, it is hard to read the reference to aloneness at this point and not hear an echo of Plotinus's famous description of the spiritual ascent of the soul: "This, therefore, is the life of the Gods, and of divine and happy men, a liberation from all terrene concerns, a life unaccompanied with human pleasures, and a flight of the alone to the alone" (Plotinus 1911, 322). Plotinus, we recall, was the late-antique philosopher who, according to his disciple Porphyry, always "seemed ashamed of being in the body" (Plotinus 1984, 1: 3), and throughout the 1830s his *Enneads* seemed to have a particular hold on Emerson's religious imagination. According to Robert D. Richardson, Emerson first took up the *Enneads* at the time of the tragic death of his first wife, Ellen, and returned to them periodically throughout much of his adult life (Richardson 1995, 345–348). *Nature,* published in 1836, contains at least three references to Plotinus, most notably in the epigraph Emerson included in the first edition. The phrase from Taylor's translation, "a flight of the alone to the alone," particularly fired his imagination. He cited it in a letter to Fuller the previous summer, and noted it again in his journal a few months after his essays were published in the following winter.[6] As if to underscore its lasting significance for him, twenty years later he returned to it yet again for the crowning vision of his essay "Illusions" (*CW* 6: 174).

It is easy enough to understand the value Emerson would have found in the ascetic and flesh-renouncing philosophy of Plotinus in the wake of Ellen's death. The shock affected him deeply, and it seems to have brought about a permanent alteration in his psychic and spiritual life, instilling a deep distrust in the stability of matter and a religiously sanctioned disposition to affirm the spiritual value of personal loss. Forever afterwards, he viewed nature appreciatively, but always as phenomenal, and not substantial; as the ephemeral, and not the real. Nature was a vast metamorphosis only, never a sure thing, and this included within it his closest friends and loved ones as well. The conversion of sorts that Emerson experienced in the months following Ellen's death in 1831 sanctioned a new spiritual outlook that appears to have prepared him for the string of horrific losses that would follow in the next several years, particularly the deaths of his brother Charles in 1836 and his son Waldo in 1842.[7] But by this time, Emerson had fully internalized his new spiritual vision, recognizing in each instance the supernatural operation of what he then termed "compensation." As he wrote in his 1841 essay of that name,

> The death of a dear friend, wife, brother, lover, which seemed nothing but privation, somewhat later assumes the aspect of a guide or genius; for it commonly operates revolutions in our way of life, terminates an epoch of infancy or of youth which was waiting to be closed, breaks up a wonted occupation, or a household, or style of living, and allows the formation of new ones more friendly to the growth of character. (*CW* 2: 73)

Plotinus was not responsible for this new spiritual outlook in its entirety, of course, but he served thenceforth as a touchstone and a kind of sanction for Emerson's vision of the winged, necessarily solitary life.

Under the circumstances, Emerson's parting defense of his insistently transcendental ideal reads like something close to a personal profession of faith:

> It is foolish to be afraid of making our ties too spiritual, as if so we could lose any genuine love. Whatever correction of our popular views we make from insight, nature will be sure to bear us out in, and though it seem to rob us of some joy, will repay us with greater. Let us feel, if we will, the absolute insulation of man. (*CW* 2: 125)

The problem with the transcendental theory, as Emerson was quick to acknowledge, is that it very nearly spiritualizes friendship out of existence:

> Late—very late—we perceive that no arrangements, no introductions, no consuetudes, or habits of society, would be of any avail to establish us in such relations with them as we desire,—but solely the uprise of nature in us to the same degree it is in them: then shall we meet as water with water: and if we should not meet them then, we shall not want them, for we are already they. (*CW* 2: 125)

This passage approximates the vision of the Upanishads with which we began, and turns essentially on the same paradox of identity—"for we are already they." It also directly confronts the paradox of *function* to which this metaphysical paradox gives rise—"if we should not meet them then, we shall not want them." When one finally rises to the exalted status of pure friendship, the *need* for it has utterly dropped away.

Emerson's essay on friendship thus lands us in paradox upon paradox, from which he apparently offers no escape. That he was cognizant of the ethical dangers and practical challenges posed by this transcendental ideal is apparent from his essay—and by all accounts, he was a much steadier and more attentive friend than this bloodless vision would lead us to expect. Yet, it says something about his character and his religious vision that, despite the limitations, he chose to let the paradoxes of true friendship stand, retreating little from even their most disturbing personal and social implications. Throughout his "Friendship" essay, at least, the antinomy between the ideal Emerson sets forth and his actual experience of friendship remains finally an intractable philosophical problem.

Flesh of My Flesh

At first blush, Thoreau's own treatment of friendship, as it is distilled for us in a long digression in the "Wednesday" section of *A Week on the Concord and Merrimack Rivers,* seems a kind of palimpsest of Emerson's essay, so frequently do we glimpse Emerson's thought immediately beneath Thoreau's (*AW* 259–289). This should probably come as no surprise, since Thoreau's text took root in the same social and imaginative soil as Emerson's had, and developed over the period of time when Emerson's influence over the younger man was most formative.[8] By the same token, Thoreau's treatment also hints at the bitterness and betrayal he felt as their friendship began to unravel in the late 1840s.[9] A closer look also suggests that Thoreau's reflections on friendship, though no less idealized, conform to a distinctly different philosophical vision than Emerson's do. We certainly find none of the Platonizing that is evident in Emerson's essay; rather, as we might expect, Thoreau adopted a rather staunchly anti-metaphysical stance in his treatment of love and friendship, in a way that is consistent with his mature thinking about the natural world. Furthermore, and this will be my final point, Thoreau's treatment here leads to a spiritual vision, only fully worked out in *Walden,* that Emerson could scarcely conceive of, much less condone.

The parallels between the two essays, first of all, are plain to see. Both writers conceive friendship in entirely ideal terms. For Thoreau, as for Emerson, friendship should be spiritual, should be ideal, and is divinely pre-ordained (*AW* 266, 267, 269). Employing language reminiscent of the Sermon on the Mount, Thoreau writes: "We do not wish for Friends to feed and clothe our bodies,—neighbors are kind enough for that,—but to do the like office to our spirits" (*AW* 266). We do not choose our friends furthermore; they are predestined for us: "We are all Mussulmen and fatalists in this respect. Impatient and uncertain lovers think that they must say or do something kind whenever they meet; they must never be cold. But they who are Friends, do not do what they *think* they must, but what they *must*" (*AW* 269). For Thoreau, as for Emerson, solitude is the ground of friendship, to which it must return periodically for health and rejuvenation: "There are times when we have had enough even of our Friends, when we begin inevitably to profane one another, and must withdraw religiously into solitude and silence, the better to prepare ourselves for a loftier intimacy" (*AW* 272). Furthermore, Thoreau writes, a "true Friendship is as wise as it is tender" (*AW* 274), unabashedly taking a page from Emerson's statement of friendship's two cardinal elements: truth and tenderness.

Thoreau's essay, as has often been pointed out, even resorts to the same rhetorical device Emerson employs—dramatizing his views through the contrivance of an apocryphal letter to a friend (*AW* 269–270). Like Emerson, Thoreau insists that friendship should be governed by only the highest standards, what he later calls "a religious demand": "The Friend asks no return but that his Friend will religiously accept and wear and not disgrace his apotheosis of him" (*AW* 279, 270). And as for Emerson, true friendship culminates in silence, not in speech: "The language of Friendship is not words but meanings. It is an intelligence above language" (*AW* 273). Thoreau's conception too is a tall order, of course, so it is not surprising that actual friendship proves just as rare for him as it does for Emerson: "Perhaps there are none charitable, none disinterested, none wise, noble, and heroic enough, for a true and lasting Friendship" (*AW* 277). And in the end, all this leads to the same sort of paradox as is found in Emerson, here showcased in Thoreau's letter to the unnamed friend: "This is what I would like,—to be as intimate with you as our spirits are intimate,—respecting you as I respect my ideal. Never to profane one another by word or action, even by a thought. Between us, if necessary, let there be no acquaintance" (*AW* 270). At this point in his treatment, following Emerson, Thoreau idealizes the friend quite to the point of irrelevance, not to say impossibility.

Despite the obvious kinship between the two essays, however, Thoreau also strikes off on his own in several important respects. To Emerson's spiritualizing of the friendship ideal, Thoreau adds his own characteristic coloring: friendship is "heroic," even "heathenish" in its stoicism and restraint (*AW* 274, 276). It is also utterly and unavoidably tragic: "No word is oftener on the lips of men than Friendship, and indeed no thought is more familiar to their aspirations. All men are dreaming of it, and its drama, which is always a tragedy, is enacted daily" (*AW* 264). Though Emerson's conception of friendship was no less conditioned by tragic loss than Thoreau's, this assertion of the necessarily tragic character of friendship reflects a more telling rhetorical difference between the two accounts, in that unlike the more broadly topical character of Emerson's essay, Thoreau conceived this digression, as he did the narrative of *A Week* generally, in broadly elegiac terms. By the mid-1840s, he had already begun to conceive of the narrative of the voyage as a memorial for his deceased brother John (Johnson 1986, 66–69). As the two brothers paddle north to Goffstown, the narrator's thoughts turn to the past, as he recalls some "distant gesture" or "kindness long passed" (*AW* 259). The poem to the young Edmund Sewall, which Thoreau inserts at this point, explicitly takes the form of an elegy reminiscent of Milton's "Lycidas," and at the close of the digression, he comes back once again to the elegiac mode and the theme of departed friends:

> Even the death of Friends will inspire us as much as their lives. They will leave consolation to the mourners as the rich leave money to defray the expenses of their funerals, and their memories will be incrusted over with sublime and pleasing thoughts, as monuments of other men are overgrown with moss; for our Friends have no place in the graveyard. (*AW* 286)

The sense of loss clearly underlies much of Thoreau's narrative in *A Week*, notwithstanding the periodic sunny stretches, and shapes his treatment of friendship profoundly. "Friendship," he writes on the heels of his elegy to Edmund, "is evanescent in every man's experience." He compares it to "heat lightning in past summers," to clouds, and to the lost islands of Atlantis (*AW* 261–262).

Thoreau's treatment of the mundane forms of friendship also seems more dismissive than Emerson's, and perhaps at points jaundiced: "What is commonly called Friendship even is only a little more honor among rogues," he proclaims (*AW* 268). If Emerson flees from intimacy, Thoreau reviles it. At points, the essay becomes an occasion for the airing of particular grievances, as in this brittle but indignant passage:

> I sometimes hear my friends complain finely that I do not appreciate their fineness. I shall not tell them whether I do or not. As if they expected a vote of thanks for every fine thing which they uttered or did. . . . What avails it that another loves you, if he does not understand you? Such love is a curse. What sort of companions are they who are presuming always that their silence is more expressive than yours? . . . They will complain too that you are hard. . . . They ask for words and deeds, when a true relation is word and deed. If they know not of these things, how can they be informed? (*AW* 277–278)

The apparently *ad hominem* character of this tirade is also not present in Emerson's essay, at least not to this extent. These comments can only reflect Thoreau's actual relationships with various particular unnamed friends and neighbors—Emerson certainly, as several commentators have suggested, but perhaps Fuller and others as well. Their tone is captious and critical, reflecting the bitterness and resentment he had experienced in his recent dealings with them. The wounds they expose have scarcely, it seems, had time to heal. Yet despite the hurt evident here, and the grim prognosis Thoreau proffers for friendship generally, he seems if anything less ready than Emerson to forgo his friendships, however vexing or imperfect, or to relax his demands on his friends. However delicate, flawed, and finally tragic, "Friendship is first, Friendship last," he insists (*AW* 265). The one thing to be feared is its loss: "The only danger in Friendship is that it will end" (*AW* 277).[10]

Yet more unsettling is the dark vision of human nature to which this critique of worldly friendship finally leads: "The lover learns at last that there is no person quite transparent and trustworthy, but every one has a devil in him that is capable of any crime in the long run" (*AW* 284). This is vintage Thoreau, actually, and calls up the vision of desolation the narrator has in *Cape Cod* when he peers into the darkened interior of a sailors' refuge, a so-called "Humane house," to see "nothing but emptiness" (*CC* 59–60). However facetious in the telling, this glimpse into a lightless human heart is also shockingly bleak. Where Emerson retreats from the guile of mundane friendships, Thoreau excoriates them, seeing nothing there but traps, offenses to his sensibility, or betrayals. Where Emerson's vision of friendship appears to lie along a gradient from lower to higher forms of friendship, Thoreau's sensibility at this point in the essay is more polarized, even Manichaean in nature.

More to my point, Thoreau will have none of the Platonism evident in Emerson's account. There is no transcendental backlight illuminating these pages, as there is in Emerson's essay, and this indicates a deeper philosophical rift than the purely personal ones indicated above. While Thoreau's view of friendship is just as idealistic as Emerson's—just as spiritualized, perhaps even more uncompromisingly so—it is also very much grounded in this world, in particular circumstances, and in actual relationships with friends. The examples he cites of flawed or prosaic friendships—of farmers and housewives, for instance—are particular examples, based in particular social contexts (*AW* 266). Thoreau's essay in general is not so philosophically invested as Emerson's. Most of the allusions here are to literature; there are none to Plato or any tradition of philosophical idealism. In fact, the only explicit religious or philosophical references notable in the essay are to Asian sources, and these are primarily to Confucianism, despite Thoreau's ongoing interest in classical Hindu texts. Even the reference to the *Vishnu Purana* in the closing pages of the essay is purely literary.

But this preference we see here for Asian rather than Western sources, and Confucian rather than Hindu ones, reflects a deeper philosophical division between the two treatments. While Emerson's vision of friendship still grows out of his early advocacy of the "Ideal theory" and his continued reliance on Plato and Neo-Platonism, Thoreau's vision is essentially anti-metaphysical. In keeping with his recourse to Confucius and Mencius, Thoreau's take on friendship is more insistently this-worldly, more intricately psychological, and consequently perhaps, more labored. If Emerson looks to Plotinus and the Platonic Ideal, Thoreau looks to Confucius and insists on a vision of *immanent* spiritual friendship *in* this world, not a friendship that transcends it. And as if to cast doubt on the entire enterprise of writing about friendship as an abstract substantive, he concludes with this anti-propositional caveat: "But all that can be said of Friendship, is like botany to flowers" (*AW* 285–286). Friendship exists in the experience of it, Thoreau seems inclined to say, and not in some remote transcendental vision.

While various persons from Thoreau's past may be discerned moving in and through these pages, it is his brother John, in the end, who comes to personify the ideal he fashions. As noted earlier, conferring this central position on John was consistent with the design Thoreau had earlier conceived for his narrative, and John's specially appointed role is made clear from the work's opening epigraph:

> Where'er thou sail'st who sailed with me,
> Though now thou climbest loftier mounts,
> And fairer rivers dost ascend,
> Be thou my Muse, my Brother—. (*AW* 1)

And as Thoreau prepares to wind up the long digression on friendship, he makes the identification explicit: "My Friend is not of some other race or family of men, but flesh of my flesh, bone of my bone. He is my real brother" (*AW* 284). Thus it appears that the "friend" for whom he had searched the world in vain resided all along at home.

> Is it of no significance, that we have so long partaken of the same loaf, drank at the same fountain, breathed the same air, summer and winter, felt the

> same heat and cold; that the same fruits have been pleased to refresh us both, and we have never had a thought of different fibre the one from the other! (*AW* 284–285)

Like the allusion to Eve's creation from Adam's rib in the immediately prior citation, Thoreau highlights here the closeness of his relationship with his brother by underscoring their physical and familial consanguinity. At the same time, there is something quite ironic about this emphasis, since throughout "Wednesday" and the narrative of *A Week* generally, John himself has been thoroughly spiritualized—and until this point, so has Thoreau's conception of friendship. This is well illustrated by the quatrain that opens the section on friendship:

> True kindness is a pure divine affinity,
> Not founded upon human consanguinity.
> It is a spirit, not a blood relation,
> Superior to family and station. (*AW* 259)

Though indispensably a friend, very likely Henry's closest friend ever, John remains throughout the narrative a mute presence, participating in the upriver voyage, but never speaking or acting on his own behalf. Brother or no, he serves as a sort of silent witness—the ideal companion, Henry's spiritual double almost—and as such, the perfect embodiment of the idealized transcendental friend. To some degree, the spiritualization of John in *A Week* reflects the way Henry actually came to grips with his brother's death in 1842, but it evidently served his larger imaginative and spiritual vision as well (*PJ* 1: 369). "Let him be to me a spirit," Emerson had written of the friend in 1841 (*CW* 2: 123), and so John has become to Henry—but with an important difference. Whereas the "spirit" Emerson envisions remains abstract, intellectual, the reflection almost of a pure Platonic ideal, we never lose sight of John's real physical existence: spirit he may be, but he is nevertheless incarnate in a way that Henry refuses to forget or do without.

In the end, the friend Thoreau conceives of in *A Week* is neither as ephemeral nor, from a spiritual point of view, as dispensable as Emerson's friends seem to be. Thoreau's friend is crucial to his very existence—"flesh of my flesh, bone of my bone" (*AW* 284). This affirmation frees him, at this point, from the paradox of *function* (reminiscent of Emerson's) that Thoreau had suggested earlier in his essay, but it opens up an *existential* paradox that is reminiscent of early Christological debates, namely: how does one conceive a person as flesh and spirit both? In the frankly mystical poem that follows the identification of his friend as his brother, Thoreau eludes this new, incarnational paradox by cosmologizing the relationship between the two brothers in the haunting image of the double sun and "the two summer days in one" (*AW* 285). At this point, the blood relationship comes to seem simply a metaphor for a more absolute spiritual relationship.

Walden, for its part, may seem at first an inhospitable site to pursue a further consideration of the friendship theme, focusing as it does on the author's solo adventure at Walden Pond; but it is here, actually, that Thoreau elaborates some of the spiritual implications of the vision of friendship adumbrated in *A Week.* As critics have recognized now for some time, despite obvious differences, these two texts are not really the disparate works they are sometimes taken to be. Rather, they are cut from the same imaginative cloth and preoccupied with many of the same themes, including Thoreau's ongoing meditations on the relationship between friendship and solitude. In point of fact, Thoreau's life at Walden was hardly the solitary existence first-time readers are apt to expect; he often found himself playing host to a lively company of friends—animal *and* human. As readers, we are afforded glimpses of the Pond's lively social scene at several points in the narrative, most notably in the chapters entitled "Visitors," "Baker Farm," and "Brute Neighbors." Although the *doppelgänger* theme of the brothers' voyage in *A Week* has obviously given way to the story of Thoreau's sedentary life at the Pond, it surfaces once again in his account of the Canadian woodchopper, Alec Therein, profiled in "Visitors"—"a true Homeric or Paphlagonian man" (*Wa* 144). Indefatigable and all but illiterate, Therein exemplifies the animal man for Thoreau, and as the similarity of their names might suggest, comes to seem almost a kind of alter ego for the more intellectually disposed author. Others too visit Thoreau at the Pond, including the "Poet" in "Brute Neighbors," and an assorted cast of birds and animals as well.

We even encounter the theme of friendship in the place we might least expect, namely in the chapter entitled "Solitude." Perhaps this should not surprise us actually, since Emerson also insisted that there was an intimate relation between society and solitude. As he noted in "Friendship": "The soul environs itself with friends, that it may enter into a grander self-acquaintance or solitude; and it goes alone, for a season, that it may exalt its conversation or society" (*CW* 2: 116–117). Society and solitude were for Emerson the two poles between which the active soul must alternately swing. But where Emerson conceived of society and solitude as poles on a continuum, Thoreau denied the opposition altogether, undercutting not only Emerson's view but also conventional notions of society and solitude in general. What passed for society was often the loneliest of all places, he argued, whereas solitude could often provide the best society yet. On the one hand, "Solitude is not measured by the miles of space that intervene between a man and his fellows. The really diligent student in one of the crowded hives of Cambridge College is as solitary as a dervish in the desert" (*Wa* 135). On the other hand, separation from human company need not be construed as solitude at all. "I have a great deal of company in my house," he noted, "especially in the morning when nobody calls" (*Wa* 137); or, indulging his penchant for paradox further: "I never found the companion that was so companionable as solitude" (*Wa* 135). Rhetorical flourishes aside, Thoreau helps us to make sense of this assertion on at least two levels, one physical, the other spiritual. In the first place, upon moving to Walden, he quickly finds himself dwelling in the midst of a lively company of friends and neighbors, a fact he underscores in this chapter, from his evocation of the opening serenade of whippoorwills and trumping of bullfrogs to the drumming of the summer rain on his rooftop. Walden is not the isolated, out-of-the-way spot his neighbors in Concord generally took it to be but rather the most convivial place imaginable, a veritable hub of the universe, and the center of a community of being stretching from the mice under the floorboards to the stars overhead. Only once, he writes, did he feel lonely at the Pond, but noting "a slight insanity" in his mood, he recovers quickly:

> In the midst of a gentle rain while these thoughts prevailed, I was suddenly sensible of such sweet and beneficent society in Nature, in the very pattering of the drops, and in every sound and sight around my house, an infinite and unaccountable friendliness all at once like an atmosphere sustaining me, as made the fancied advantages of human neighborhood insignificant, and I have never thought of them since. Every little pine needle expanded and swelled with sympathy and befriended me. I was so distinctly made aware of the presence of something kindred to me, even in scenes which we are accustomed to call wild and dreary, and also that the nearest of blood to me and humanest was not a person nor a villager, that I thought no place could ever be strange to me again. (*Wa* 131–132)

But the narrator's paradoxical assertion of the sociality of solitude has a spiritual rationale as well. For all Thoreau's evident naturalism, *Walden* is also the expression of a thoroughly spiritual vision of life, and "Solitude" offers one of its clearest manifestations. We are reminded of this dimension of the narrator's experience with the quaint, mock-religious introduction at the end of the chapter of "an old settler and original proprietor, who is reported to have dug Walden Pond," and of the "elderly dame" tending its gardens with the "genius of unequalled fertility" (*Wa* 137). On a more reflectively theological note, he asks, what is it, after all, that "we want most to dwell near to"? And the answer he offers is not this or that village edifice, but "the perennial source of life" (*Wa* 133). Such answers place us of course in a more overtly religious atmosphere, and the reference to the source of life, though non-theistic, has a family resemblance to similar conceptions of God as friend or lover, such as we find in the Christian tradition.[11] But Thoreau was no Christian, at least not in any orthodox sense, and probably never much of a theist either: divinity was for him now and here, or it was nowhere. The "source of life" he seeks in "Solitude," it turns out, surrounds him on all sides and culminates in the life of the wakeful mind.

> Any prospect of awakening or coming to life to a dead man makes indifferent all times and places. The place where that may occur is always the same, and indescribably pleasant to all our senses. For the most part we allow only outlying and transient circumstances to make our occasions. They are, in fact, the cause of our distraction. Nearest to all things is that power which fashions their being. *Next* to us the grandest laws are continually being executed. *Next* to us is not the workman whom we have hired, with whom we love so well to talk, but the workman whose work we are. (*Wa* 134)

The climax, however, of Thoreau's religious reflections in "Solitude" is the memorable passage of contemplative self-spectatorship I have elsewhere referred to as an expression of Thoreau's ecstatic witness.

> With thinking we may be beside ourselves in a sane sense. By a conscious effort of the mind we can stand aloof from actions and their consequences; and all things, good and bad, go by us like a torrent. We are not wholly involved in Nature. I may be either the drift-wood in the stream, or Indra in the sky looking down on it. I *may* be affected by a theatrical exhibition; on the other hand, I *may not* be affected by an actual event which appears to concern me much more. I only know myself as a human entity; the scene, so to speak, of thoughts and affections; and am sensible of a certain doubleness by which I can stand as remote from myself as from another. However intense my experience, I am conscious of the presence and criticism of a part of me, which, as it were, is not a part of me, but spectator, sharing no experience, but taking note of it; and that is no more I than it is you. When the play, it may be the tragedy, of life is over, the spectator goes his way. (*Wa* 135)

If Thoreau "never found a companion so companionable as solitude," as he goes on to aver, this passage of ecstatic self-communion would appear to suggest one reason why. Here the trope of the two brothers—one active, the other silently looking on—has been psychologized and reconstituted in entirely contemplative terms. The doubleness of which he speaks grounds and contains the relation between friends, of self and other, within the settled experience of the meditative mind. And as the reference to Indra, the Vedic storm god, serves to suggest, Thoreau's reading of certain classical Hindu texts shaped such representations of ecstatic self-witnessing, but his conception of it also apparently reflected his own spiritual experience and characteristically disjunctive imagination.[12] That this experience of contemplative nonattachment was not a complete substitute for more ordinary forms of companionship, Thoreau concedes with the disclaimer with which he concludes this epiphany: "This doubleness may easily make us poor neighbors and friends sometimes" (*Wa* 135). By the same token, the charm of this meditative self-awareness clearly vies with the pleasures of actual friendship—perhaps at some level, even portends its actual fulfillment. Later in the narrative, we find a similar ambivalence reflected in the reservations expressed by the "hermit" about abandoning his solitary meditations—and perhaps a "budding ecstasy"—to join his friend, the "poet," to go fishing (*Wa* 223–225).

In view of the frustrations and discord we saw reflected in Thoreau's treatment of friendship in *A Week,* it is tempting to construe Thoreau's inward turn here, and perhaps his retreat to Walden generally, as a form of escape, a sort of compensation, perhaps, for eroding personal relationships. His disenchantment with Emerson and the Transcendentalist social scene may well have contributed at some level to his recourse to nature (Sattelmeyer 1995, 34). But if so, it was a remarkably productive and long-lived response—as Thoreau's late journals massively attest, its echoes endured till the end of his life and channeled all his creative energies. If, indeed, his life in the woods was only a response to such personal disappointments, it is hard to see how it would have prospered the way it did, unless in some sense he found there what he was looking for. In theory at least, for Thoreau no less than for Emerson, the key to ideal friendship was to be found, ironically enough, in solitude. But where Emerson conceived solitude as a stepping-stone in his ever-mounting vision of spiritual transformation, one swing of the pendulum of human growth, Thoreau looked to solitude to instantiate friendship in the here and now, in the depth and substance of his own inward, contemplative experience.

Notes

1. The epigraphs are from *Bṛhadāraṇyaka Upaniṣad* 2.4.5, my rendering (but see Radhakrishnan 1994, 197); Plato 1961, 562–563; and Emerson's citation of Goethe's phrase in his essay "Love," *CW* 2: 105 (and cf. 2: 244 n). Emerson probably found this rendering of the German in Austin 1833, 2: 195.

2. Cf. Plato 1961, 496.

3. Jeffrey Steele provides a particularly succinct and comprehensive reading of the problem of transcendental friendship; see Steele 1999, 121–139.

4. Emerson quotes the full phrase in the companion essay, "Love." Cf. *Hamlet* 3.4.68–70: "You cannot call it love, for at your age / The hey-day in the blood is tame, it's humble, / And waits upon the judgment." Cited as above in *CW* 2: 243. The story of the intense relations during this period of time between and among Emerson and an enthusiastic circle of young friends, consisting especially of Margaret Fuller, Caroline Sturgis, Anna Barker, and Samuel Ward, has been the subject of much critical interest. See *CL* 2: 323ff.; cf. Slater's "Historical Introduction," *CW* 2: xvii–xx; and also Steele 1999.

5. On Emerson's lifelong interest in Plato, see Richardson 1995, 65–66.

6. *CL* 2: 328; *JMN* 7: 430.

7. For a telling account of Emerson's immediate reactions to these losses and their long-term repercussions, see Sebouhian 1989, 219–239.

8. On the history and evolution of Thoreau's essay on friendship, see Johnson 1986, 66–69. For a particularly sensitive reading of this essay, see Robinson 2004, 64–72.

9. For a careful reconstruction of the vicissitudes of this famous relationship, see Sattelmeyer 1995, 25–39.

10. Cf. Yarbrough 1981, 67: "For Emerson friendship is an ideal impossible to attain and perhaps not even desirable ideal; for Thoreau, friendship in its ideal form becomes the ultimate end of his quest, and in its actual form becomes a necessary constituent of reality."

11. One thinks here of the Catholic mystical tradition of Jesus as lover and the ubiquitous expression in Protestant hymnody of Jesus as friend, though Thoreau's stolid Unitarian background would have inclined him to neither of these.

12. See Hodder 2001, especially chapter 5.

PART FOUR

Giving Friendship for Life

EIGHT

Giving Friendship: The Perichoresis of an All-Embracing Service

JAMES CROSSWHITE

Emerson's and Thoreau's explorations of friendship take place against the background of the philosophical treatment of friendship in Plato and Aristotle. Emerson and Thoreau do not simply inherit the problems of classical accounts of friendship; they also inherit the ontology and the theology that create those problems and the terms with which writers on friendship have attempted to address them. While the traditional ontotheological framework of the tradition mostly overwhelms Emerson, Thoreau breaks out of it in some notable passages in the "Wednesday" section of *A Week*. I explain these passages by referring to a major alternative to the inherited ontotheological framework, the idea of *perichoresis,* and I show that perichoretic thinking is present in all but name in Thoreau's account of friendship. Although "ontotheology" and "perichoresis" are not common terms in the literature on Emerson and Thoreau, their appropriateness for illuminating what is distinctive about Thoreau's conception of friendship will become clear toward the end of the essay.

Plato: Love, Friendship, and Ascent

I will linger at the start with Plato because his dialogues are always subtler and more complex than any abstract summary of his "beliefs," and because capturing the thinking of the dialogues requires noting some of their dramatic energies. Registering these subtleties and energies will allow a more revealing and productive reading of Aristotle on friendship, make visible the framework in which Emerson performs "Friendship," and clarify the Platonic challenges that later writers face.

Plato's early dialogue, *Lysis,* is his sole dialogue focused on friendship. The action of this dialogue occurs in a newly constructed "wrestling school" in which young men not only study wrestling but also try to win one another's friendly affections. In questioning the boy Lysis in front of the other boys (207d–211a), Socrates slowly reveals that, despite his wealth and attractiveness, Lysis is not really very useful to anyone else because he has very little knowledge of anything that would make him useful. This conversation uncovers a basic principle explored by every later writer in this tradition: people form friendships only with those who are in some way capable of benefiting them.

The next section of the dialogue continues the humbling exposé of the boys' ignorance of and incapacity for friendship, and in the course of the discussion Socrates probes a number of issues that will determine the agenda of the philosophy of friendship from Aristotle onward. Socrates' first query is concerned with who the true friend is: whether it is the lover or the beloved (212a–213c). Menexenus, another boy, gives the obvious reply that friendship is mutual, reciprocal. The rest of this first discussion is taken up with exploring the paradoxes of mutuality and ends with a failure to resolve them. Reciprocity seems to be implicit in the idea of friendship, and yet there seem to be friendships that do not meet this standard.

Socrates then examines Lysis as to whether friends are drawn to one another because they are like one another (213d–216b). The framework for this discussion is a naturalistic understanding of attraction in which "like attracts like." Lysis goes along with the idea, but it leads to the difficulty that such friends are not going to be very useful to each other since they will not add anything to what the other already has. This leads the interlocutors to entertain briefly another naturalistic hypothesis, namely that "likes repel" and "opposites attract," but the consequence that the just are attracted to the unjust or the friendly to the hateful is not acceptable to either of them.

At this point, Socrates changes the terms of the discussion. They have taken it for granted that the befriender and the befriended have certain traits in common, and that a natural affiliation of the two will depend on those traits. Socrates now suggests that the friend of the good and beautiful will be neither good nor bad, but will rather be defined by a *lack* of these traits. Socrates develops an analogy (218a–b): what is neither good nor bad but is a *friend* of the good and beautiful is analogous to the ignorance that belongs to lovers of wisdom. Those who take possession of wisdom will no longer love or desire it, since they already have it; but those who are ignorant through evil or stupidity will not love wisdom either, since it holds no attraction for them. Only those who are honestly and studiedly ignorant, will love and long for wisdom. They do not possess it; they comport themselves toward it, and their entire existence opens up and organizes itself as a project that moves toward wisdom. They become what Socrates calls "philosophers," friends of wisdom or lovers of wisdom. The discussion has shifted from the question of how two individuals with specific traits can come to affiliate naturally, to a question of how one can oneself become a friend of the beautiful and good.

Socrates said that he would be a "diviner" in his speech (216d), and at the end of it he acknowledges that its results are only a dream (218c). Immediately, then, he returns to the naturalistic (or ontic) framework of the previous discussion. He asks: what is the purpose of friendship? Why is it valuable? The dialogue continues, but it ends with everyone a little out of sorts and confused. In fact, Socrates says to Lysis and Menexenus that the three of them together are laughable, since they consider themselves to be friends but they do not understand the first thing about friendship.

Plato addresses these problems by abandoning them for a set of issues that revolve around the question of *eros* and erotic desire. On the one hand, this is not so drastic a maneuver. The love between friends and the love between lovers are both parts of a complex field of affiliations in Plato and Aristotle, and in ancient Greek experience generally. *Philia* is not a concept that is strictly distinguished from *eros* or from desire. In Plato's *Symposium,* love and friendship take center stage in the discussion, and although the focus is on love (*eros*), a great deal hangs on the proper understanding of the relation of love and friendship. In fact, the *Symposium* and Plato's *Phaedrus* can be read as together making a case that philosophical friendship is a highly developed form of erotic conduct. On the other hand, the abandoning of a *philia*-focused discussion of the issues raised in the *Lysis* for *eros*-based discussions of the relation between love and philosophy puts the idea of friendship in a drastically different light.

In the *Phaedrus,* young Phaedrus has become enthralled with the speechwriter Lysias, who has written Phaedrus a speech that argues that one should give one's favors to a non-lover rather than a lover because this will give the beloved more benefits and incur fewer costs and risks. Phaedrus is dazzled by the attention given him by the famous speechwriter, and Socrates' activity in the dialogue is to woo Phaedrus away from Lysias and win him for philosophy. This requires a serious befriending of the young man by

Socrates. He engages in erotic competition with Lysias, not for his own sake or benefit, but for the sake of Phaedrus, to lead him away from utility-based assessments of affiliation and toward a more philosophical understanding of love. For Phaedrus, this means awakening from an erotic enthrallment to Lysias and becoming a friend of wisdom. The loving friendship between Phaedrus and Socrates is thus grounded not in the positive pleasures they can exchange, but in a shared "lack," in their love for something else.

This idea is reinforced in Plato's *Symposium,* in which a number of noteworthy Greek men spend an evening giving speeches in praise of *Eros,* the god of love. Each spins out an indirect defense of his own erotic desire, disguised in a universalizing, mythologizing speech in praise of this god. Most of the speeches revolve around the question of Athenian pederasty, in which a man loves a young teenage boy and takes on an obligation to benefit him. When it is Socrates' turn to speak, he begins with ironic praise for the *style* of the others' speeches, and then relays—in stark contrast—the erotic teachings of Diotima, his own teacher and a woman (201c–212a). *Eros,* she says, is not a god at all but a spiritual force that inhabits the sphere between the human and the divine. Its virtue is to carry the divine and human across their borders to each other. As such, *eros* stands, like the philosopher, midway between ignorance and wisdom. Gods do not seek wisdom, and so they do not practice philosophy, because they are already wise. Love, though, is *philosophical,* a "friend" of wisdom, and thus lovers are by nature friends of wisdom, *philosophers.*

In response to Diotima's account, Socrates raises the obvious utility question: then what is the use of love for human beings (204c)? Diotima acknowledges that this is the next question, but she does not give a direct reply. Instead, she moves gradually into a very different discussion of the "ladder" of *eros* and the ascent of a human being toward the beautiful. Along this ascent, she characterizes friendship in some surprising ways. She begins by changing our minds about what it is that love desires: it is not simply the beautiful or good thing or person that we desire, but it is also not the beautiful or the good itself that we perceive in the thing or person. Instead we desire to magnify, amplify, replicate, recreate, or "engender and beget upon" the beautiful. We want the beautiful to *be,* and we want *more* of it to be. In fact, we long not just for the beautiful, but for the immortality of beauty, for the good and beautiful not to perish from the earth (206e–207a).

The first erotic step, then, lies in the attraction to other beautiful bodies, to "beget upon them" and reproduce their beauty in children, and so make it less perishable. However, the logic of the ladder leads one to notice that the beauty found in one other body is common to many, and this leads to a diminishment of the erotic energy focused on another body. Instead, *eros* moves up a rung of the ladder to love the beauty of souls. If fortunate, one finds a beautiful soul in the beautiful body one knows, and a special relationship of mutual education develops in the dialogue of the souls. This intercourse, says Diotima, generates a stronger commonality because its offspring—good and beautiful works of the soul, for example, in poetry—are more deathless than human children.

Such friendship (209c) is grounded in the creative and productive desire to preserve and protect in time what is beautiful and good—to pass it on to others, to prevent it from dying, to give it life. This attempt to cooperate in order to serve what is best draws both souls more deeply toward each other—but as a side effect of their each trying to amplify and preserve what is good. So here, finally, is Diotima's response to Socrates' question about the utility of love and friendship: *eros* not only leads us to magnify and preserve what is best, it also leads us into deeper friendships. And these two mutually support each other: it is necessary for friendship to develop for souls to be able to generate what is best in each other, and it is necessary for there to be an erotic longing to make the good and beautiful immortal for this kind of friendship to develop. This is obviously an abandonment of ordinary notions of utility. *Eros* is not satisfied with sexual reproduction; the more erotic one is, the less satisfied one is. *Eros* pushes on; and friendship is its companion and co-laborer.

A further rung in the ladder is the development of a love for the laws and customs of a city, for their improvement and preservation. After laws come the branches of knowledge, which are also spheres of beauty, and which must be kept from being destroyed or from perishing through decline. Finally, through philosophical discourse and contemplation, one catches a vision of imperishable beauty, the source and sustenance of such beauty as is found in all the previous cases. At the culmination of Diotima's speech, she suddenly addresses Socrates directly: "In this state of life above all others, my dear Socrates . . . a man finds it truly worthwhile to live" (211d). Here Diotima is "begetting" on Socrates by reproducing in him this vision of *eros* and beauty, training his desire toward what is best, and so befriending him in the profoundest way. Her speech ends with one final over-the-top remark on friendship. When one has made this ascent, she says, one is disabused of illusions and lesser images of beauty and finally cultivates in oneself (begets) true virtue, wins the "friendship of heaven," and becomes the most deathless of persons (212a). *Eros* has now completed its work, and carried the human and the divine to one another.

So Plato dramatizes the tensions in the concept of friendship. Although there is an assumption or pretense that friendship is supposed to be advantageous or useful in some ordinary sense for people as they actually are, there is also a radical overthrowing of ordinary notions of advantage and utility for ideas of ascent and transformation. These ideas are figured as a dream breaking into ordinary life (in *Lysis* and *Phaedrus*), or as the voice of someone else (Socrates in *Phaedrus,* Diotima in *Symposium*). Aristotle will do everything he can to temper this Platonic dreaming, and to contain the energies of friendship in more familiar and terrestrial forms, but in the end he will come up against some of the same tensions. Whereas Emerson will later absorb Aristotle, and struggle with this conflicted inheritance, Thoreau will stir up Plato's dream again—and go Plato one better.

Aristotle

Aristotle begins his discussion of friendship in the *Nicomachean Ethics* by remarking—as any sane person would—on the broad acknowledgment that friendship is of practical, material benefit. Yet Aristotle also recognizes that there are disagreements and questions about friendship. To address these questions, he establishes a number of principles, in large part by making distinctions. Early on, he distinguishes between goodwill and friendship by pointing out that one can have goodwill toward someone without its being returned (1155b–1156a). But friendship, in contrast, is necessarily mutual; so goodwill cannot constitute friendship if it is only one-sided. Aristotle here continues the concerns in Plato's early treatment of friendship in the *Lysis:* mutuality, reciprocity, equality.

He answers the question of whether there are different kinds of friendship by distinguishing among the three kinds of things that people desire and exchange in friendship: what is useful, what is pleasurable, and what is good. Most of books 8 and 9 of the *Nicomachean Ethics* is taken up with discussions of utility and pleasure and of the difficulties in achieving equality and reciprocity in the exchange of benefits. Aristotle provides in these passages an interesting comment on Athenian pederasty. The mutual complaints between the man who loves and the boy who is loved result when the man loves the boy on account of pleasure and the boy loves the man because of his usefulness, and neither truly has and gives that for which he is loved (1164a).

Aristotle says that all friendships which are based on giving and receiving what is useful and pleasurable are "accidental," because they are based on the changeable circumstances of another person and not on the person himself (1156a). These friendships last only as long as the friend is useful and provides pleasure, since the friendship is founded on that exchange. The goal is to get into a sustainable exchange relation with a friend in order to get optimal benefits. However, Aristotle goes to great lengths to show how difficult it can be to achieve fair exchange and equality in ordinary friendships. Friendships demand justice and equality (1159b), but since this is practically impossible to achieve, they are constantly threatened with complaints and dissolution (1162b). In a discussion of the way in which friendships based on mutual usefulness deal with giving and receiving, while yet no formal record is kept, he insists that exchange is nevertheless supposed to be *quid pro quo:*

> Friendship . . . is not on explicit terms; rather, each gives a gift . . . as to a friend, yet he expects to get back either the equivalent or more . . . and when he does not . . . he will complain. This happens because . . . people . . . wish noble things but choose beneficial ones; and treating someone *well,* not in order to be repaid, is noble, but being the recipient of a good service is beneficial. (1162b)

The conditions of equality and sustainability are difficult enough to achieve, but a special stress is put on these friendships by the fact that while they give an appearance of being formed by an interest in what is good for the other for his own sake, this is rarely true.

That rare friendship that is formed by giving and receiving reciprocally, each for the sake of the other, is a friendship based on virtue. Aristotle's challenge in describing it is to keep it as materially and terrestrially grounded—and to make it as rich—as his discussions of the lesser kind of friendship. Aristotle calls the friendship of good people who are equally virtuous "complete" or "fulfilled" friendship (1156b). Such a friendship is temporally stable and complete in that fully virtuous people are not virtuous simply on occasion: virtue is itself a stable thing, an enduring disposition and not a passing act. It is also "complete" in that it is perfectly mutual: each friend gives no less than he receives. Aristotle gives two reasons for the rarity of this kind of friendship. First, it takes a long time and lots of companionship to develop, since it is difficult to gain knowledge of another person's profoundest dispositions. Second, very few people turn out to be virtuous to the requisite degree (1156b25–35).

An essential Aristotelian idea, and one that will return in an interesting form in Emerson, is that self-love is prior to and is the source of friendship. Virtuous people love themselves and are friends with themselves:

> A friend is most of all someone who wishes, or someone to whom are wished, good things for that person's sake . . . but these belong most of all to a person in relation to himself . . . so he should also love himself most of all. . . . If someone happened to be always eager that he, above all others, did just actions . . . and if . . . he was always acquiring what is noble for himself, no one would . . . find fault with him . . . [for] he gratifies the supreme element in himself and complies with it in everything. (1168b)

This love is analogous to the Platonic desire for the beautiful not to perish. In this case, virtuous people cherish the virtues. They are friends to themselves for the sake of sustaining and furthering the virtue in themselves.

This friendship with oneself is the model and source for friendship with others: "But as a good person is related to himself, so [must he be] also to his friend, since a friend is a different self" (1170b). That is, a good person desires to be useful to herself, to benefit herself, to take pleasure in herself, and especially to take pleasure in and be a servant of her own goodness. In the same way, when she comes to experience the goodness of a friend, she also desires to be useful to that friend and to take pleasure in that friend and serve that friend for the sake of the goodness of that friend—that is, for the sake of the friend herself, since virtue is not an accidental feature of a person, but a disposition to action that has become consistent. In the virtuous in general there is a kind of equality in identity, since virtue is character. Thus, the virtuous friend of a virtuous person is a "different self."

Many readers experience some discomfort with this idea, since it seems to say that a virtuous person discovers in all his friends simply another version of himself. Aristotle himself has trouble with this idea. Why, he asks, should the virtuous then need friends at all? If virtue is the completion of friendship, and if the mother of all friendship is friendship with oneself, why isn't the happily virtuous person self-sufficient? Aristotle even adds that friends seem useless: "A friend, since he is another self, provides things that one is unable to provide for oneself" (1169b), but the virtuous person *is* able to provide *virtue* for himself, and does not need it from another.

One answer is in the passages cited above, to the effect that friendship with other virtuous people is natural once one discovers their virtue. However, this does not answer the question of whether one *needs* friends. Aristotle argues that the idea of a happy life without friends defies common sense—and a virtuous person is a happy person (1169b9). Yet he is concerned that common sense may be an expression of the common attitude that friendships are for utility and pleasure (1169b10–15). He gives another argument that the virtuous are beneficent and so need friends to treat beneficently, but this kind of friendship hardly meets the reciprocity condition. Aristotle also tries a more general argument: happiness is an activity, and thus the virtuous need friends in relation to whom they can actualize their virtues (1169b–1170a). However, this argument also fails to meet the usual expectations of reciprocity and mutuality.

We can now summarize the achievements and quandaries of classical philosophy's framework for illuminating the dynamics of friendship. Plato's *Lysis* uncovers the basic natural assumption that friendships give pleasure and utility. The boys at the wrestling school naturally assume this, and in the *Nicomachean Ethics* Aristotle just as consistently affirms this. The *Lysis* also introduces the problem of reciprocity, and in that dialogue, as in Aristotle, the idea seems to create most of the problems for understanding the failures and successes of friendships. The question of whether we are naturally attracted to people who are like us or unlike us is also introduced in the *Lysis.* Aristotle repeats the same question, but develops a powerful argument in favor of the idea that virtuous friends are not only profoundly alike: one's friend is even "another self." The *Lysis* also presents us with the first of a series of what we might call "abandonments," in Socrates' "dream," in which we suddenly no longer consider friends as individuals with traits, but in which we instead consider how seeking the beautiful and good would affect the forming of friendships. And so we have the development of the fundamental split between ordinary utility-based friendships and a "higher" kind of friendship.

This basic split is carried out in radically different ways in Plato and Aristotle. For Plato, the turn to philosophical friendship is an abandonment of the preoccupations of utility-based friendship. In the *Phaedrus,* the two kinds of friendship are in competition with each other for the soul of a young man, and they are presented as irreconcilable. In both the *Phaedrus* and the *Symposium,* this abandonment is also presented by way of steps in a kind of ascent or ladder, or as a kind of growth in which friendship plays an important role. Aristotle, on the other hand, presents the split between the "kinds" of friendship in terms of the differences between common people and rare virtuous people. Importantly, the move away from utility friendships in the *Phaedrus* requires the love and care of a Socrates, a philosopher, in a friendship that takes the form of a dialogue. In the *Symposium,* Socrates' growth in the love of what is most worth loving comes only in his friendship with Diotima, his own philosophical teacher. In Plato, the philosophical friend—one who loves you for your own sake and not for your usefulness or for the pleasure you can give—seems to be a requirement for your own development into someone who is capable of the higher kind of friendship, the kind Aristotle calls a "fulfilled" one.

Emerson

In the famous essay on "Friendship," Emerson is at his most Emersonian. Pouring all the ingredients of the classical view of friendship into the caldron of an essay, he manages to create an aesthetic and rhetorical unity out of conflicting judgments on the received problems, and comes close to vaporizing friendship at the end. He begins his essay at the most abstract level, describing human affiliation in the first two paragraphs in very general terms as "kindness . . . love . . . affection . . . benevolence and complacency . . . good will." These are the natural ground of friendship, and they are universal: "The whole human family is bathed with an element of love like a fine ether" (*CW* 2: 113). This is Aristotelian *philia* in a Transcendentalist register, which goes so far as to restate Aristotle's naturalistic account of like seeking like between the virtuous: "My friends have come to me unsought. The great God gave them to me. By oldest right, by the divine affinity of virtue with itself, I find them, or rather not I, but the Deity in me" (*CW* 2: 115). The tension here between the divine naturalistic intelligence that allows virtue to find virtue, but that also unfolds itself in the differentiations that allow no two individuals to be alike, sets an important part of the agenda for Emerson's efforts in the essay.

At the beginning, Emerson explains the benefit of friendship in clearly Aristotelian terms as its capacity for strengthening our natural virtues, enhancing our feeling of life, and giving pleasure: "Our intellectual and active powers increase with affection" (*CW* 2: 113). In a friend's presence, we feel "a lively surprise at our unusual powers" (*CW* 2: 114).

Throughout the essay, Emerson makes several efforts to describe the "high friendship" that produces these results more or less consistently. It is difficult to give an account of this friendship because he keeps interrupting his own exposition to protest and lament the impossibility of what he is explaining, so I will (in an anti-Emersonian way) separate his encomium and his lament here. High friends are gods and poets who enlarge the self and the world (*CW* 2: 115). Our relation to them is "select and sacred," even "absolute" and "divine" (*CW* 2: 118). We all pass our lives in search of this kind of friendship (*CW* 2: 117). Friendship is the cosmic center: the sincerity of joy and peace we draw from friendship "is the nut itself whereof all nature is but the husk and shell." And in a wonderful juxtaposition, Emerson immediately exclaims: "Happy is the house that shelters a friend" (*CW* 2: 119), as if such a house were a microcosm of nature and contained nature's whole purpose.

Emerson also moves well beyond the classical analysis and into some distinctively Emersonian perspectives. He attempts to analyze high friendship into its elements, and finds two: "truth" and "tenderness." By "truth" he means truthfulness and the falling away of all pretense. In the presence of a high friend, we can at last be honest and sincere, with no need of the conformity that rules in common social life. We drop all "dissimulation," and return to "simplicity" and "wholeness" (*CW* 2: 119). A friend "exercises not my ingenuity but me" (*CW* 2: 120). It is as if friendship were another form of self-reliance, which turns out to be not far from the truth. "Tenderness" receives only very brief treatment, and it seems to bear the meaning of both "givingness"—in that the friend is the only one to whom we can really give or tender ourselves—and kindness, in that when every more external and accidental bond is stripped away by truthfulness, what remains is the simpler but more profound love of friendship, the giving of kindness beyond any exchange of benefits.

Throughout the development of the idea of high friendship, Emerson alternates between extolling and lamenting the possibility of high friendship. But just before the end, when the encomium rises to unsustainable heights, he sketches a three-part analysis and stumbles upon a mid-world of friendship, although it is announced in a collision of possibility and impossibility. First, the two rejected ideas of friendship: "We chide the citizen because he makes love a commodity. It is an exchange of gifts, of useful loans . . . yet, on the other hand, we cannot forgive the poet if he spins his thread too fine, and does not substantiate his romance." Emerson proposes instead that:

> The end of friendship is a commerce the most strict and homely that can be joined. . . . It is for aid and comfort through all the relations and passages of life and death. . . . We are to dignify to each other the daily needs and offices of man's life, and embellish it by courage, wisdom, and unity. (*CW* 2: 121)

Here is the joining of the transcendentally high ("strict") with the common ("homely"), the practice of the highest virtues in the commonest joys and sufferings of life.

However, this mid-world evanesces even before it can take shape. The complete version of the sentence that introduces it, with emphasis added, reads thus: "The end of friendship is a commerce the most strict and homely that *can* be joined; *more strict than any of which we have experience.*" While the first clause announces the possibility of this friendship, the second all but takes this possibility away. Thus, exactly where Emerson comes closest to resolving the classical tension between common friendship and ideal friendship, he also magnifies that tension to one of its most extreme forms.

Anxiety about the possibility of friendship is everywhere evident in the essay. The idea of a logical or argumentative or dialectical resolution would be profoundly anti-Emersonian. Consider that while the essay opens with five paragraphs in praise of friendship, it takes only a paragraph of doubt for Emerson to unravel the whole ball, announcing then in the seventh paragraph:

> Friendship, like the immortality of the soul, is too good to be believed. . . . In strictness, the soul does not respect men as it respects itself. In strict science all persons underlie the same condition of an infinite remoteness. I cannot deny it, O friend, that the vast shadow of the Phenomenal includes thee also . . . (*CW* 2: 116)

There is nothing like this notion of radical isolation in Aristotle, who acknowledges the rarity of high friendship but never questions its possibility.

Emerson describes many different problems with friendship, including the difficulties in achieving reciprocity and equality in exchanges; but in the end it is the self-sufficiency and radical solitude of the Emersonian soul that makes high friendship impossible. If we always "descend to meet," as Emerson suggests, then friendship is tethered to the opposite of a Platonic "ascent." And near the end of "Friendship," at the point of his most unrestrained praise, friendship becomes spiritualized into something that does not seem like friendship at all—at least not to the ancients or most writers on friendship: "The condition which high friendship demands, is, ability to do without it"; "Friends, such as we desire, are dreams and fables"; "It has seemed to me lately more possible than I knew, to carry a friendship greatly, on one side. . . . It never troubles the sun that some of his rays fall wide and vain into ungrateful space, and only a small part on the reflecting planet" (*CW* 2: 123, 125, 127). By the last paragraph of the essay, necessarily lesser friends have become analogous to frogs and worms.

However, the most intoxicating and withering of Emerson's difficulties is his radical transcendentalizing of Aristotle's perspective on the friend as being "another self." For ultimately, the lesser character of all friends is a result of the special relationship one has with one's own soul. This idea receives different expressions in "Friendship." In the dialectically engineered seventh paragraph, Emerson says that we become aware that we project or "bestow" greatness on our friends, and that their light is thus a "reflection" of our own light. There is a kind of necessity to this: "I *cannot* choose but rely on my own poverty more than on your wealth. I *cannot* make your consciousness tantamount to mine. Only the star dazzles; the planet has a faint, moon-like ray" (*CW* 2: 116, emphasis added). It is necessary to project friends—and then to realize that they are not the friends one supposed, but rather one's efforts to understand one's own powers and virtues. The repetition of "cannot" in the passage expresses the necessity of its development, but it is difficult to make such a double-necessity precise in Emerson. It could be the necessity of Emersonian spiritual experience, which includes projecting external realities and then coming to realize that they are not external and independent realities, but expressions of the soul. Or it could be the necessity of needing a knowledge and measure of virtue before one can even recognize it in others, and so always being the ultimate measure of virtue oneself, with no possibility of a measure's overwhelming one from without. However, there also seems to be the idea that the sense of the overwhelming "magnificence" of one's own soul is all one can ever really know, that others are conceived and experienced on the basis of this, and that as "copies" of this they are necessarily less vivid, less real. This is the line of thinking that aligns with the ideas of friendship's being "too good to be true," with our always "descending to meet," and with the idea of "infinite remoteness."

However, even this melancholy sense of the infinite remoteness of others does not prevent Emerson from trying to find a way forward. The only solution is to find in others—myself. Such identity has a distinctly Aristotelian cast of virtue meeting virtue, and yet the Emersonian self seems at last to love its own soul *more* than the virtue it shares with another:

> if we should not meet them . . . we shall not want them, for we are already they. In the last analysis, love is only the reflection of a man's own worthiness from other men. Men have sometimes exchanged names with their friends, as if they would signify that in their friend each loved his own soul. (*CW* 2: 125)

This magnificent soul that must "descend to meet" or to converse rises in love only to itself.

In short, Emerson continues the Aristotelian quandary about self-sufficiency and the need for friends, but intensifies and magnifies it. For

Aristotle, this quandary is addressed—though not settled—in three ways: by consulting common sense and recognizing that utility and pleasure are not only the bases of *kinds* of friendship, but are dimensions of all friendships; by a conception of the love of virtue that loves virtue in others as well as in oneself; and by the introduction of the dangerous and complex idea of the friend's being "another self." Emerson's problem is more difficult, for besides magnifying the tensions in the idea and experience of friendship, he at times completely obliterates them by dismissing the need for anything like friendship altogether. For the love of friend *is* self-love. There might be a long discussion here, sympathetic to Emerson, about the complexity of this self-love and its social dimensions and realities. However, there is another way to address the instabilities in friendship, one that abandons this circle and suggests a different frame altogether.

Theological Interlude

Before moving ahead to Thoreau's abandonment of the Aristotelian/Emersonian horizon, a theological interlude is in order, for a theological background has been active in the development of all these perspectives on friendship. As Hans-Georg Gadamer claims, Aristotle's model for thinking of friendship, the one inherited by Emerson, is a fundamentally theological one. The difficulty is that while the divine is an ideal, "the god who is complete in himself has no friends" (1999, 137). A god is "superior to the need for uniting with something beyond himself" (1999, 138). The Aristotelian/Emersonian challenge is thus to reconcile the self-sufficiency of the virtuous person with that person's need of friendship. Gadamer addresses Aristotle's problem in a Heideggerian reading of Aristotle's conception of human sociality, though this conflicts with Aristotle's theological frame. This is a corrective and creative interpretation. (As David Vessey puts it, Gadamer's reading of Aristotle "seems both selective and without precedent—certainly it is at odds with the dominant readings of Aristotle on this point" [2005, 67].) Gadamer claims that for Aristotle the activity of life always has the character of "being-with" in Heidegger; cognition is always "perceiving-with, knowing-with, thinking-with—that is, living-with and being-with (*Mitsein*)." He finds in Aristotle's observation that "the essence of a friend consists in someone's being able to understand his neighbor more easily than himself" (1999, 137) the New Testament idea that we see the speck in another's eye and not the plank in our own. Thus, Gadamer finds that this Aristotelian dictum amounts to an assertion that self-knowledge is always incomplete. He uses this idea to valorize Aristotle's contrast of divine self-sufficient happiness with the human need for friends. In this happy Aristotelianism, the friend is both a mirror that reveals those aspects of myself which I have difficulty understanding, and a model of what I am becoming: my "better self." In short, Gadamer not only gives Aristotelian *philia* a Heideggerian cast, but he also Platonizes Aristotle by creating an ascent out of ignorance and misplaced desire by way of a friend.

A similar conception of friendship is developed by Stanley Cavell, who credits Emerson's "perfectionism" with including a notion of friendship that fulfills Gadamer's longings. In Cavell's version, there can be nothing like self-sufficiency or completion for human beings. Instead, perfectionism requires a more or less permanent dissatisfaction with oneself (one's present attainments) in favor of one's "next self" (which is unattained but attainable). Cavell takes the perfectionist friendship dramatized in the Platonic dialogues to be exemplary here. He finds in Plato's *Republic:*

> (1) a mode of conversation, (2) between (older and younger) friends, (3) one . . . authoritative because (4) his life is somehow exemplary . . . and (5) in the attraction of which the self recognizes itself as enchained . . . and (6) removed from reality, whereupon (7) the self finds that it can turn (convert, revolutionize itself) and (8) a process of education is undertaken . . . in which (10) each self is drawn on a journey of ascent to (11) a further state of that self, where. . . . (Cavell 1990, 6–7)

Cavell goes on for twenty-eight numbered items. Here the essential role of friendship in *becoming oneself* is added to the Gadamerian observations that friends are mirrors (we see ourselves as enchained) and models (the attraction to the friend as exemplary). This notion of needing friends to advance or return to oneself, of a friend as a friend-enemy (enemy of my present attainments, friend of my next self), is perfectly aligned with Emerson's "beautiful enemy" passage in "Friendship" (*CW* 2: 124), where the idea is an essential but minor variation on the theme of love of one's own magnificence. However, to make these Cavellian moves requires a larger break with Aristotelian theology and in fact with all ontotheology than Emerson can manage.

Breaking the Theological Frame: Perichoresis and Thoreau

Traditional ontotheological thinking conceptualizes the divine as a self-sufficient being: deity is perfect and complete, unchanging, without lack or need. Human beings at their best are understood as approaching or aiming toward—or as capable of realizing at extraordinary moments—just this kind of completion. They are also entities-with-traits, like divine entities; however, unlike divine entities, they are in their usual state notoriously unfulfilled. Nevertheless they have their individual being independently of their friendships. However, the main problems of friendship arise in the questions of (1) how human individuals can sustain optimal exchanges of benefits with other individuals, (2) how to characterize the relationship between this "low" exchange-of-benefits friendship and the "high" friendship that goes beyond it, and (3) how virtuous human beings—who resemble the divine being—could have any need of friendship whatsoever. And these questions are all concerned with giving and receiving. Because Transcendentalists are oriented by the ontotheological idea of self-sufficiency, they are caught in an unstable tension between the ideal of a fully developed individual and the receiving of gifts. The ontotheological/economic model equates receiving a gift with putting the recipient in debt to the giver. One must pay the debt to recover one's status as a self-sufficient individual; if one cannot pay the debt, then one has been diminished. This demand of self-sufficiency can be exacting; even gratitude can seem like a debt that can never be paid off, and so be experienced as an intolerable diminishment.

The idea of perichoresis suggests a different model of giving and receiving, one that disrupts the ontotheological model and opens the door to a better appreciation of Thoreau's accomplishments in the "Wednesday" section of *A Week*. "Perichoresis" is the old theological word for that relation among the members of the Christian Trinity which is sometimes called "indwelling" in English. The conceptual space it opens is the site of classic theological contests between Eastern and Western Christianity, as well as over impressive words like "hypostases" and "energies," "circumincession," "homoousios," and "filioque." In recent years the idea has been strongly shaped by new philosophical developments, especially Jean-Luc Marion's notion of "God without Being." Very briefly, the idea here is that God is not a being: God is giving. In fact, God is the giving of being. (Marion, following Heidegger, crosses through the "is" here to emphasize the point and tame the grammatical paradox.) As Stephen H. Webb puts it in a gloss on Marion, "God is not the essence of being, but the beginning of giving" (1996, 130). The Trinity is one site for making sense of this. The individual members of the Trinity do not first exist independently and then enter a relation with one another. Some do not exist first such that others then proceed from them in time. Instead, the members of the Trinity give being to one another and receive being from one another *as* givers and receivers of being in a perichoretic procession—and in all sorts of doctrinal and heretical and controversial ways. Marion's account of giving is appropriate here: "Love gives itself only in abandoning itself, ceaselessly transgressing the limits of its own gift, so as to be transplanted outside of itself" (Marion 1991, 48). In recent uses of the idea, this giving and receiving also characterize creation and human being; we give and receive our human being, such as it is, to and from one another. We are a giving and receiving before (and while) we are what we are independently as individuals. Giving is prior to being; being itself is an effect. Thus, the "onto-" of ontotheology vanishes—as does the ontically conceived "theo-" that determines it. Giving and receiving take the place of any once-vaunted self-sufficiency. The idea is complicated, and sorting it out creates enormous controversies, but its attractions are clear for anyone concerned about the way ontotheological frameworks seem to prevent us from expressing what we experience as true.

I want to show the special appropriateness of perichoresis for thinking about friendship by showing how it illuminates some of Thoreau's most important remarks in "Wednesday." First, as Thoreau notes, friendship does not exist as a thing: it is, as he says, "evanescent" (*AW* 261). He does not mean simply that it appears and then disappears; he means that it is *always* on the point of vanishing. He is observing that it does not have a secure ontological basis: if the idea of *perduring* is constitutive of "substance," then friendship is literally *insubstantial*. There is no institution to secure it a habitat, no religion to shelter it, no scripture or temple to circumscribe it (*AW* 263). Marriage preserves itself through explicit vows, laws, rituals, and fairly formal conventions. Friendship has none of these guarantees. This is why it is so difficult, why part of its nature is to start and stop and start and stop—and why after it has stopped, one can no longer be sure whether it is there, or indeed whether it ever was. In light of the perichoretic insight, we would say that friendship *is* only in its being given and received. It has no other being. This means, too, that friends *are friends* only in the giving and receiving of friendship.

Thoreau goes out of his way to clear the ground of the traditional model so that the appropriate reality of friendship can show itself:

> Most contemplate only what would be the accidental and trifling advantages of Friendship, as that the Friend can assist in time of need, by his substance, or his influence, or his counsel; but he who foresees such advantages in this

> relation proves himself blind to its real advantage, or indeed wholly inexperienced in the relation itself. Such services are particular and menial, compared with the perpetual and all-embracing service which it is. (*AW* 266)

This "service" is, in light of perichoresis, the giving of being to a friend—or more specifically, the giving of a *way* of being called "friendship." Thoreau's figures for this service—it is "perpetual" and "all-embracing"—signify that it is not susceptible to economic measurement and control. Friendship is not at all concerned with "substance." In friendship, "substance" is quite precisely rendered "accidental"; and thus the service which friendship *is* becomes—when juxtaposed to an exchange model—excessive, beyond measure, and strictly *incalculable.*

It is a claim of perichoretic friendship that without it we would not be able to become ourselves; we would not be given our being. "To his Friend a man's *peculiar character* appears in *every* feature and in *every* action, and it is thus *drawn out* and *improved* by him" (*AW* 266–267, emphasis added). The Friend both knows our individual character, and aids in its continuing creation, expression, growth, improvement; that is, the Friend knows how to help in the attainment of our next self. This is the significance of Thoreau's insistence on the importance of friendship in education. The service of friendship precipitates, in Cavell's words, the "friend-enemy" known to Nietzsche and Emerson. In Thoreau's words: "Friends . . . when they treated us not as we were, but as we aspired to be"; "A friend is one who incessantly pays us the compliment of expecting from us all the virtues" (*AW* 259, 267). In Cavell's writings this is the friend not of our attainments (as in the traditional model) but of our next self, our beyond: the self that makes us uncomfortable with our conformity. In other words, this is the perichoretic friend from whom we receive our *being as* someone capable of change, movement, learning, onwardness.

Thus, Thoreau ridicules the idea that one "selects" such friends (*AW* 269). This would be to enter an instrumental relationship based on the knowledge made available by one's current attainments. But friendship is not voluntary. It is not a willing but a giving and a receiving. Friends call us away from our current self-understanding to a new one. This can come by chance. It can be a kind of suffering. In its involuntary insistence it can come to be figured as chains. Rebirth is hardly a simple pleasure.

This power of friendship to give being should not be understated, and Thoreau is in no danger of doing so in "Wednesday." Indeed, the love of friendship is said to be capable of giving existence to a "new world." Just after Thoreau says that much that is called friendship "is only a little more honor among rogues," he writes:

> But sometimes we are said to *love* another . . . so that we *give* the best, and *receive* the best . . . There are passages of affection in our intercourse with mortal men and women, such as no prophecy had taught us to expect, which transcend our earthly life. . . . What is this Love that may come right into the middle of a prosaic Goffstown day, equal to any of the gods? that discovers a new world, fair and fresh and eternal, occupying the place of the old one, when to the common eye a dust has settled on the universe? which world *cannot else be reached, and does not exist.* (*AW* 268, emphasis added)

This Thoreauvian extravagance in which friendship becomes equal to any god is certainly a reference to its divine capacity for creation—for without it the new world literally does not exist, has not been given being. (And the best is given, and the best is received, only in love.) We are in the realm of what has being *only* in being given and being received.

This friendship also has an unusual relation to temporality. As cited, Thoreau writes of the "perpetual" service of friendship, and says that a Friend is one who "incessantly" pays us the compliment of expecting from us all the virtues. However, these references to eternity are not only indicators that the economic model cannot capture the event; they are also figures of the ontogenetic power of friendship. In their suggestions of timeless being, they move the consideration from the transitory and practical to the ontological. Our excessive temporal duty is a function of friendship's having no other substrate than our service, no endurance outside of our timely giving and receiving of it.

And finally, friendship of this kind is symmetrical, and addresses the classical questions of reciprocity and equality not on the exchange model but, as Thoreau says, in "the state of the just dealing with the just, the magnanimous with the magnanimous, the sincere with the sincere" (*AW* 267). The symmetry here is not in the ontic exchange of benefits, but in the perichoretic form and manner of giving and receiving: justly, magnanimously, sincerely, on all sides. This is incommensurate with the usual quantitative ways of measuring exchange. And neither are the only *challenges* of friendship on the ontic level of exchange—for gifts become gifts at all only when they are received, in an activity of giving to others their own giving, allowing them into the perichoretic currents of education and change by accepting what they have to give. To cease the giving of this giving is not simply to unbalance a friendship. It is to extinguish its only being.

An ontic, utilitarian conception of friendship is relatively easy to grasp and analyze. One focuses on the traits of existing individuals, and these traits are for the most part open to observation. One then develops a framework for understanding the kinds of mutual exchanges that take place in relations of friendship. Socrates' figure of a "dream" of friendship was his way of marking the break between this ontic, utilitarian conception of friendship and a conception of friendship that would not rely on an observable exchange of benefits, but rather would be an effect of a profound kind of love. Thoreau also marks this break, but instead of speaking of a "dream," he remarks on the "evanescence" of friendship, its not being completely under our control, and its being a "perpetual and all-embracing service" instead a merely temporal exchange of specific benefits. For Thoreau, too, this friendship that conflicts with ordinary expectations is connected with a love that gives and receives the best. For the Socrates of the *Symposium* this kind of friendship culminates in a friendship with the divine that, according to Diotima, is purified of anything having to do with the human body (211e). This is part of what gives this friendship its dreamlike quality. For Thoreau, however, the abandonment of a purely ontic, utilitarian conception of friendship leads not *out* of the world but back *into* a new world, *with* "mortal men and women." It leads to a friendship fulfilled not in heaven but in a world that occupies the same place as the old one. Despite its theological resonances and dimensions, this friendship's habitat is among mortals, in their waking lives, and it arrives in the course of their prosaic days.

From this point of view, it would be dangerous to set up a perichoretic ideal against which the economic model looks like a "fall," and so to address one of the traditional questions of the philosophy of friendship by speaking of two essentially different kinds of friendship. For perichoretic giving necessarily takes place in a context with ontic content; it is never free of the real circulation of gifts within concrete economies. And perichoresis is not a theory that could in any simple way guide practice and cure friendship of its instabilities. The idea of perichoresis does shed light on dimensions of friendship that the old model leaves in darkness, and it does allow us to address old problems in new ways. But it is not a simple ideal.

The most radical point about perichoresis relative to Thoreau is that from this perspective individuality and self-sufficiency are *achievements* of friendship, made possible by a befriending that is prior to whatever we call self-sufficiency—a befriending that generates self-sufficiency, and sustains it. The problem faced by Aristotle and Emerson is how the virtuous, self-sufficient individual could possibly need friends or be motivated to make friends and sustain friendships. What they fail to remember consistently, or what they fail to grasp as an ontological issue, is that self-sufficient individuals who can form friendships with themselves are not self-generating and self-sustaining. They have already been befriended by family members and by their other friends along the way. They can thus carry on the conversations with themselves about how virtuous fathers, sons, neighbors, and citizens should conduct themselves because their family members, neighbors, and fellow citizens acknowledge them (give them their being) *as what they are: as* members of a family, *as* neighbors and fellow citizens. If they did not—if these relatives, friends and neighbors did not sustain them in a practical and ongoing recognition of their social identities, in the beneficial transactions of daily life and economic life, in their own ethical and political behavior toward them, and in their shared form of life in a language spoken together almost incessantly—there would simply be no "virtuous" individual who, forgetting his provenance, could wonder what need he has for friends.

But in "Wednesday," Thoreau awakens from this forgetfulness and writes about friendship in a very different light. What is more, he also acknowledges and practices his provenance, consciously, deliberately, fluently, in the giving and receiving of friendship that is the composition of *A Week*. He is, in the very activity of writing, John's brother—and this brother's beauty, as Diotima would say, illuminates *A Week*.

NINE

Leaving and Bequeathing: Friendship, Moral Perfectionism, and the Gleam of Light

NAOKO SAITO

> It is foolish to be afraid of making our ties too spiritual,
> as if so we could lose any genuine love.
>
> EMERSON

Emerson and Thoreau are generally known as representatives of American individualism, that is, as proponents of the strongly self-reliant individual. George Kateb, however, raises the question: "Does the self-reliant individual need others?" His answer is positive, but with a recognition of the "difficulty of connection." His ensuing question is then: how, even if Emerson is unable to close the "gaps between persons," can he at least narrow them (2000, 96, 97)? Striking a similar note, Lawrence Buell points to an "affective deficit" in Emerson's notion of friendship with its "disregard for the body" (2003, 82, 92). The use of negative words in their appraisals suggests that Kateb and Buell find a dilemma or paradox in Emerson's concept of the self, especially in relation to the connection with others—a price that the independent self must pay for the sake of sustaining its own integrity. It is to this paradox—or to put it more strongly, to the sense of guilt that this price exacts—that I would like to respond in this essay, with a view to giving it a positive turn. Through a reconsideration of the idea of friendship in Emerson and Thoreau, I shall try to identify a kind of self-reliance that is sustained in a relation *with* others but *without* "deficit."

To accomplish this task, the central theme I shall address is the nature of friendship in *Emersonian Moral Perfectionism*—Stanley Cavell's representation of Emerson and, by implication, Thoreau. Cavell points us toward a way of thinking that enables us to transcend the diverse dichotomies that lie behind the foregoing dilemma; and his approach can help us revive the voices of Emerson and Thoreau today, in such a way as to respond to a need of our times. In the face of the world-wide dominance of "Americanization," which amounts to the negative apotheosis of American individualism; and in the face of the assimilation of difference into the same in the name of globalization and multiculturalism, this is the need for alterity through self-transcendence. To this end, one of the aspects in Emersonian moral perfectionism to which I shall pay attention is the inseparable relationship between friendship and education: the idea of *mutual education*—of education as the ongoing and endless process of perfecting a relationship itself. This brings with it a concomitant notion of mutuality: mutuality not in the sense of equivalency, but rather a mutuality that is not fully rewarded. To illustrate this, I shall examine the essential role of the friend who leaves us with an awakening such that we may pursue our own "gleam of light." This is the imagery of Emerson's self-reliance. In conclusion, and in resistance to the characteristic discourse of cosmopolitan education and of the love of humanity that transcends national and cultural borders, I shall propose an Emersonian and Thoreauvian vision of citizenship education.

Friendship and Emersonian Moral Perfectionism

When we read Emerson and Thoreau, we are struck by apparent contradictions in their ideas of friendship: affinity and radical difference between the self and the other; the intense moment of encounter and the undeniable sense of eternal distance. In Emerson's words, there are both aspects of "deep identity" and "disparities" in friendship (*CW* 2: 123); and in Thoreau's: "our spirits are intimate," while at the same time friendship "is not so kind . . . it has not much human blood in it" (*AW* 270, 275). For both Emerson and Thoreau, solitude is a mark of the self-reliant individual. As Emerson puts this: the "soul environs itself with friends that it may enter into a grander self-acquaintance or solitude" (*CW* 2: 116–117); and Thoreau, in his solitary life at Walden Pond, claims: "I have found that no exertion of the legs can bring two minds much nearer to one another" (*Wa* 133). There is an undeniable sense of "distance" at work in both their concepts of friendship (Kateb 2000, 108). Readers of Emerson and Thoreau, then, cannot help but question: Why does a *self*-reliant individual need *others*?

In response to this question, Kateb's answer is that friendship "alone helps to do the work of solitude, and that, because friendship alone assists both self-acquaintance and (without paradox, without compromise) self-reliance" (2000, 114). In order to sustain relationships of this kind, "friends have to remain somewhat strange to each other," retaining "an aura for each other": both "tension" and "affection" are necessary (Kateb 2000, 112, 110). In his literal interpretation of self-reliance, there still remains a question (and perhaps a possible criticism with a more moral accent) of whether the other is needed by the self only for its self-serving goal. Furthermore, a kind of skepticism of other minds seems to be retained: the mind of the self eternally sustains a realm that is unapproachable for and unknowable by others. With the sense of imperfectability in our understanding of the other, our sense of guilt then continues to mount. Because of the imbalance involved in one's relation to one's own self and to others, there arises the negative feeling that one aspect (attention to or care for the self) is emphasized at the expense of the other (regard for others)—the latter is sacrificed for the former.

To untangle these riddles, Stanley Cavell's idea of Emersonian moral perfectionism offers an alternative approach to Emerson's and Thoreau's ideas of friendship. He reinterprets Emersonian self-reliance from the standpoint of his moral perfectionism. In response to the charge that Emerson's thought is elitist, Cavell says that Emersonian moral perfectionism is not only "compatible with democracy, but [is] its prize": it is essential to the "criticism of democracy from within" (1990, 3, 28). Cavell shifts our attention from the idea of the self-serving goal of self-reliance to Emerson's call upon the potential nobility of the self, which Emerson names "genius." Genius is not the privilege of a few individuals, but the "sound estate of every man" (*CW* 1: 56–57). In the context of democracy as a way of living that involves the question of how we should live, each individual has a responsibility to contribute *her* own response to *her* own society. This Cavell calls the Emersonian (as opposed to the Rawlsian) version of the "conversation of justice"; in this sense "the capacity for self-reliance . . . is universally distributed" (1990, 27, 26). While the perfection *of the self* is the undeniable component of Emersonian moral perfectionism, the transformation of the self in itself is not self-contained: it is inseparable from the betterment of society.

As another distinctive trait of *Emersonian* moral perfectionism (in contrast particularly to Plato's and Aristotle's), perfection is the endless journey of self-overcoming and self-realization, whose central focus is on the here and now, and in the process of attaining a further, next self, and not the highest self. Drawing on Emerson's idea of the "unattained but attainable self," Cavell writes: "The self is always attained, as well as *to be* attained" (1990, 12). Emersonian perfectionism is characterized by "goallessness": it refuses final perfectibility (Cavell 1990, xxxiv). This implies that though Emerson uses the phrase "self-acquaintance," the perfection of the self is not geared toward a final grasp of the self as the object of knowledge.

The goal-less-ness, however, does not mean a boundless or laissez-faire quest for self-satisfaction. Emerson's self-reliance necessitates the other as the essential condition—say, as the criterion—for sustaining and revising the sense of the better in perfection. Recognition of "my attained perfection (or conformity)" requires "the recognition of an other—the acknowledgment of a relationship" (Cavell 1990, 31). Echoing Emerson's idea of representativeness (*CW* 2: 27), Cavell states: "this other of myself—returning my rejected, say repressed, thought—reminds me of something, as of where I am, as if I had become lost in thought, and stopped thinking" (1995, 26–27). Cavell says that for Emerson, moral constraint is not given by the universal moral law of an "ought," but by a friend as an attraction—a friend who reminds us of the state of our conformity and thanks to whom we "*are* drawn beyond ourselves"; the "friend (discovered or constructed) represents the standpoint of perfection" (1990, 58–59). Here is the inevitable connection of friendship with education—"we are educations for one another" (1990, 31). This implies that perfection as a matter of education involves a certain kind of mutuality. The educative relationship itself is always in process of perfecting. As Emerson himself says, friendship "cannot subsist in its perfection" (*CW* 2: 121); and as Thoreau says, "Friendship is never established as an understood relation" (*AW* 272).

The Friend as the Other of Myself

Though Cavell's Emersonian moral perfectionism demonstrates the need of a friend, there still remains a series of points that need to be clarified in order to address the question with which we started: does the self-reliant individual need others? What does *mutual* perfection mean if it is a mark of Emersonian friendship? What is it that distinguishes Cavell's Emersonian idea of the simultaneous perfection of the self and the other, from the conventional understanding of mutual benefit? Furthermore, in order to address the apparent contradiction of affinity and distance in Emersonian friendship, a Cavellian approach needs to say more, to show persuasively that the other is already a constituent of the self—that is, to sustain the paradox. Let us further explore, therefore, the question of what *kind* of other is needed for the self as a friend.

Both Emerson and Thoreau suggest that as friends the self and the other are *equal*. Thoreau says that friendship is a "relationship of perfect equality" (*AW* 271). Similarly, Emerson says that a friend is a "man so real and equal" to oneself that he can be encountered just like "one chemical atom meets another" (*CW* 2: 119). Equality, however, does not connote here equivalency or exchange. In their descriptions, there is simultaneously the sense of the *gap* that exists—the unreachable or the unredeemed in the moment of the self's encounter with the other. In Emerson's words, a friend is a "beautiful enemy, untamable" (*CW* 2: 124). In Thoreau's: "It may be that we are not even yet acquainted" (*AW* 276).

In Emersonian moral perfectionism, the encounter with another constitutes the moment of turning, a point of departure from the existing circle of the self, not only in joy and hope, but with a strong sense of "shame"—shame at the self in its conformity (Cavell 1990, 16, 30). Cavell says that the role of friendship in moral perfectionism is both "recognition and negation": there are simultaneous movements of being "[t]oward and away" (1990, 59). The other of myself appears here, as it were, as a force of approval which is exercised through negation. Friendship is a reminder that we should "never fall into something usual and settled" (*CW* 2: 21). In Emersonian *moral* perfectionism, the moral task of a friend is not the full grasp of the other, but remembrance of the other in the realm of the yet-to-be known—in "a positive depth of silence, never to be revealed" (*AW* 278).

This is echoed in Cavell's idea of *acknowledgment* in *The Claim of Reason*—of accepting the unknowability of the other but still searching for connection with the other. This is Cavell's unique way of responding to the anxiety manifested in the skeptical question: can I know the mind of the other?—an ill-conceived question that reflects the fatal tendency of the human being to deny the existence and real sense of the other. The quest for intimacy and closeness is transformed into a quest for absolute knowledge of the other. With a reactionary turn, a radical skepticism occurs: you can never really know. Cavell's take on friendship can be considered as his alternative approach to our chronic obsession with the complete understanding of the other. It is from this perspective that the paradox of closeness and distance in Emerson's and Thoreau's friendship can be seen in a new light. Significantly, Cavell shifts the focus of the question onto the other: how can we transform the nature of our quest for being (re)united with the other even after acknowledging the unfilled gap between the self and other?

Friendship and the Politics of Interpretation

The relationship of the self and the other, and concomitantly the nature of friendship in Emersonian moral perfectionism, are inseparable from the medium of language, especially from the act of reading and writing. Cavell suggests: "Emerson offers his writing as representing this other for his reader" (1990, 32). One of the central tasks of Emersonian moral perfectionism is the entering of "my" voice into the conversation of justice, my participation in the "city of words," which is the language community (1990, 8, 12). The *moral* force of perfection, then, according to Cavell, hinges not on judgment (as in conventional moral theories) but on "every word." Despite the focus on the singularity of the self ("the infinitude of the private man"), Cavell reminds us that "we need not, we should not, take [Emerson] to imagine himself as achieving a further state of humanity in himself alone" (1990, 10–11).

Cavell's earlier work, *The Senses of Walden*—which in its 1981 expanded version includes two essays on Emerson—as well as his essay on "The Politics of Interpretation" help us here to develop retrospectively, as it were, the theme of friendship and Emersonian perfectionism in connection with language, reading, and writing. Cavell's idea of the politics of interpretation, adumbrated in *The Senses of Walden,* shows that the focus on language is not merely a literary matter or private activity. Rather, participation in the language community is a crucial condition for the realization of authentic political action.

In resistance to the professionalization of Anglo-American philosophy, Cavell sees in Emerson's and Thoreau's devotion to the "common, the familiar, the everyday, the low, the near" what it is that underwrites his quest for an ordinary language philosophy: the recovery of the human voice (1984, 31–33, 48–49). He considers "their interpretation of what you might call the politics of philosophical interpretation as a withdrawal or rejection of politics, even of society, as such." In this light Thoreau's *Walden,* Cavell claims, is "an act of civil disobedience," one that is effected or realized through "silence" (1984, 50–51). The foremost task in the politics of interpretation is to regain the autonomy of language and of ourselves, by returning ourselves and language back to the ordinary, to let them rediscover their place in the world. The politics of interpretation brings us back at this point to a central task of Emersonian moral perfectionism: "whether the voice I lend in recognizing a society as mine, as speaking for me, is my voice, my own" (1990, 27). Finding "my voice" involves asking where this "I" stands in the world, and it is this question of standing that emerges as the essential condition for political participation. By understanding *Walden* as outlining "an epistemology of conscience," Cavell indicates that conscience is not something which is fully encapsulated in a private realm, but rather the crucial beginning of public participation from within, a significant source of internal as well as social transformation; and such participation requires initiation into the language community, as well as a turning away from it. The movement from the private to the public is not one-directional; privacy is always an *achievement,* and its terms are public.

The relationship between the writer and the reader in the "politics of interpretation" exemplifies the presence of the other as another of myself in Emersonian moral perfectionism, and illustrates the value of friendship beyond any concept of "affective deficit" as in Buell. The politics of interpretation illustrates how the encounter with this other takes place through the medium of language, particularly through written words. Cavell here refers to what Thoreau calls the "father tongue" (*Wa* 101)—"a reserved and select expression, too significant to be heard by the ear, which we must be born again in order to speak" (Cavell 1992, 15). The father tongue is used here in contrast to the mother tongue—which is the native, the natural, and the familiar. The mother tongue is the essential starting point of one's being initiated into the language community, and is characterized by immediate, intimate relationships. The idea of the father has nothing, however, to do with notions of authoritarianism or doctrinaire dogmatism. The relationship with the father here suggests a need to deliberately create a distance within familiarity. While the mother tongue, with its emphasis on speech, suggests a relation of immediacy, the written word enables a reflective, indirect relationship with what is native. Indirectness in the act of writing (and reading) gives us the time to think, to deliberate, and to readjust our relationship with the world. Indeed, the "father tongue" in Thoreau and Cavell is characterized by receptivity, silence, and patience—the reader's relation to the text and the writer revealed in its feminine aspect. In our common quest for immediacy and direct, face-to-face contact, we are given, as it were, proof of our knowledge and understanding of the other: we are fated to conformity—conformity to the familiar and the native. This obliterates the space for the unknowable, causing us to fall into the illusion that we understand everything in our grasp. It is in resistance to this danger of conformity that the father tongue is needed as much as the mother tongue.

To emphasize the father tongue is not, however, to deny the role of the mother. Nor is the relationship between the mother and the father simply a matter of staged development in a kind of unitary trajectory, from the immature to the mature. Rather what is needed is to "keep faith at once with the mother and the father, to unite them, and to have the word born in us" (Cavell 1992, 16). The union of the mother and the father is not a unification, but a union which has issue. That is, we need both mother and father in order to experience the world in its full-blown form: we need always both an initiation *into* and departure *from* the language community. The emphasis is on the dual elements of the "into" and of the "from" in movement, as well as a turning point from the familiar to the strange. This brings us back to Cavell's Emersonian perfectionist call: "the self is always attained, as well as *to be* attained" (1990, 12). These turning points (in the plural) are the moments of "crisis" throughout one's life: "for the child to grow he requires family and familiarity, but for a grownup to grow he requires strangeness and transformation, i.e., birth" (Cavell 1992, 60). Just as Emersonian perfectionism is lifelong, so too is "the education of grownups" (Cavell 1979, 125).

The act of reading demonstrates the way in which these turning points are created in the reader's encounter with the writer. Words inscribed in the text are a kind of juncture at which the reader and writer "conjecture"—"casting words together and deriving the conclusions of each" (Cavell 1992, 28–29). This is a relationship of mutual "trials" (1992, 12)—of testing what counts, of finding our criterion in the words we use. The reader is "convicted" by the text in that she is caught in a position of responsibility: responsibility is her necessary response (and that is, the necessity of a response) to the text that she reads (1992, 34). It is through this testing relationship with the writer that the reader's power of words is tried—in a trial that is weighted with the "power of life and death," and through which the reader undergoes a kind of rebirth (1992, 32). This involves a relationship of intensive confrontation and aversion, which Cavell calls Thoreauvian and Emersonian friendship in the "shock of recognition" (1992, 32).

In sum, the politics of interpretation as engaged in the relationship between the reader and the writer suggests the dual nature of closeness and distance in Emersonian friendship. Encounter with this other of myself, with the "*not mine* [*as*] *mine*" (*CW* 2: 122), is an essential component of Emersonian perfectionism.

The Friend Who Leaves and Bequeaths

The other as a friend is essential to my own perfection. What kind of influence then can the friend have on me in this shock of recognition? If "we are educations for one another," as Cavell says, then what kind of educative influence can there be? Cavell's account of Emerson's idea of representativeness offers a good start in answering these questions:

> Emerson's study is of this (democratic, universal) representativeness—it comes up in my first lecture under the head of "standing for" ("I stand here for humanity")—as a relation we bear at once to the other and to ourselves: if we were not representative of what we might be . . . , we would not recognize ourselves presented in one another's possibilities: we would have no "potential." (1990, 9)

Cavell here suggests that the relationship between the self and the other in terms of representativeness is not only the matter of the self and the other outside myself, but also that of the self to the self inside itself. It is this entanglement between the intra- and inter-dimensionality of the self that is unique to Cavell's interpretation of Emersonian and Thoreauvian friendship, and that enables Cavell's perfectionist stance to transcend the conventional framework of Emersonian *self*-reliance.

His account of Thoreau's idea of neighborhood and nextness helps us here. Cavell says that Thoreau's reencounter with the world is for the achievement of "outsideness" or "outwardness" (1992, 55). Thoreau articulates the "externality of the world as its nextness to me" (1992, 106–107). He finds in Thoreau a clue to the human being's imaginative power to reveal the reality of the world outside, starting from within one's consciousness. Cavell and Thoreau rebuild, even overturn, the relationship between inside and outside, not as two separate realms of experience, but as the interaction of the two. This is the experience of the strange and unfamiliar within oneself—an encounter with otherness not only without but also *within* the self, and an acquisition of the standpoint of outsideness within the familiar. Cavell calls this "sense of distance from self" a relationship of "perpetual nextness" (1992, 107–108). "This other of myself" is manifested within the self in the way that outsideness is constructed within the same. Thoreau calls this a condition of "doubleness," the state of being "beside ourselves in a sane sense" (*Wa* 134). In Emersonian moral perfectionism, the relationship is more *indirect*—it is symbolized by a relationship through the father tongue, through the opacity of written words. In observing the way that the other confronts his own self, his language, his culture, the self is turned back upon her own self, now as a stranger.

Both Emerson and Thoreau suggest that an educative influence is exercised through *leaving*—another significant theme in their idea of friendship. Let us begin with Thoreau's words: "The Friend is a *necessarius,* and meets his Friend on homely ground: not on carpets and cushions, but on the ground and on rocks they will sit, obeying the natural and primitive laws. They will meet without any outcry, and part without loud sorrow" (*AW* 274). Here is an apparent paradox again. On the one hand, Thoreau refers to a friend with the imagery of home and the necessities of life—of things typically associated with our quotidian domestic regimes; but on the other, he depicts friends as meeting on rough ground—not a place of comfortable settlement, but perhaps somewhere to push off from. Emerson also suggests the "evanescent" nature of friendship: "We will meet as though we met not, and part as though we parted not" (*CW* 2: 126). Friendship never stays the same; it is always in process of perfecting. In Thoreau's words, friendship is "a miracle which requires constant proofs" (*AW* 272). A friend is a necessity of our lives, but necessary neither a priori nor in any final sense. Friendship in this sense is a primordial site of its enactment.

But a question may be raised here: how can you then achieve friendship as the state of being at home yet at the same time not being fully at home? In *The Senses of Walden,* Cavell captures this evanescent sense through Thoreau's idea of leaving and its consequent implications for home—home is not a permanent shelter or a place to settle down. In this respect Cavell contrasts Thoreau to Heidegger: "The substantive disagreement with Heidegger, shared by Emerson and Thoreau, is that the achievement of the human requires not inhabitation and settlement but abandonment, leaving" (1992, 138). Leaving Walden is as hard—and is perhaps the same—as entering it (1992, 116). Thoreau was "at home" at Walden, but home is the place where Thoreau learns "how to sojourn, i.e., spend his day" (1992, 52). It is a place where you learn to reestablish your relationship with the familiar, and hence, necessarily, a place that you must leave. Cavell finds in Thoreau's idea of leaving a key to deconstructing, indeed, to destabilizing, the concept of home.

More recently, Cavell restates the theme as follows:

> The concept of letting things be what they are—as it were leaving things to themselves, but at the same time letting them happen to you—is pervasive in *Walden,* enacted in the main action of learning to leave Walden (the place

and the book, most notably figured in the double concept of mo(u)rning). (2005, 217)

Ultimately, Thoreau must leave the reader too, and the reader must move on from *Walden* and whatever light it has conferred. But through the act of leaving, the other does not simply leave us behind: he leaves us with the act of pursuing our own light. Images of light appear frequently in Emerson's and Thoreau's writings. In "Self-Reliance" Emerson says: "A man should learn to detect and watch that gleam of light which flashes across his mind from within. . . . In every work of genius we recognize our own rejected thoughts" (*CW* 2: 27). The gleam of light is the metaphor of self-reliance, the inner being of the self. It is, however, anything but substantial: neither the self nor the other can grasp it. In the sentences just cited, Emerson implies that it is through the *mutual* reflection of the genius of the other (as a friend) that the self remembers its own genius. The friend speaks to me here and now, saying: do not forget the intensity of your light. Emerson says: "I fear only that I may lose them receding into the sky in which now they are only a patch of brighter light" (*CW* 2: 126). Thoreau says: "the sunset in my latest November shall translate me to the ethereal world, and remind me of the ruddy morning of youth" (*AW* 285). Though the light is transitional and evanescent, it always awaits itself to be expressed through your own words. The light in Emersonian moral perfectionism is thus not solely a metaphor for the inner self or self-contained privacy. It is the embodiment of the life of the self, always awaiting to transcend itself outward from within.

By exemplifying the possible state of further perfection, while at the same time awakening the senses of both shame and hope, the friend who comes from a distant land rekindles my extinguished light: a prophet of the possibility of my own light, he witnesses the moment of the rebirth of my self. Here again the idea of a friend as a mirror comes back—as the other who reminds me of my own extinguished light, a kind of light that only this "I" can remember, sustain, and cultivate. As Emerson says: "love is only the reflection of a man's own worthiness from other men" (*CW* 2: 125).

Though the moment of encounter is evanescent, even after parting from the friend, "thou art enlarged by thy own shining" (*CW* 2: 125). The friend is a "*necessarius*" for the self to keep intensifying its light and to help it "draw a new circle" (*CW* 2: 190). He represents, however, the paradox of the necessity—the necessary other—by acknowledging the fact that we "must be our own before we can be another's" (*CW* 2: 124). Once he exercises such influence, the friend leaves: "The Friend asks no return" (*AW*

270). A friend thus exercises an influence through absence and leaving, and even, in the most extreme form, through dying.

Where Is Your Home?

> I have implied that the time of crisis depicted in [*Walden*] is not alone a private one, and not wholly cosmic. It is simultaneously a crisis in the nation's life. And the nation too must die down to the root if it is to continue to recognize and neighbor itself.
>
> STANLEY CAVELL

This essay started with the questions of whether the Emersonian and Thoreauvian strong self requires the other, and if so, in what sense. The examination thus far has shown that the answer to the first question must be "yes." But to clarify the second question and further enrich the implications of this "yes," there is a need to address another related question: how can friendship in interpersonal relationships extend beyond home? Is friendship in Emersonian moral perfectionism only the story of an interpersonal encounter and a personal conversion? In response to these questions, and as a conclusion, I would like to show that Cavell revives Emerson's and Thoreau's voices today as a call for attaining an outward-turning friendship while starting at home, and that Emersonian moral perfectionism is filled with the possibilities of an alternative conception of citizenship education. This involves an idea of citizenship that takes the friendship of the neighbor as a necessary condition for realizing democracy as a way of life, through dialogue between different people and nations—a neighborliness beyond national and cultural boundaries.

Cavell's "politics of interpretation" provides us with an alternative standpoint from which to be critically aware of the pitfalls in a prevalent language and way of thinking—those which characterize, for example, any politics of recognition: the danger of the unconscious assimilation of the different into the same, the illusion of a full understanding of the other, and consequently the possibility of blindness to the foreign in what is near. Cavell awakens us to this illusion of immediacy and helps us release the voice of the different within the same, including (or perhaps, first and foremost) within one's own self. This is a recognition of space for the otherness which eternally escapes our full grasp. The obliteration of this space does not necessarily take the obvious form of oppression; a more subtle but more pervasive crisis may encroach upon us through the benign language of "co-existence" or "mutual understanding."

The Emersonian perfectionist approach thus encompasses an aspiration toward the cosmopolitan. This is not, however, the kind of transcendental cosmopolitanism that moves in a unitary, one-directional trajectory from partiality to impartiality. It rejects any borderless cosmopolitanism that purports to supersede the complexity of this relation to home. Kateb, for example, in his interpretation of Emerson's transcendentalism, suggests the possibility of such borderless cosmopolitanism. He cites the following words from Emerson's 1838 essay, "Home": "I have said that a true Culture goes to make man a citizen of the world . . . at home in nature. . . . Now that he has learned to associate himself by affinities and not by custom he finds himself a stranger under his own roof" (*EL* 3: 31; Kateb 2000, 130).

Kateb interprets this passage in the following manner: "We cannot love the world as we love what we know close to hand and is ours, but we can develop the imagination of love and take to heart the fact that anyone known well can be loved well" (2000, 130). He implies that Emerson's idea of "impartiality" is the opposite of partiality, which, on the face of it, may seem hard to resist but which misses the multiple senses of the latter term that prevent its resting as a simple opposite to "impartial"—senses, that is, of being a part of a whole and, crucially, of having a proclivity toward something. Without this proclivity, without this asymmetry between the terms, the political force of the gleam of light is lost. In a similar tone Buell, in opposition to "Americanist readings of Emerson," suggests that Emerson's transcendentalism points us to "cosmopolitan detachment," to a detachment that is not reducible to "Americanness" (2003, 48, 51, 56). Buell seeks a vision of the united world, one that dissipates all differences beyond the "particularistic cultural context" (2003, 55). For both Kateb and Buell the concept of impartiality in Emerson's transcendentalism is a matter of going beyond Americanness.

In contrast to this type of reading, Cavell maintains Emerson's and Thoreau's Americanness all the way through, trying to recover their distinctively American voices. Despite his call for departure and abandonment, leaving one's primordial home does not mean becoming either an exile or, by blurring the boundaries of nations or cultures, a citizen of the world. Cavell's message is that we can never negate our original connection with home. In other words, he does not start with the proposal of cosmopolitanism if cosmopolitanism entails a bypassing of the depth of one's encounter with one's own culture and language. This is not, however, to represent Emerson and Thoreau as figures of merely local significance. Their Americanness—their ways of confronting their native culture—

demonstrates the Emersonian perfectionism of "this yet unapproachable America," and creates a gateway to an outward-turning friendship. Cavell calls for "shunning the cosmopolitan and embracing the immigrant in yourself" (1992, 158). In short, in the case of Cavell, impartiality and partiality, native culture and cosmopolitan world are not contradictory forces, but the dual aspects of human perfection.

Cavell also reinterprets Emerson's and Thoreau's searching for "a common origin" (1992, 160) as ends ever to be achieved as we "have yet '*to get our living together,*' to be whole, and to be one community" (1992, 96; citing *Wa* 72). Cavell does not seek immediate bonds or commonality, but rather "isolation" as the sincerest way of building neighborhood with others. Citizenship education is thus an eternal process of learning to be a neighbor not only to the outside other but also to one's own self. In this sense alone, Cavell says *Walden* is a book on "education for citizenship," one that "identifies citizens as 'neighbors'" (1992, 85–86). This will guide us to education for national citizenship—in the sense that it endorses a hope for the best of one's own culture. It does not, however, point us to patriotism in any aggressive sense—to a love that cannot tolerate irritation, that cannot face (self-)criticism, and that allows the self to slumber in its mother tongue and native culture. It is rather the case that the flowering of a just *national* citizenship necessarily includes stirrings of *global* citizenship. And friendship is a precondition for the kind of ethical and political relationships that are appropriate to the achievement of such a citizenship.

The epigraph at the head of the essay is from Emerson, *CW* 2: 125; the epigraph at the head of the concluding section is from Cavell 1992, 116.

WORKS CITED

Alcott, A. Bronson. 1938. *The Journals of Bronson Alcott.* Ed. Odell Shepard. Boston: Little, Brown.

Allen, Margaret Vanderhaar. 1979. *The Achievement of Margaret Fuller.* University Park: Pennsylvania State University Press.

Aristotle. 1962. *Nichomachean Ethics.* Trans. Martin Oswald. Indianapolis: Bobbs-Merrill.

———. 1998. *Nicomachean Ethics, Books VIII and IX.* Trans. with comm. Michael Pakaluk. Oxford: Oxford University Press.

———. 2002. *Nichomachean Ethics.* Trans. Joe Sach. Newbury Port: Focus.

Attig, Thomas. 1996. *How We Grieve: Relearning the World.* New York: Oxford University Press.

Augustine, Saint. 1991. *Confessions.* Trans. Henry Chadwick. Oxford: Oxford University Press.

Austin, Sarah. 1833. *Characteristics of Goethe.* 3 vols. London: E. Wilson.

Blake, William. 1970. *The Poetry and Prose of William Blake.* Ed. David V. Erdman. Garden City: Doubleday.

Bloom, Harold. 1976. *Figures of Capable Imagination.* New York: Seabury.

Bolotin, David. 1979. *Plato's Dialogue on Friendship.* Ithaca, N.Y.: Cornell University Press.

Booth, Wayne. 1988. *The Company We Keep: An Ethics of Fiction.* Berkeley: University of California Press.

Bosco, Ronald A., and Joel Myerson. 2006. *The Emerson Brothers: A Fraternal Biography in Letters.* Oxford: Oxford University Press.

Brain, Robert. 1976. *Friends and Lovers.* London: Hart-Davis, MacGibbon.

Buell, Lawrence. 1973. *Literary Transcendentalism: Style and Vision in the American Renaissance.* Ithaca, N.Y.: Cornell University Press.

———. 2003. *Emerson.* Cambridge, Mass.: Harvard University Press.

Cameron, Sharon. 1986. "Representing Grief: Emerson's 'Experience.'" *Representations* 15: 15–41.

Canby, Henry Seidel. 1939. *Thoreau.* Boston: Houghton Mifflin.

Capper, Charles. 1992. *Margaret Fuller: An American Romantic Life. The Private Years.* Oxford: Oxford University Press.

———. 2007. *Margaret Fuller: An American Romantic Life. The Public Years.* Oxford: Oxford University Press.

Carlson, Marvin. 1996. "What Is Performance?" *The Twentieth-Century Performance Reader.* 2nd ed. Ed. Michael Huxley and Noel Witts. London: Routledge. 146–153.

Cavell, Stanley. 1979. *The Claim of Reason: Wittgenstein, Skepticism, Morality and Tragedy.* New York: Oxford University Press.

———. 1981. *Pursuits of Happiness: The Hollywood Comedy of Remarriage.* Cambridge, Mass.: Harvard University Press.

———. 1984. "The Politics of Interpretation (Politics as Opposed to What?)." *Themes Out of School: Effects and Causes.* Chicago: University of Chicago Press. 27–59.

———. 1988. *In Quest of the Ordinary: Lines of Skepticism and Romanticism.* Chicago: University of Chicago Press.

———. 1990. *Conditions Handsome and Unhandsome: The Constitution of Emersonian Perfectionism.* Chicago: University of Chicago Press.

———. 1992. *The Senses of Walden.* Chicago: University of Chicago Press.

———. 1995. *A Pitch of Philosophy: Autobiographical Exercises.* Cambridge, Mass.: Harvard University Press.

———. 2003. "Finding as Founding: Taking Steps in Emerson's 'Experience.'" *Emerson's Transcendental Etudes,* ed. David Justin Hodge. Stanford, Calif.: Stanford University Press. 110–140.

———. 2005. *Philosophy the Day After Tomorrow.* Cambridge, Mass.: Harvard University Press.

Channing, William Ellery, II. 1966. *Thoreau the Poet-Naturalist.* Rev. ed. Ed. F. B. Sanborn. New York: Biblo and Tannen.

Cicero, Marcus Tullius. 1923. *De Amicitia.* Trans. William Armistead Falconer. Cambridge, Mass.: Harvard University Press.

———. 1971. *On the Good Life.* Trans. Michael Grant. New York: Penguin.

Cohen, Rachel. 2004. *A Chance Meeting: Intertwined Lives of American Writers and Artists, 1854–1967.* New York: Random House.

Coleman, Deirdre. 1988. *Coleridge and 'The Friend' (1809–1810).* Oxford: Clarendon Press.

Coleridge, Samuel Taylor. 1969. *The Friend.* 2 vols. Ed. Barbara E. Rooke. Princeton, N.J.: Princeton University Press.

Constantinesco, Thomas. 2008. "Discordant Correspondence in Ralph Waldo Emerson's 'Friendship.'" *New England Quarterly* 81: 218–251.

Cox, James M. 1975. "R. W. Emerson: The Circles of the Eye." *Emerson: Prophecy, Metamorphosis, and Influence,* ed. David Levin. New York: Columbia University Press. 57–81.

Crain, Caleb. 2001. *American Sympathy: Men, Friendship, and Literature in the New Nation.* New Haven, Conn.: Yale University Press.

Delano, Sterling F. 2004. *Brook Farm: The Dark Side of Utopia.* Cambridge, Mass.: Harvard University Press.

Dennis, Jeffery P. 2007. *We Boys Together: Teenagers in Love Before Girl-craziness.* Nashville, Tenn.: Vanderbilt University Press.

Derrida, Jacques. 1997. *The Politics of Friendship.* Trans. George Collins. London: Verso.

Durning, Russell E. 1969. *Margaret Fuller, Citizen of the World.* Heidelberg: C. Winter.

Emerson, Edward Waldo. 1917. *Henry Thoreau as Remembered by a Young Friend.* Boston: Houghton.

Emerson, Ralph Waldo. 2008. "Thoreau." *Walden, Civil Disobedience, and Other Writings*, ed. William Rossi. New York: W. W. Norton. 394–409.

Enright, D. J., and David Rawlinson, eds. 1991. *The Oxford Book of Friendship*. Oxford: Oxford University Press.

Esterhammer, Angela. 2000. *The Romantic Performative: Language and Action in British and German Romanticism*. Stanford, Calif.: Stanford University Press.

Fielding, K. J. 1996. "Carlyle and the Americans: 'Eighteen Million Bores.'" *Carlyle Studies* 16: 55–62.

Fink, Steven. 1992. *Prophet in the Marketplace: Thoreau's Development as a Professional Writer.* Princeton, N.J.: Princeton University Press.

Francis, Richard. 1997. *Transcendental Utopias: Individual and Community at Brook Farm, Fruitlands, and Walden*. Ithaca, N.Y.: Cornell University Press.

Friedman, Marilyn. 1993. *What Are Friends For? Feminist Perspectives on Personal Relationships and Moral Theory.* Ithaca, N.Y.: Cornell University Press.

Fuller, Margaret. 1841. "Goethe." *Dial* 2: 31–33.

———. 1983. *The Letters of Margaret Fuller.* 6 vols. Ed. Robert N. Hudspeth. Ithaca, N.Y.: Cornell University Press, 1983–1994.

———. 1991. *These Sad but Glorious Days: Dispatches from Europe, 1846–1850*. Ed. Larry J. Reynolds and Susan Belasco Smith. New Haven, Conn.: Yale University Press.

———. 2001. *"My Heart Is a Large Kingdom": Selected Letters of Margaret Fuller.* Ed. Robert N. Hudspeth. Ithaca, N.Y.: Cornell University Press.

Gadamer, Hans-Georg. 1992. *Truth and Method*. 2nd rev. ed. New York: Crossroad.

———. 1995. With Christiane Gehron and Jonathan Rée. "Interview: Hans Georg Gadamer: Without Poets There is No Philosophy." *Radical Philosophy* 69: 27–35.

———. 1999. "Friendship and Self-Knowledge: Reflections on the Role of Friendship in Greek Ethics." *Hermeneutics, Religion, and Ethics*, trans. Joel Weinsheimer. New Haven, Conn.: Yale University Press.

Garvey, T. Gregory, ed. 2001. *The Emerson Dilemma: Essays on Emerson and Social Reform*. Athens: University of Georgia Press.

Goodman, Russell. 1997a. "Emerson's Mystical Empiricism." *The Perennial Tradition of Neoplatonism*, ed. John J. Cleary. Leuven: Leuven University Press. 456–478.

———. 1997b. "Moral Perfectionism and Democracy in Emerson and Nietzsche." *ESQ: A Journal of the American Renaissance* 43: 159–180.

———. 2009 (forthcoming). "Paths of Coherence in Emerson's Philosophy: The Case of 'Nominalist and Realist'." *The Other Emerson: New Approaches, Divergent Paths*, ed. Branka Arsic and Carey Wolfe. Minneapolis: University of Minnesota Press.

Gougeon, Len. 1990. *Virtue's Hero: Emerson, Antislavery and Reform*. Athens: University of Georgia Press.

Gould, Stephen Jay. 1987. *Time's Arrow, Time's Cycle: Myth and Metaphor in the Discovery of Geological Time*. Cambridge, Mass.: Harvard University Press.

Hawthorne, Nathaniel. 1972. *Mosses from an Old Manse*. Ed. Roy Harvey Pearce, et al. Columbus: Ohio State University Press.

Hodder, Alan D. 2001. *Thoreau's Ecstatic Witness*. New Haven, Conn.: Yale University Press.

Hunt, Mary E. 1991. *Fierce Tenderness: A Feminist Theology of Friendship*. New York: Crossroad.

Hyatte, Reginald. 1997. *The Arts of Friendship: The Idealization of Friendship in Medieval and Early Renaissance Literature*. Leiden and New York: E. J. Brill.

James, William. 1983. *The Principles of Psychology.* Cambridge, Mass.: Harvard University Press.

Johnson, Linck C. 1980. "Historical Introduction." *A Week on the Concord and Merrimack Rivers,* ed. Carl F. Hovde, William L. Howarth, and Elizabeth Hall Witherell. Princeton, N.J.: Princeton University Press. 433–500.

———. 1986. *Thoreau's Complex Weave: The Writing of A Week on the Concord and Merrimack Rivers with a text of the First Draft.* Charlottesville: University Press of Virginia.

Kant, Immanuel. 1996. *Practical Philosophy,* ed. and trans. Mary J. Gregor. Cambridge: Cambridge University Press.

Kateb, George. 2000. *Emerson and Self-Reliance.* Walnut Creek, Calif.: Altamira Press.

Langer, Ulrich. 1994. *Perfect Friendship: Studies in Literature and Moral Philosophy from Boccaccio to Corneille.* Geneva: Librairie Droz.

Lawrence, Kathleen. 2005. "'The Dry-Lighted Soul' Ignites: Emerson and his Soul-Mate Caroline Sturgis as Seen in her Houghton Manuscripts." *Harvard Library Bulletin* 16: 37–67.

Lebeaux, Richard. 1978. *Young Man Thoreau.* New York: Harper.

———. 1984. *Thoreau's Seasons.* Amherst: University of Massachusetts Press.

Levine, Philippa. 1990. "Love, Friendship, and Feminism in Later 19th-century England." *Women's Studies International Forum* 13: 63–78.

Lingeman, Richard R. 2006. *Double Lives: American Writers' Friendships.* New York: Random House.

Luciano, Dana. 2007. *Arranging Grief: Sacred Time and the Body in Nineteenth-Century America.* New York: New York University Press.

Lysaker, John T. 2008. *Emerson and Self-Culture.* Bloomington: Indiana University Press.

Marion, Jean-Luc. 1991. *God Without Being.* Trans. Thomas A. Carlson. Chicago: University of Chicago Press.

Maynard, W. Barksdale. 2004. *Walden Pond: A History.* New York: Oxford University Press.

McAleer, John. 1984. *Ralph Waldo Emerson: Days of Encounter.* Boston: Little, Brown.

McGuire, Brian Patrick. 1988. *Friendship and Community: The Monastic Experience, 350–1250.* Kalamazoo, Mich.: Cistercian Publications.

Michelfelder, Diane P., and Richard E. Palmer, eds. 1989. *Dialogue and Deconstruction: The Gadamer-Derrida Encounter.* Albany: SUNY Press.

Miller, William I. 1993. *Humiliation and Other Essays on Honor, Social Discomfort, and Violence.* Ithaca, N.Y.: Cornell University Press.

Milton, John. 1968. *The Poems of John Milton,* ed. John Carey and Alistair Fowler. London: Longman; New York: W. W. Norton.

Montaigne, Michel de. 1958. "Of Friendship." *The Complete Essays of Montaigne,* trans. Donald Frame. Stanford, Calif.: Stanford University Press.

———. 1991. *The Complete Essays,* trans. M. A. Screech. London: Penguin Press.

Monteith, Sharon. 2000. *Advancing Sisterhood? Interracial Friendships in Contemporary Southern Fiction.* Athens: University of Georgia Press.

Neimeyer, Robert A., ed. 2001. *Meaning Reconstruction & the Experience of Loss.* Washington, D.C.: American Psychological Association.

Nietzsche, Friedrich. 1974. *The Gay Science,* trans. Walter Kaufmann. New York: Vintage.

———. 1982. *The Portable Nietzsche,* ed. and trans. Walter Kaufmann. New York: Viking.

———. 1986. *Human, All Too Human,* trans. R. J. Hollingdale. Cambridge: Cambridge University Press.

Packard, Chris. 2005. *Queer Cowboys and Other Erotic Male Friendships in Nineteenth-century American Literature.* New York: Palgrave Macmillan.

Packer, Barbara L. 1982. *Emerson's Fall: A New Interpretation of the Major Essays.* New York: Continuum.

Pakaluk, Michael. 1991. *Other Selves: Philosophers on Friendship.* Indianapolis: Hackett.

Plato. 1961. *Plato: The Collected Dialogues,* ed. Edith Hamilton and Huntington Cairns. Princeton, N.J.: Princeton University Press.

———. 1979. *Lysis: Plato's Dialogue on Friendship,* trans. with interpretive essay by David Bolotin. Ithaca, N.Y.: Cornell University Press.

———. 1998. *Phaedrus.* Trans. with notes and interpretive essay by James H. Nichols, Jr. Ithaca, N.Y.: Cornell University Press.

———. 2001. *Symposium. Lysis, Symposium, Gorgias,* trans. W. R. M. Lamb. Cambridge, Mass.: Harvard University Press.

Plotinus. 1911. *Select Works of Plotinus,* trans. Thomas Taylor. London: G. Bell & Sons.

———. 1984. *Enneads.* 7 vols. Trans. A. H. Armstrong. Cambridge, Mass.: Harvard University Press, 1984–1990.

Pochmann, Henry A. 1957. *German Culture in America.* Madison: University of Wisconsin Press.

Porte, Joel. 1966. *Emerson and Thoreau: Transcendentalists in Conflict.* Middletown, Conn.: Wesleyan University Press.

Radhakrishnan, Sarvepalli, trans. 1994. *The Principal Upanishads.* New Delhi: Harper Collins.

Ramazani, Jahan. 1994. *The Poetry of Mourning: The Modern Elegy from Hardy to Heaney.* Chicago: University of Chicago Press.

Reynolds, Larry J. 1988. *European Revolutions and the American Literary Renaissance.* New Haven, Conn.: Yale University Press.

Richards, Robert J. 2002. *The Romantic Conception of Life: Science and Philosophy in the Age of Goethe.* Chicago: University of Chicago Press.

Richardson, Robert D., Jr. 1986. *Henry Thoreau: A Life of the Mind.* Berkeley: University of California Press.

———. 1995. *Emerson: The Mind on Fire.* Berkeley: University of California Press.

Robinson, David M. 1982a. *Apostle of Culture: Emerson as Preacher and Lecturer.* Philadelphia: University of Pennsylvania Press.

———. 1982b. "Margaret Fuller and the Transcendental Ethos: *Woman in the Nineteenth Century.*" *PMLA* 97: 83–98.

———. 1993. *Emerson and the Conduct of Life: Pragmatism and Ethical Purpose in the Later Essays.* Cambridge: Cambridge University Press.

———. 1997. "Thoreau's 'Ktaadn' and the Quest for Experience." *Emersonian Circles,* ed. Wesley T. Mott and Robert Burkholder. Rochester, N.Y.: Rochester University Press. 207–223.

———. 2004. *Natural Life: Thoreau's Worldly Transcendentalism.* Ithaca, N.Y.: Cornell University Press.

Ronan, John. 2006. "Thoreau's Declaration of Independence from Emerson in *Walden.*" *Nineteenth Century Prose* 33: 1–34.

Rossi, William. 1994. "Poetry and Progress: Thoreau, Lyell, and the Geological Principles of *A Week on the Concord and Merrimack Rivers*." *American Literature* 66: 275–300.

———. 2008. "Performing Loss, Elegy, and Transcendental Friendship." *New England Quarterly* 81: 252–277.

Rotundo, E. Anthony. 1989. "Romantic Friendship: Male Intimacy and Middle-Class Youth in the Northern United States, 1800–1900." *Journal of Social History* 23: 1–25.

Rusk, Ralph L. 1949. *The Life of Ralph Waldo Emerson*. New York: Columbia University Press.

Sacks, Peter M. 1985. *The English Elegy: Studies in the Genre from Spenser to Yeats*. Baltimore, Md.: Johns Hopkins University Press.

Sanborn, F. B. 1895. "Thoreau's Poems of Nature." *Scribner's Magazine* 17: 352–355.

Sattelmeyer, Robert. 1988. *Thoreau's Reading: A Study in Intellectual History with Bibliographical Catalogue*. Princeton, N.J.: Princeton University Press.

———. 1989. "'When He Became My Enemy': Emerson and Thoreau, 1848–1849." *New England Quarterly* 62: 187–204.

———. 1995. "Thoreau and Emerson." *The Cambridge Companion to Henry David Thoreau*, ed. Joel Myerson. Cambridge: Cambridge University Press. 25–39.

Schweitzer, Ivy. 2006. *Perfecting Friendship: Politics and Affiliation in Early American Literature*. Chapel Hill: University of North Carolina Press.

Sebouhian, George. 1989. "A Dialogue with Death: An Examination of Emerson's 'Friendship.'" *Studies in the American Renaissance, 1989*, ed. Joel Myerson. Charlottesville: University Press of Virginia. 219–239.

Shamir, Milette. 2006. *Inexpressible Privacy: The Interior Life of Antebellum American Literature*. Philadelphia: University of Pennsylvania Press.

Slater, Joseph. 1979. "Historical Introduction." *The Collected Works of Ralph Waldo Emerson*, vol. 2: *Essays: First Series*, ed. Alfred R. Ferguson, et al. Cambridge, Mass.: Harvard University Press.

Smith, Harmon. 1999. *My Friend, My Friend: The Story of Thoreau's Relationship with Emerson*. Amherst: University of Massachusetts Press.

Standish, Paul. 2006. "Who is My Neighbor? Skepticism and the Claims of Alterity." Paper presented at the International Network for the Philosophers of Education, August 2006.

Steele, Jeffrey. 1999. "Transcendental Friendship: Emerson, Fuller, and Thoreau." *Cambridge Companion to Ralph Waldo Emerson*, ed. Joel Porte and Saundra Morris. Cambridge: Cambridge University Press. 121–139.

———. 2001. *Transfiguring America: Myth, Ideology, and Mourning in Margaret Fuller's Writing*. Columbia: University of Missouri Press.

Strauch, Carl F. 1968. "Hatred's Swift Repulsions: Emerson, Margaret Fuller, and Others." *Studies in Romanticism* 7: 65–103.

Taussig, Gurion. 2002. *Coleridge and the Idea of Friendship, 1789–1804*. Newark: University of Delaware Press.

Thoreau, Henry David. 2001. *Thoreau: Collected Essays and Poems*. Ed. Elizabeth Hall Witherell. New York: Library of America.

Trillin, Calvin. 2006. "Alice, Off the Page." *The New Yorker* (27 March): 44–57.

Van Leer, David. 1986. *Emerson's Epistemology: The Argument of the Essays*. Cambridge: Cambridge University Press.

Vessey, David. 2005. "Gadamer's Account of Friendship as an Alternative to an Account of Intersubjectivity." *Philosophy Today* 49/5: 61–67.

von Frank, Albert J. 1994. *An Emerson Chronology.* New York: G. K. Hall.
Von Mehren, Joan. 1994. *Minerva and the Muse: A Life of Margaret Fuller.* Amherst: University of Massachusetts Press.
Wadell, Paul J. 1989. *Friendship and the Moral Life.* Notre Dame, Ind.: University of Notre Dame Press.
Walls, Laura Dassow. 1995. *Seeing New Worlds: Henry David Thoreau and Nineteenth-Century Natural Science.* Madison: University of Wisconsin Press.
———. 2003. *Emerson's Life in Science: The Culture of Truth.* Ithaca, N.Y.: Cornell University Press.
Walter, Tony. 1996. "A New Model of Grief: Bereavement and Biography." *Mortality* 1: 7–25.
Webb, Stephen H. 1996. *The Gifting God: A Trinitarian Ethics of Excess.* New York: Oxford University Press.
Weil, Simone. 1951. *Waiting for God,* trans. Emma Craufurd. New York: Harper.
Weiss, Penny A., and Marilyn Friedman, eds. 1995. *Feminism and Community.* Philadelphia: Temple University Press.
Welty, Eudora, and Ronald A. Sharp, eds. 1991. *The Norton Book of Friendship.* New York: W. W. Norton.
Wittgenstein, Ludwig. 1963. *Tractatus Logico-Philosophicus.* Trans. D. F. Pears and B. F. McGuinness. London: Routledge & Kegan Paul.
Yarbrough, Stephen R. 1981. "From the Vice of Intimacy to the Vice of Habit: The Theories of Friendship of Emerson and Thoreau." *Thoreau Journal Quarterly* 13.3–4: 63–73.
Zwarg, Christina. 1995. *Feminist Conversations: Fuller, Emerson, and the Play of Reading.* Ithaca, N.Y.: Cornell University Press.

CONTRIBUTORS

Lawrence Buell is Powell M. Cabot Professor of American Literature at Harvard University. He is author of *Emerson; Writing for an Endangered World: Literature, Culture, and Environment in the United States and Beyond; The Environmental Imagination: Thoreau, Nature Writing, and the Formation of American Culture;* and *New England Literary Culture: From Revolution through Renaissance.*

James Crosswhite is Associate Professor of English and Director of Composition at the University of Oregon. He is author of *The Rhetoric of Reason: Writing and the Attractions of Argument* and "Rhetoric in the Wilderness: The Deep Rhetoric of the Late 20th Century" in *A Companion to Rhetoric,* edited by Walter Jost and Wendy Olmsted.

Russell B. Goodman is Regents' Professor in the Philosophy Department at the University of New Mexico. He is author of *American Philosophy and the Romantic Tradition* and *Wittgenstein and William James.* He is also editor of *Pragmatism: A Contemporary Reader; Pragmatism: Critical Concepts in Philosophy;* and *Contending with Stanley Cavell.*

Alan D. Hodder is Professor of Comparative Religion at Hampshire College, where he teaches courses on the history of religion and American literature. He is author of *Emerson's Rhetoric of Revelation* and *Thoreau's Ecstatic Witness.* He is also editor, with Robert Meagher, of *The Epic Voice.*

John T. Lysaker is Professor of Philosophy at Emory University. He is author of *Emerson and Self-Culture; You Must Change Your Life: Poetry,*

Philosophy, and the Birth of Sense; and, with Paul Lysaker, of *Schizophrenia and the Fate of the Self.*

Barbara Packer is Professor of English at the University of California, Los Angeles. She is author of *Emerson's Fall: A New Interpretation of the Major Essays* and *The Transcendentalists.*

David M. Robinson is Distinguished Professor of American Literature, Oregon Professor of English, and Director of the Center for the Humanities at Oregon State University. He is author of *Natural Life: Thoreau's Worldly Transcendentalism; Emerson and the Conduct of Life;* and *Apostle of Culture: Emerson as Preacher and Lecturer.*

William Rossi is Associate Professor and Director of Undergraduate Studies in English at the University of Oregon. He is editor of Henry D. Thoreau, *Walden, Civil Disobedience, and Other Writings; Wild Apples and Other Natural History Essays;* and, with Heather Kirk Thomas, of Henry D. Thoreau, *Journal 6: 1853.*

Naoko Saito is Associate Professor of Education at Kyoto University. She is author of *The Gleam of Light: Moral Perfectionism in Dewey and Emerson* and has translated Stanley Cavell's *The Senses of Walden* into Japanese.

INDEX